NOW I KNOW WHO MY COMRADES ARE

NOW I KNOW WHO MY COMRADES ARE

VOICES FROM

THE INTERNET UNDERGROUND

EMILY PARKER

SARAH CRICHTON BOOKS
FARRAR, STRAUS AND GIROUX   NEW YORK

Sarah Crichton Books
Farrar, Straus and Giroux
175 Varick Street, New York 10014

Published in 2014 by Sarah Crichton Books / Farrar, Straus and Giroux
First paperback edition, 2015

The Library of Congress has cataloged the hardcover edition as follows:
Parker, Emily, 1977–
    Now I know who my comrades are : voices from the Internet underground /
Emily Parker. — First edition.
        pages   cm
    Includes bibliographical references (p.).
    ISBN 978-0-374-17695-2 (hardcover) — ISBN 978-0-374-70934-1 (ebook)
    1. Internet—Social aspects—Communist countries.   2. Internet—Social
aspects—Former communist countries.   3. Blogs—Political aspects—
Communist countries.   4. Blogs—Political aspects—Former communist
countries.   5. Intellectual freedom.   6. Political participation.   7. Social
change.   I. Title.

HN962.I56 P37 2014
302.23'1—dc23

                                                            2013035399

Paperback ISBN: 978-0-374-53551-3

Designed by Abby Kagan

Our books may be purchased in bulk for promotional, educational, or business
use. Please contact your local bookseller or the Macmillan Corporate and
Premium Sales Department at 1-800-221-7945, extension 5442, or by
e-mail at MacmillanSpecialMarkets@macmillan.com.

www.fsgbooks.com
www.twitter.com/fsgbooks • www.facebook.com/fsgbooks

P1

Some names and identifying characteristics have been changed.

For my parents

CONTENTS

NOW I KNOW WHO MY COMRADES ARE

INTRODUCTION

THE STORY WE MISSED IN EGYPT

In 2011, ordinary Egyptians, many armed with little more than social media, helped topple a thirty-year dictatorship in eighteen days. But Egypt's real "online revolution" began years before. During the darkest hours of the Hosni Mubarak regime, when much of Egyptian society had essentially given up on political change, radically different citizens were emerging. They came to life on the Internet, which was the closest you could get to a free space. These citizens were fearless, densely networked, and ready to fight. And when Egypt was finally ready for revolution, these were the people who were poised to lead the way.

So why didn't anyone see it coming? In November 2010, a mere two months before revolution broke out, Reuters published an article headlined "Egypt Dissent Yet to Get from Facebook to the Streets." It said that social media was unlikely to provoke real change in Egypt. This reflected the conventional wisdom at the time. By late 2010 the idea of social media revolutions was out of vogue. Excitement over Iran's 2009 so-called "Twitter Revolution" was hard to maintain when Iranian authorities had basically snuffed out the protest movement.

As Internet dissent spread, repressive governments ramped up their attempts to rein it in. They censored words, blocked websites, arrested bloggers, and surveilled dissidents. Commentators mocked the idea that social media could pave the way for revolution. A vibrant online community, the theory went, would not change bleak off-line realities.

But such critics underestimated the psychological impact of the Internet in Egypt in the years leading up to the revolution. Change begins with individuals. Over the years, blogs and social media helped to transform cowed, powerless individuals into revolutionaries.

In the years leading up to 2011, Egypt's off-line life was bleak. The country had been living under emergency law since 1981, when Anwar Sadat was assassinated and Hosni Mubarak took power. The law severely restricted freedom of speech and assembly, and it afforded the police limitless powers. Dissidents risked arrest or torture by the state security services.

This all took a severe psychological toll. Many Egyptians were terrified of criticizing the government in public, let alone of forming a viable opposition force. Almost all broadcast and print media were controlled or owned by the Mubarak government or the ruling National Democratic Party. Worst of all, there was little reason to believe that anything would change. Mubarak had tenaciously held on to power for three decades, and elections were widely perceived as neither free nor fair. Faced with their apparently immutable fate, many Egyptians withdrew from politics.

Although Egyptian authorities targeted individual bloggers, they didn't seem to see the Web as a serious threat. Thus, the Internet offered possibilities that didn't exist in "real" life. When state media presented a distorted version of reality, bloggers reported on events themselves. They took photographs and posted videos on YouTube. They fiercely debated, signed petitions, and organized street demonstrations.

The now famous "We Are All Khaled Said" Facebook page, named after a blogger who was beaten to death by police, played a key role in organizing the January 25, 2011, protests. But the ability to mobilize citizens via social media did not materialize overnight. Previous Internet campaigns helped build networks and trust. In a country where you needed a permit to gather more than five people, tens of thousands of individuals were joining forces online. In 2009 Rasha Abdulla, a professor at the American University in Cairo, described such sites as Facebook as "virtual nations, a place where members can roam freely without worrying about the restrictions their own countries and political systems might be imposing on them."

On the Internet, ordinary Egyptians began to overcome the isolation, fear, and apathy that are the lifeblood of authoritarian regimes.

ISOLATION, FEAR, AND APATHY

Most authoritarian regimes would not survive a sustained mass uprising. Lucky for them, such uprisings may never come to pass. Their populations are too paralyzed by various psychological obstacles, which in turn are deftly manipulated by authorities. The first is isolation. Regimes will strive to isolate potential dissenters from one another, both physically and psychologically. Those who don't agree with the party line feel powerless and alone. When protests are small and scattershot, they are both ineffective and dangerous for those involved. It's much easier for authorities to target a few dissidents, as opposed to a large crowd.

The second obstacle is fear. People are scared that if they dissent, they could lose their livelihoods or even go to jail. Networks of citizen informers lead people to fear one another, and society is flooded with risk aversion and distrust. A population that is crippled by paranoia, distrust of neighbors, and fear of state reprisals is not likely to band together in protest.

The third obstacle is apathy, an authoritarian government's best protection. Apathy often sets in once fear and isolation have done their damage. It may appear as if the average citizen doesn't care about politics or is more concerned about his daily bread, but often people don't protest because they have nothing to protest for. The state has marginalized potential opposition so effectively that the ruling regime truly looks like the best option. If there are no viable alternatives, and demonstrations are dangerous and won't change anything anyway, then what's the point? So people stay home.

Isolation, fear, and apathy keep authoritarian regimes in power. So what happens when people overcome these feelings? Governments can manipulate mass psychology to a certain degree, but when that stops working, their regimes are in serious trouble. As Gene Sharp wrote in his seminal work *From Dictatorship to Democracy*, even dictators require the assistance of the people they rule, and the degree of liberty or tyranny in any government is largely "a reflection of the relative determination of the subjects to be free."

THE NEW CITIZENS OF THE WEB

Repressive governments have long tried to control the spread of information, and ordinary citizens have long used creative ways to get around these controls. In eighteenth-century France, people criticized King Louis XV by spreading poems that were copied on pieces of paper or set to the tunes of popular songs. In the early 1980s, workers in Soviet-era Poland spread news via mimeographs and cassette tapes. Technological progress has only increased the breadth and speed of this phenomenon. As Albert Wohlstetter said in his 1990 speech "The Fax Shall Make You Free," "isolating and suppressing dissidents are incompatible with using . . . decentralizing information technologies."

The same is true about the Internet, only on a much grander scale. In China, there are hundreds of millions of *wangmin*, or netizens, which is another way of saying "citizens of the Web." And these are very different kinds of citizens. They are surrounded, at least virtually, by like-minded individuals. They learn the power of collective action. They become parts of networks that extend outside their country's borders. This affords some protection: Once, authorities could simply make troublemakers disappear. Now they face the wrath of domestic public opinion or even the rebukes of the outside world.

Nations are largely defined by stories and collective memory. Regimes that thoroughly control access to information end up narrating the past, present, and future of the country. By telling their own versions of events, bloggers reclaim the national narrative. They write descriptions, take photos, and shoot videos of what's happening outside their windows. They are no longer passive subjects in surveillance photos.

Over time, their collective voice grows louder and stronger. Charismatic figures emerge online, suggesting future alternatives to the current leadership. Netizens start winning small but real victories. They write the truth, and the domestic media often have no choice but to follow. They call attention to injustice and attract the interest of the outside world. They raise a racket, and detainees are freed. And success is the best antidote to apathy.

Of course, governments fight back. They censor content and block entire websites. They try to influence online discussions. They spy on troublemakers and intimidate and arrest bloggers. But these efforts are not nearly enough to reverse the psychological transformation taking place among citizens of the Web.

Does this psychological transformation automatically lead to revolution? Of course not. It still takes a spark to compel a critical mass to take to the streets. This spark can be a split in the political elite or an economic crisis. In Egypt, where hope had been suffocated for so long, there had to be an indicator that change was within reach. In that case, the spark was Tunisia.

In December 2010 Mohamed Bouazizi set himself on fire to protest the confiscation of fruit from his vendor cart and his mistreatment by Tunisian police. Protests erupted, and state media tried to play them down. But it was too late; images of the protests lit up social media. On January 14, 2011, Tunisian president Zine El-Abidine Ben Ali, who had held on to power for more than two decades, fled the country. People in Egypt took note. Or as the Cairo-based journalist and blogger Issandr El Amrani said that same month, "The first lesson from Tunisia is that revolution is possible."

There was already discussion of taking some kind of action on January 25, Police Day, on the "We Are All Khaled Said" Facebook page. But after events in Tunisia, Egyptian interest in a protest soared.

THE NEW FRONTIERS: CHINA, CUBA, AND RUSSIA

We often react to stories after they happen rather than chart their development. This book is based on the personal stories of bloggers and Internet activists in China, Cuba, and Russia, the next battlegrounds between netizens and the state. These countries, to varying degrees, bear similarities to Egypt circa 2009. Despite intense government repression, parallel universes are emerging on the Web.

China, Cuba, and Russia all bear the distinct scars of Communist authoritarianism. Over the years, networks of citizen informers have broken down solidarity and trust among the people. The Communist Party decided how history was taught and reported. Mainstream media existed to serve the Party, not the people, and in all three countries the media remain largely controlled by the state. Russia no longer has a Communist government, but nonetheless it has no tolerance for real political opposition.

I have been working on this project in some form since 2004, when I started writing about China and the Internet for *The Wall Street Journal*. Since then, I have spent extensive time in all three countries. For the most part I have tried to focus on the Internet foot soldiers rather than on bloggers who are already celebrated by the international media. In some cases, bloggers featured here, such as Russia's Alexey Navalny, grew exponentially more famous during the time this book was being written. It may seem that Internet activists in Beijing, Moscow, and Havana don't represent the masses. But sometimes a relatively small group of people can provoke wider change.

In all three countries the Internet is helping ordinary citizens overcome the challenges of isolation, fear, and apathy. In China, netizens are overcoming feelings of isolation and forming vibrant communities online. In Cuba, a small but fierce group of bloggers are overcoming their fears. And in Russia, netizens are finally beginning to move past deep-rooted feelings of apathy.

Some will point to censorship, surveillance, and arrests to argue that in all three cases, the governments are "winning." They'll say that online critics don't have a critical mass, and that opposition is only virtual. But those very same arguments were made about Egypt, right up to the eve of revolution.

Wael Ghonim, the administrator of the "We Are All Khaled Said" Facebook page, used to argue about the power of the Internet in Egypt. "The Internet is not a virtual world inhabited by avatars," he declared. "It is a means of communication that offers people in the physical world a method to organize, act, and promote ideas and awareness." Not long before revolution broke out, Ghonim wrote on Facebook and Twitter that the Internet would change politics in Egypt. But few believed him, and he was hit by a wave of cynical responses.

I am not predicting revolutions in China, Cuba, and Russia. But there's no question that citizens of the Web are eroding the foundations of authoritarian rule. This book is an attempt to tell their stories.

PART ONE

CHINA (ISOLATION)

"NOW I KNOW WHO MY COMRADES ARE"

"Wo ku le yi ge wanshang," Michael Anti told me. "I cried all night." In 1999 Anti saw something on the Internet that turned his world upside down.

Michael Anti is a pen name. Pronounced "Ahn-tee" in Chinese, Anti comes from the word "anti"—to oppose. His real name is Zhao Jing. Anti, once fiercely loyal to the Communist Party of China, used to believe everything he saw on television. In 1989 the People's Liberation Army opened fire on the pro-democracy protesters who had been swarming Tiananmen Square and its surrounding areas. At the time, Anti was living in Dongshan, a suburb of Nanjing. His only information came from official state media, which portrayed the protests as a violent uprising by counterrevolutionary mobs. Anti thought that reports of the army killing peaceful student protesters were malicious rumors spread by foreign media.

Ten years later, Anti was working as a hotel receptionist in Wuxi, in China's eastern Jiangsu Province. One night he was at home, in a small rented apartment, with a female friend who worked at the same hotel. Anti had not fully abandoned communism, but he was starting to have doubts. He had studied in Nanjing, and some of his classmates came from Beijing. He heard people referring obliquely to the 1989 killings, and on the Internet, where he spent much of his time, people discussed Tiananmen more directly. So in 1999, driven by a sense that something was not quite right, he downloaded a newsletter from an overseas dissident website. The site was blocked in China, but Anti used a proxy server. He saw first-person testimonies and photographs that claimed to be from the 1989 Tiananmen crackdown. He saw photos of dead bodies and a picture of flesh that appeared to have been crushed by a tank.

Anti couldn't stop crying. He felt cold, betrayed, and completely alone. He exclaimed, "How could they do this!" But he didn't tell his friend why he was crying, and she probably didn't care. The daughter of a rich businessman, Anti's friend was far more interested in Gucci and Louis Vuitton than in politics. She later went on to work for Apple, Asia Pacific.

Nor did Anti feel comfortable talking about his discovery with his other friends. And when I asked him if he talked about Tiananmen with his parents, he looked up at me sharply. "Never," he said. "They're Party members." Besides, they were from a different generation; they would never understand. "I never talk about serious things with my mother and father," he said.

So he turned to the Internet. In a later post on an online discussion forum Anti described how he cried that night. He avoided such direct references as "Tiananmen Massacre" or "June 4," the date the tragedy occurred. Instead, he invoked *1984*, George Orwell's dystopian novel about totalitarian life.

"Before going online," Anti wrote, "for 20 years I lived in 1984. I absolutely didn't know what really happened in the world, I only knew what they wanted me to know." He continued to describe the night when his illusions about communism were broken by images he saw online. In those moments, he wrote, "everything was destroyed. My dreams about my country and my society were all destroyed."

When I first met Michael Anti, in 2004, he was in his late twenties. He was skinny, with thin arms, delicate wrists, and skin pulled taut over a wide face and square jaw. His black hair lay close to his skull, and his willowy frame quivered with energy and ambition.

Once, Anti brought me to his apartment. We sat at his desk in the pale glow of his computer monitor. There were books and clothing strewn everywhere. Behind us was a light wood bookshelf that contained computer books and a Chinese version of the Cambridge philosophy series. Anti had ordered the volumes from a Chinese website, and the philosophers' names were written on the covers in Chinese characters. The text inside was in English. One time, Anti came to meet me proudly bearing a copy of *"Bolatu,"* or Plato, which he ultimately found too boring to finish.

At the time, I was writing a *Wall Street Journal* column about China and the Internet. I was living in Hong Kong, but I flew to Beijing on weekends, where I would see Anti fairly regularly. He was far less famous than he is now, and therefore much less busy. We would buy a bag of oranges and stroll through the narrow paths that lined Beijing's Houhai Lake. I would toss the fruit into the air and catch it in my palm, the orange bright against the polluted chalk-white sky.

Even on those casual afternoons, I would glimpse Anti's iron determination. Once we rented a kayak. I sat in front, Anti in back. I paddled slowly, taking in the thatched roofs, stone bridges, and trees whose leafy branches arched lazily toward the water. But Anti was on a mission. We had to defeat the other boaters. He wanted to do a clean circle around an island in the lake. My lackadaisical paddling infuriated him. "Turn right!" "Now left!" "Go straight!" he shouted at me from the back of the boat.

In 2004 Anti was already a journalist and, he liked to say, a *huaidan*, a bad egg, or dissident. But above all, he was a *wangmin*, a citizen of the Web. "The Internet is everything," he once told me. "The Internet made me know who I am."

Roughly every two months, the same two people from the

Public Security Bureau would invite Anti to "drink tea," which was a way of letting dissidents know they were being watched. The first time, a woman called him on his cell phone to fix a time to chat. When the call first came, Anti felt "damned." He remembers a meeting at Starbucks. The woman showed up with another man. Neither was wearing a uniform, and they spoke with Beijing accents, quickly praising some of Anti's earlier reporting. The message was clear: we are polite, and we know everything about you.

The tea invitations began after the pro-democracy activist Jiang Qisheng was released from jail in 2003. Jiang had been sentenced to four years in jail for writing and distributing an open letter that commemorated the victims of the 1989 crackdown at Tiananmen Square. Following Jiang's release, Anti and others went to meet him in a public park. Anti presented Jiang with two gifts: a DVD of the famous prison movie *The Shawshank Redemption* and a DVD player to watch it on. To Anti, the movie represented hope and breaking out of prison. Anti believed that authorities were watching the park and listening to his phone calls. When his tea companions asked him why he gave Jiang this present, Anti said that he respected his elders. They responded, There are so many people in jail, why don't you show your respect and give all of them DVD players? Anti said that he didn't know anyone else in jail.

Since then, the Chinese authorities have been on his case. "You can't get rid of them," he said. "I know they know everything." Anti believed that his phone was tapped. I was somewhat unnerved by this and tried to avoid calling him from my own cell phone, but he didn't seem concerned. He eventually came to find the tea-drinking sessions more tedious than intimidating, just "wasting everyone's time." Beneath his passionate exterior was a sharp political acumen. He was immensely confident in his ability to identify the Communist Party's "bottom line" and then carefully dance around it.

When Anti told me, "The Internet made me know who I am," he was speaking literally. The Internet made him realize that he was no longer a Communist and, more important, that he was not alone. Before the Internet era, opponents of the Party were effectively isolated from one another. In 1989, hundreds of thousands of demonstrators gathered all over the country, threatening the very existence of the Party. Beijing was not about to let that happen again.

It may look as though China's leaders are terrified of freedom of speech. But they are far more threatened by a basic liberty that many in the West take for granted: freedom of assembly. Falun Gong, a religious group that emphasizes meditation and physical exercises, learned this the hard way. Falun Gong's real troubles began in April 1999, when some ten thousand believers surrounded the Chinese government compound in Zhongnanhai, Beijing. Their main request was that Chinese state media stop referring to them as a superstitious cult.

The protesters were generally peaceful and polite. Before quietly dispersing, the mostly middle-class, middle-aged crowd spent much of the time meditating. All they really did was *assemble*. But this was enough to spook the Chinese government. In July 1999 Beijing formally banned Falun Gong, denouncing it as an "evil cult." Over the years, Falun Gong members in China have been arrested, beaten, and even killed.

So it was no small event that millions of Chinese gathered every day on the Internet. Anti's online universe was split into rightists and leftists, liberals and democrats, opinion leaders and followers. "You can see the beginning of political parties!" he exclaimed. On the Internet, Anti knew who was on his side. That's why, when he learned about Tiananmen, he turned to netizens before he turned to anyone else.

Anti talked about the Internet with a devotion that bordered on evangelism. His words were electric. He once explained to me, in one short phrase, how the Internet changed his life. And over the years I've heard his words echoed, in some form or other, in conversations with Internet dissidents from all over the world.

Anti said, "Now I know who my comrades are."

"CHINESE PEOPLE DON'T READ PERSONAL STORIES"

Michael Anti was born as Zhao Jing in 1975 in Dongshan. He hates talking about his childhood, mostly because he sees it as completely irrelevant. "Chinese people don't read personal stories," he explained. "History books are always about big events, not personal stories." It took years of perseverance to piece together the basic facts of Anti's early life.

In early childhood he lived with his grandfather because his parents didn't have a babysitter and weren't able to take care of both him and his sister. He described 1970s China as being like "North Korea." His family had no telephone. His parents' family was one of the first in the neighborhood to have a black-and-white television. He doesn't remember any cars on the street, just a pond near his parents' house. "I have a lot of memories of ducks," he said.

Anti's worldview was largely shaped by his grandfather, an intellectual who was well respected in the community. He taught Anti how to write Chinese calligraphy. But when I asked Anti to describe his grandfather's physical appearance, he was exasperated by such a pointless question. "Typical Chinese grandfather!" he snapped.

Anti's grandfather grew up in Nanjing, formerly known as

Nanking, which was the capital of the Kuomintang government at various points in the first half of the twentieth century. He was part of the Kuomintang Youth League, and he also had a brother who was a Kuomintang soldier. Mao Zedong defeated the Kuomintang in the Chinese civil war, which ended with the founding of the People's Republic of China in 1949. So during Mao Zedong's 1966 to 1976 Cultural Revolution, Anti's grandfather was on the wrong side of politics, and despite his extensive learning, he dyed textiles for a living, ultimately getting ill from the chemicals in the dye. Instead of going to high school, Anti's mother was sent to the countryside.

The Cultural Revolution was Mao's massively destructive campaign to rid the nation of traditional or cultural influences that were harmful to communism. Mao worried that the ideals of the Russian Revolution had gone astray and that China risked following the same path. He was also concerned about the level of socialist commitment among his own Party officials. So in 1966 he launched an attempt to solidify both communism and his own historical legacy.

The Cultural Revolution that spanned the last decade of Mao's rule was a period of collective madness marked by purges, beatings, and executions. At the forefront was a massive, overzealous army of youths, called Red Guards, who set out to attack all that was traditional or bourgeois. Schools were shut down and intellectuals were sent to labor camps. The general Western supposition is that the Cultural Revolution caused somewhere between five hundred thousand and a million deaths, but the Harvard University professor Roderick MacFarquhar has said that responsible former Chinese officials have suggested that 10 million would be closer to the truth.

Citizen turned against citizen to prove loyalty to Mao. Those who showed any signs of political incorrectness risked being subjected to public "struggle sessions" where they would endure verbal and even physical abuse until they confessed their crimes. The writer Kang Zhengguo, whose defiant nature quickly made him an outcast in Mao's China, describes a series of incidents in 1968. A middle-aged administrator aimlessly picked up a pin and pricked a few holes in a Chinese newspaper; when he went to the bathroom, one of his colleagues went through the paper and found that a pinprick had penetrated Mao's photo on the back page. The colleague reported this to the Party, and the offender was charged with a "vicious attack on the Great Leader," locked up in a cow pen, and beaten. Then he was sentenced to four years in prison.

Kang also tells the story of a factory worker who accidentally shattered a Mao figurine while dusting a table. In a panic, he wrapped the shards in newspaper and threw them into the garbage. Unfortunately, the chairwoman of the neighborhood committee had seen it all. She took the pieces from the trash and brought them to the police. The factory worker was sentenced to six years in prison for trashing Mao's image.

As these examples illustrate, an informer could be anyone. Kang writes in his memoir, "Human relationships are impermanent, and politics can destroy even the closest of friendships." The Cultural Revolution gave millions of Chinese a window into the darkest corners of humanity.

In the preface to Kang's memoir, *Confessions*, the China scholar Perry Link describes the Cultural Revolution as a thoroughly alienating movement: even though the collectivism of the Mao era was officially portrayed as "idealistic group-mindedness," the Party's power engineering created very nearly the opposite. "It focused sharply on the individual person, you are wrong, you are alone." Link added that Kang and most of the people he describes "are isolated as individuals, or at most in families or small circles of friends—and they perceive the larger society as a majority arrayed against them, while in fact that majority is a sea of people who are similarly frightened and isolated."

Anti's mother talked to him about her suffering during the Cultural Revolution, when she was forced to work on a farm rather than study in a classroom. Anti's grandfather was more laconic. His refusal to criticize the Party after all he had been through made Anti later suspect him of Stockholm syndrome, wherein hostages feel sympathy for their captors. Anti's grandfather taught him first and foremost that he should love the country and love the people. Anti doesn't remember his grandfather specifically saying that he should love the Communist Party, but for young Anti, Party and country were one and the same.

Anti's grandfather taught him Confucian values: take care of the elderly, help the weak. He heard the same things in school, although those ideas were framed in the language of communism. So he decided that he would be a good Communist. One of his earliest heroes was the legendary Lei Feng, a squad leader in the People's Liberation Army. The actual facts of Lei Feng's life remain somewhat murky, but his symbolic import is not. Soon after his death, in 1962 (he was hit by a falling telephone pole), he became the hero of a Communist propaganda campaign, "Learn from Comrade Lei Feng." He was the model of selflessness, altruism, and devotion to Mao Zedong. His diary became a kind of Communist textbook.

Anti's family was poor, and he was embarrassed to wear patched clothes in front of his classmates. But he got high scores on tests and already possessed a keen political instinct. He was even appointed by the teacher to be the class leader. "I was born a leader," he told me.

In 1987, when Anti was twelve, the spirit of Lei Feng inspired him to help a younger, disabled student who hobbled around on a stick. Anti called on his classmates to pool money to buy him a wheelchair. "I totally used Lei Feng language, of course," he remembered. *"Bangzhu renmin!"* he implored, help the people! His plea was effective, and a combination of school funds and individual donations were pooled to buy the wheelchair. Anti already had the power of persuasion. What's more, he added proudly, "I already knew how to fundraise."

Anti's father was an engineer, and his mother worked as an accountant for a department store. Anti didn't like to read novels, because his grandfather didn't approve of them. During the Cultural Revolution, writers and artists worked within clear political guidelines. Those who fell afoul were severely punished. Don't become a writer, Anti's mother warned. She said that writing was *weixian*, dangerous. So as soon as Anti could buy his own books, he bought books only about science.

"I SUPPORT THE PARTY . . . BUT WHAT ABOUT OTHER PEOPLE?"

Anti was still a true Communist believer in 1989, the year protests swept across China. He was fourteen years old. The 1989 Tiananmen demonstrations are generally thought of as student protests, but the masses of protesters across China included a broad spectrum of the population, from doctors to journalists to members of the military. Uprisings were in hundreds of cities, with demonstrators calling for both economic and political reforms.

There was a sense that anything could happen, and some seemed to really believe that the regime would fall. The spread of the protests from intellectuals to workers and peasants struck fear in the hearts of China's leaders. It seemed to be a direct threat to the stability of the nation. Over the past decade, some living standards had improved but were marred by inflation and corruption. People had political grievances as well. Although the 1980s were defined by greater freedom and openness, the Party came to fear that this freedom could go too far, and so in 1986 and 1987 the authorities cracked down on the largely student demonstrations that called for greater individual rights. One casualty of this crackdown was the Communist Party general secretary Hu Yaobang, who was in favor of greater openness in China. Hu was forced to resign from his post in 1987, and his death in April 1989 helped spark the Tiananmen protests. The national protests were centered in Beijing's main square, Tiananmen, where tens of thousands of students camped out for weeks, with demands that included an end to corruption and expanded rights to free speech.

In a meeting on June 2, 1989, the Party decided to clear Tiananmen Square of the students who were occupying it, and they would use force if necessary. People's Liberation Army soldiers and tanks were sent in to restore order to Beijing. As the troops approached the square, people tried to block them. The crackdown was well before the age of cell phone cameras and Twitter real-time reports, which added to the challenges of getting an accurate sense of what happened on the days surrounding June 4, 1989. Officially, the government reported that more than two hundred died, emphasizing the death of soldiers. According to other accounts, the number of casualties was significantly higher, and the majority were unarmed civilians.

Contrary to popular perception, it now appears that the student protesters in Tiananmen Square itself were not the primary victims of the violent crackdown. Jay Mathews, a *Washington Post* reporter who covered the 1989 crackdown, wrote in the *Columbia Journalism Review* almost a decade later, "All verified eyewitness accounts say that the students who remained in the square when troops arrived were able to leave peacefully. Hundreds of people, most of them workers and passersby, did die that night, but in a different place and under different circumstances." He continued by saying that "many victims were shot by soldiers on stretches of Changan Jie, the Avenue of Eternal Peace, about a mile west of the square, and in scattered confrontations in other parts of the city, where, it should be added, a few soldiers were beaten or burned to death by angry workers."

It now seems that many of the killings took place in the western roads to the city leading to the square, as people tried to protect the protesters by setting up roadblocks to stop the tanks' approach. Soldiers responded with live ammunition. Some protesters threw stones and Molotov cocktails.

The description by Nicholas Kristof, who was the *New York Times* Beijing bureau chief in the spring of 1989, sums it up this way:

> There is no massacre in Tiananmen Square, for example, although there is plenty of killing elsewhere. Troops frequently fire at crowds who are no threat to them, and at times aim directly at medical personnel and ambulances. Some of those who are shot have been threatening the troops—for while the students have generally urged nonviolence, many young workers carry firebombs or pipes, and they manage to kill more than a dozen soldiers or policemen. But many other civilians are casually slaughtered for no apparent reason.

In 1989 Anti's access to information mainly came from government propaganda. But it was clear that something big was happening. Anti wrote in his diary that this was the first time he experienced national turmoil and upheaval. He heard news that most of China's big cities were in a state of chaos, with marches, hunger strikes, and riots.

Anti's relatives who lived in the city of Nanjing had a different perception of what was happening. Student protests were happening there, as they were in various other Chinese cities. They also listened to the Voice of America, a U.S.-government radio broadcast that aimed to present an alternative to Chinese official propaganda.

Anti listened primarily to his grandfather. And his grandfather believed that the protesting students didn't love China. Anti wrote in his diary, "I am a member of the Communist Youth League of China, loyal to my doctrine, naturally I support the correct, incorruptible Party and government of the motherland. But what about other people? According to my observation, except for the people over forty years old and students in middle school or lower than middle school who support the government, most youths believe the news of 'Voice of America.'"

Anti went on to describe the Voice of America broadcasts, noting that you could hear the following statements in the doorways at homes and small businesses: "'The Beijing government heavily and harshly suppressed students; workers, students and farmers are in a rage—about 6 million people are on a strike now . . .' 'President Bush expressed regret that China used force to brutally harm students.' 'Fight for a free China!'"

Meanwhile, the Chinese official media offered a radically different version. Anti's diary described a video on CCTV, the main state-television channel. He saw images of violence and chaos, writing, "The behavior of the counterrevolutionary and violent criminals makes every Chinese with a conscience's hair stand on end." He learned that two People's Liberation Army soldiers were beaten to death. There were armed soldiers, but they did not even fight back! He also heard of a violent criminal who threw a soldier from an overpass, doused the body with gasoline, set it on fire, and then hung the burned body to show the crowd. "These outstanding people's soldiers didn't die in battle gloriously, but sacrificed their lives in the great capital of the Republic," Anti wrote. "People cry for you, the Republic won't forget you."

And yet, despite this televised evidence, people persisted in believing the insidious American reports! Anti was flummoxed by the gap between the wildly diverging accounts of the Americans and his own government. Are the people in Beijing "students," or are they "rioters"? Are they patriotic or counterrevolutionary? The vocabulary was so different that one side must be lying. Anti had no reason to doubt the Party. So he decided the culprit was VOA and its malicious "rumors."

Anti addressed his invisible countrymen in his diary, his writing style hinting at the online opinion leader he would eventually become. "I don't understand these people who attentively listen to VOA. Are you Chinese? Do you want Bush to teach you how to walk? Do we have white skin, blond hair and blue eyes?" Don't forget, Anti reminded his disloyal compatriots, no matter what you do, "the United States immigration service still won't give you a passport."

Even after the crackdown, when order appeared to have returned to the capital, Anti's indignation remained. "Now that calm has descended on Beijing, the rumor creator company 'VOA' can take a rest. But if VOA can no longer create rumors, it can't even survive for one more day."

Soon after the Tiananmen crackdown, Anti's uncle, a lieutenant in the People's Liberation Army, returned from Beijing. Anti's mother's brother was stationed in Xuzhou, in the north of Jiangsu, and had been sent to Beijing several days after the crackdown to help secure martial law.

On July 29, 1989, Anti wrote in his journal, "Today, my lieutenant uncle suddenly appeared in front of us, like the return of a victorious warrior, and I felt an inexplicable pride inside my chest." His uncle brought some of the food he had been eating—canned vegetables and compressed biscuits. The people of Beijing, he told Anti, were "too awful." Anti's uncle said that they put poison in tap water.

Anti now believes that his uncle, who was in Beijing for only a short time, may not have known what really happened. But at the time of his uncle's visit Anti felt vindicated, and infuriated anew. The facts were so clear now. He just couldn't understand his countrymen. He wrote in his diary, "Why is it that as soon as there is a rumor they will listen, believe it and spread it, and yet they somehow don't trust our own army?"

"MY WORLD WAS SO SMALL"

After the upheaval of Tiananmen, a kind of silence descended over the country. The novelist Yu Hua described watching Chinese television immediately after the crackdown. He saw "the despairing looks on the faces of the captured students and heard the crowing of the news announcers." Then one day the picture on his TV totally changed. "The images of detained suspects were replaced by scenes of prosperity throughout the motherland. The announcer switched from passionately denouncing the crimes of the captured students to cheerfully lauding our nation's progress."

This progress wasn't immediately apparent in 1995, when I first landed in Beijing to study Chinese. That summer, and then for a longer stint in 1998, I lived on the same basic campus. I was barely out of high school. The dormitories were squat and brick, and there was a small courtyard with a table and white stone stumps for chairs. The dormitory toilet was a hole in the ground, with the shower right above it. When the weather was cold, we wore our winter coats to class.

Yet in those same classrooms we learned to chant, like a

mantra, *"Zhongguo jingji fazhan hen kuai!"* The Chinese economy is developing very fast! And it was true. Construction cranes seemed to be everywhere. China's transition to a market economy began with Deng Xiaoping's 1978 reforms, and the 1990s were marked by a period of rapid growth. In 1995 China's GDP per capita was $604. In 2011 it was $5,442.

But in the 1990s all this development seemed a long way off, at least to me. People still gawked at foreigners at train stations. I had access to one telephone, located at the little campus store, from which I would very occasionally call my parents in the United States. I wrote and received handwritten letters.

China's first "email" was sent in 1987, via an academic network, by German scholars in Beijing. The message said, "Across the Great Wall we can reach every corner in the world." In 1994 China built the first cable connection to the Internet. Nobody could have imagined that one year later ordinary Chinese would use the Internet to save a young woman's life.

This particular drama starred one of Anti's friends, Bei Zhicheng. In 1995 Bei was a twenty-one-year-old student at Peking University, where he studied mechanics. He heard that his former high school classmate Zhu Ling was suffering from a strange illness.

Bei didn't know Zhu all that well. She was a round-faced chemistry student who was pretty and smart. Bei's main memory of Zhu was when he tried to convince her to cheat with him on a politics exam. She was very uncomfortable with the idea, Bei recalled. Bei and Zhu ended up at two of the best Chinese universities: Bei went to Peking University, or Beida, while Zhu attended the nearby Tsinghua University.

In early 1995 Bei heard that Zhu Ling had been hospitalized. Starting in late 1994, she had been feeling sick and her hair had fallen out. Zhu was eventually treated at the well-respected

Peking Union Medical College Hospital (PUMCH), but doctors didn't know the cause of her symptoms.

One Saturday, Bei and a group of other students went to visit her in the hospital. They went into her room one person at a time. When it was Bei's turn, he found his former classmate lying in bed half naked, with tubes attached to her body. He was stunned. At age twenty-one, Bei recalled, "the death of our peers seemed very distant." He wanted to leave but couldn't move.

At the hospital, Bei observed the sadness of Zhu's parents. The doctors were stumped. Bei suddenly remembered someone in his dormitory talking about this thing called the Internet, via which you could communicate with the whole world. Even though China had very little Internet connectivity at that time, some academics used it for work-related purposes. Bei's dorm mate, Cai Quanqing, had Internet access via one of his professors. The Internet connection was actually not at Beida, but at nearby Tsinghua. Beida's computer lab was close enough to Tsinghua that Cai's professor was able to snake a cable through a fence.

Cai had access to Bitnet, a computer network that was founded in 1981 by professors at American universities. By 1989 Bitnet extended to hundreds of educational organizations and thousands of nodes all over the world. Cai also had access to Usenet, a computer network that was similar to modern bulletin board systems (BBS).

As Bei was leaving the hospital, he searched for something to talk about with Zhu's anguished parents. He mentioned that he had heard of this thing that allows "any person to seek help from the entire world." Zhu's parents were skeptical, but they didn't have much to lose. They printed out a copy of their daughter's medical report and gave it to Bei. As he was leaving, one of the students cried out to him, "You must try and think of a way!"

———

Bei Zhicheng comes from a powerful family. In the 1930s his grandfather was a high-ranking military official. But from a young age he found himself strongly drawn to the idea of American democracy. His unlikely inspiration was the 1984 movie *Protocol*, starring Goldie Hawn. In the American comedy Hawn plays Sunny Davis, a bubbly cocktail waitress who somehow becomes a protocol officer at the U.S. State Department. In one of the film's scenes, Hawn reads aloud from the Declaration of Independence. Bei saw the film on video, subtitled in Chinese. His parents, whose work was related to foreign affairs, were able to get their hands on these kinds of treats.

Bei watched the pretty blond actress speak the words of the Declaration: "We hold these truths to be self-evident, that all men are created equal . . ." He was electrified. Communist political rhetoric touched him in a very different way. To Bei, Communist rhetoric evoked the might of the Party, appealing to people's anger and indignation and compelling them to do the "correct" thing. He had a different reaction to the Declaration, which spoke the words "that you feel in your heart, but can't express."

These words were in Bei's mind when he, along with Cai, set out to write a letter to the outside world seeking help for the sick Zhu. An American friend helped them translate the letter into English. Bei thought that Americans particularly loved to talk about freedom and democracy, so he figured that opening the letter with such vocabulary would be the best way to convince Americans that this was an important request. The letter began, in rather imperfect English: "Hi, This is Peking University in China, a place those dreams of freedom and democracy. However, a young, 21-year-old student has become very sick and is dying. The illness is very rare. Though they have tried, doctors at the best hospitals in Beijing cannot cure her; many do not even know what illness it is. So now we are asking the world—can somebody help us?"

The letter proceeded to describe Zhu's symptoms in detail. It listed the tests that the doctors had done, as well as their results. The doctors thought that Zhu might be suffering from acute disseminated encephalomyelitis, or lupus, the letter said, but the data from the tests did not support those conclusions. The letter provided a list of the antibiotics the doctors were using to treat Zhu, noting that none were pulling her out of her "vegetative state." If anyone knows what the illness might be, the letter implored, please tell us. It concluded, "This is the first time that Chinese try to find help from Internet, please send back E-mail to us."

Cai Quanqing was one of the few students at Peking University who had an email address. Although he was supposed to be using the Internet for academic purposes, there can't be any rule against trying to help a friend, Bei figured. They went to the university computer room and located several "sci.med" newsgroups in an online directory. They then posted the letter on Bitnet and Usenet.

The letter was transmitted via satellites and telephone circuits to computers at hospitals and universities everywhere from Ohio to Germany to India. Before long, responses arrived in Cai's email account. "That day was the first time I felt the power of the Internet," Bei said.

At the time, Bei was using a Unix operating system. "You look at a green screen, no graphics, just characters. It's like something you'd see in a hacker movie," Bei told me. "Before that, you could not imagine there are nearly two hundred doctors all over the world who could diagnose this girl and make the right diagnosis and give treatment advice. It's impossible to imagine; it's like a dream." Bei was so excited that he stayed up until five in the morning watching new messages pop up on the green screen. By morning there were some hundred messages. He saved them on a floppy disk and brought it back to his dormitory.

One of the recipients of Bei and Cai's plea was a doctor named

John Aldis, who had worked as a U.S. embassy physician in Beijing. He knew and respected the doctors at PUMCH. Aldis forwarded the letter to State Department doctors and other colleagues, asking for their help. Several wrote back, and Aldis replied directly to Bei and Cai. Bei says that in total he received around three thousand messages. Many of them said that Zhu had likely been poisoned by thallium, a very toxic heavy metal.

Bei printed out the diagnoses he received from all over the world and brought them to the hospital. At first the Beijing doctors weren't thrilled about having a student tell them how to do their jobs, nor did they have time to go through a stack of messages coming in from abroad. But the students persisted. An X-ray of Zhu's brain was put onto a server at the University of California, as was a CT scan of her nervous system. Foreign doctors also wanted to know on what basis thallium had been eliminated. It finally emerged that PUMCH hadn't even conducted a laboratory test for thallium, because they didn't have the right equipment.

When Bei and his friend posted this particular piece of information to their international network, a small commotion ensued. Finally, some young PUMCH doctors agreed to break hospital rules and give Zhu Ling's parents the blood, urine, and hair samples they needed for heavy metal tests at a disease prevention center.

Soon after, Zhu Ling's father contacted Bei. Zhu's father said in a low, sad voice that the thallium diagnosis was correct. Li Xin, a Chinese graduate student at UCLA's medical school who had also seen Bei and Cai's call for help, consulted other specialists. They said that Prussian blue, a kind of dye, was the right antidote for thallium poisoning. Li emailed a detailed treatment plan to Dr. Aldis, who faxed it to a friend at the U.S. embassy in Beijing, who got it to the hospital.

In the spring, a month after posting their original message, Bei and Cai sent an update to the medical community:

> With the help of the warmhearted people all over the world including you, the doctors of Zhu Ling now are sure that her illness is the result of THALLIUM POISONING. Now a group of toxicologists are working for Zhu through the internet with PUMC . . . Thank you very much for all you did for Zhu which have encouraged us, friends of her, to go ahead in the endless night with you. We believe that Zhu Ling has been the most lucky girl in the world for all your kindness from the internet.

Finally, Prussian blue was administered to Zhu. Soon after, her thallium levels went down and she slowly emerged from her coma. In August she squeezed her mother's hand. One doctor, Rich Hamilton, wrote of the incident, "I sit here at my computer and type recommendations, and they make life a little better for someone on the other side of the world. Truly humbling. It may be that Zhu Ling's illness has helped change the way medicine will be practiced."

At that time, Bei, who later went on to start his own software development company, only partly grasped the potential of the Web. "Internet telemedicine had become a reality. But not one person among us seemed to imagine that the Internet could yield great riches." Some pointed to the Zhu Ling case to highlight the potential of the Internet in China. "Many start-up companies tried to introduce the Internet to China. This is their case to explain what the Internet can do," Bei said. He also said that Chinese media articles would cite the story of Zhu Ling in an attempt to introduce the concept of the Internet to general readers. Bei would sometimes be interviewed for articles about science and technology.

The Zhu Ling case marked one of the earliest instances of Chinese Internet activism. And even back then, Chinese officials apparently divined the threat that the Web would pose to their control over information. Bei says that a year or so after the incident, Chinese reporters no longer wanted to interview him. Several journalists told him that there was an order from above to stop covering this story. He believes that the Chinese authorities didn't totally understand what had happened. He had said that he received nearly three thousand responses from abroad, but he thinks someone in power thought that he had sent thousands of emails or had thousands of exchanges. In Bei's view, that official would have said, This is a student who sent thousands of letters abroad, without our knowing about it. This is a big problem.

Bei unequivocally believes that the Internet saved Zhu's life. Unfortunately, her story doesn't have a very happy ending. By the time she began her recovery, too much physical damage had been done. Today she is alive but remains paralyzed and mentally disabled, relying on her parents for care. Furthermore, nobody has been convicted of the poisoning. The only suspect in the case was Zhu's roommate, Sun Wei, who happened to be the granddaughter of a senior official. This has led to intense netizen speculation that Sun Wei's family connections saved her from prosecution.

Bei, now in his mid-thirties, has the appearance of a wealthy investor. He is well traveled and cosmopolitan. He has a sunny disposition and political views that Anti describes as "Fox News Republican." In 2012 I had dinner with Bei, his wife, and two of their friends at Bouley, a posh restaurant in Tribeca, New York. He and his wife asked me to recommend New York stores that sold accessories and clothing for pets.

Bei also says that the Internet helped him find his "comrades." He was a businessman, and in off-line life people wanted to talk about making money, not politics.

Bei now looks back at his life before the Internet and thinks that China was so cut off from the world that he didn't even realize he was isolated. He says it was only after many years, and so much new information, that he could look back at his previous life and think, My world was so small.

"I THOUGHT, I CAN REALLY CONTROL THE WORLD"

In 1998 Anti got his first computer. Buying an actual machine was too expensive, so he put one together himself. He went to the Wuxi electronics market, which was teeming with wires and electronic components. He bought a central processing unit, a screen, a keyboard, a mouse, a main board, a hard drive, and other parts. He found pirated Windows 98 software as well as someone who could assemble the computer for him. The whole enterprise cost a few hundred dollars. When he saw the finished white box, he later told me, "I thought, I can really control the world."

Technology presented the Communist Party with a real dilemma. This wasn't the Mao era, when the country could slam its door to the outside. In 1978 the Chinese leader Deng Xiaoping began liberalizing the economy and opening it up to foreign investment. In 2001 China joined the World Trade Organization, helping the country become the economic juggernaut it is today. And yet China remained essentially a one-party state, with zero tolerance for serious political opposition.

This tension between economic growth and political freedom played out in the struggle over the Internet. China's leaders understood that the Web was necessary for the country's growth and modernization. In January 1999 there were some 750,000 computers connected to the Internet. By January 2002 that number had shot up to more than 12 million. By mid-2005 China had a little over 100 million Internet users, with half of them on broadband, accounting for about 8 percent of the population. Even in the big cities Internet users were less than 50 percent of the population. People tended to use computers at home or at Internet cafés. One study found that a typical Chinese Internet user was "young, male, well educated and well paid."

But the numbers were growing, and fast. By the end of 2007 there were 157 million urban netizens and more than 52 million rural netizens. By the end of 2011 there were 377 million urban netizens and 136 million rural netizens, with almost 90 percent of netizens accessing the Internet from home. By the end of 2012 China had a total of more than 564 million Internet users.

As the Internet increased access to knowledge, the Party strove to retain control. The Great Firewall of China, or GFW, blocked access to foreign Web content related to the Tiananmen Square crackdown, Falun Gong, Tibetan independence, or other sensitive topics. Most Internet traffic between China and the outside world was routed through a small number of fiber-optic cables that connected to the country at several international gateways. At each of these gateways, content was reflected back to surveillance computers that determined whether it should enter the country.

But the Great Firewall blocked content only from outside China. Much domestic content never made it online in the first place. Internet service providers filtered key words along the lines of "human rights" and "democracy." Chinese search engines removed search results, and blog service providers barred posts with sensitive key words or edited them out of the posts.

Companies also employed people to actively monitor content. A study by the Harvard researchers Gary King, Jennifer Pan, and

Margaret E. Roberts found that individual sites privately employed up to a thousand censors. The study said that "approximately 20,000–50,000 Internet police . . . at all levels of government—central, provincial, and local—participate in this huge effort." The Chinese Internet expert Guobin Yang described studying a large Internet firm that in 2010 had thirty editors monitoring the content of its website. Yang wrote, "About 80 percent of the messages are posted after being screened by the firm's filtering software. If the software gives a red light to a certain posting, an editor will immediately block it. After a message is posted, it is up to the editor to monitor it. If it is found to have sensitive content, or if the firm receives a call from government authorities about a specific posting, then it will be deleted." According to a more recent report, China had some 2 million people monitoring online opinion.

Efforts were not limited to blocking content and deleting. There are also members of the Wu Mao Dang, or 50 Cent Party, who are hired by the government to influence online discussions by posting pro-Party positions. (The party's name comes from the widespread belief that commenters are paid 50 cents for each post.) According to some estimates, there are up to three hundred thousand members of the 50 Cent Party.

China had a complex system of laws and regulations that monitored Internet use. The General Administration of Press and Publication licensed and monitored publications, including websites. China's State Administration of Radio, Film, and Television regulated Internet broadcasts. In 2013 the two merged into the State General Administration of Press, Publication, Radio, Film and Television. The Ministry of Industry and Information Technology controls the licensing of Internet content providers while the Ministry of Public Security oversees regulation of Internet access. The Propaganda Department of the Communist Party's Central Committee coordinates and guides Internet ideology.

But these government bodies weren't necessarily the ones

exercising censorship on a day-to-day basis. Regulation happened at the level of Internet content providers, Internet services providers, and online editors. State Council Order No. 292, promulgated in September 2000, further established that Internet content providers are responsible for ensuring that the information disseminated through their services is in keeping with the law. Internet access providers are required to make a record of such user information as Internet addresses and domain names.

And yet the most effective means of controlling the Chinese Internet remains invisible: self-censorship. Often, editors will delete content before anyone orders them to do it. They rely on their instinct to decide what is most likely to ruffle the government's feathers. The Party's bottom line is not only murky, it is constantly shifting. In a 2002 essay in *The New York Review of Books*, "China: The Anaconda in the Chandelier," Perry Link described Beijing's censors as a great snake, coiled above. "Normally, the great snake doesn't move," he wrote. "It doesn't have to . . . Its constant silent message is 'You yourself decide,' after which, more often than not, everyone in its shadow makes his or her large and small adjustments."

The most sensitive posts tend to be calls to assembly. The Harvard researchers mentioned earlier devised a system to analyze millions of social media posts. They compared the content of the posts that were censored to the ones that were not. The study concluded that attempts to organize on the Chinese Internet were the quickest paths to trouble.

"When the Chinese people write scathing criticisms of their government and its leaders, the probability that their post will be censored does not increase," the study said. Instead, "the purpose of the censorship program is to reduce the probability of collective action by clipping social ties whenever any collective movements are in evidence or expected." Authorities are particularly concerned about instances in which "a locus of power and control, other than the government, influences the behaviors of masses of Chinese people."

People like Anti had ways to get around almost every level of Chinese censorship. To get to blocked overseas websites, he would "jump" the firewall by connecting to proxy servers that allowed him to browse the Internet as if he were outside of China. After 2001, simple proxies became less easy to access. So Anti started using Freegate, a "proxy hunter" that helped locate available proxies. Freegate was controversial, as it was founded by members of Falun Gong and also received funding from the U.S. government. Although Anti approved of Freegate on a technical level, he didn't like the fact that when he used it, a Falun Gong home page would pop up. "We dissidents really hate propaganda," he explained.

Proxy servers wouldn't help with filters for key words, but Chinese netizens got around those by writing in code. As far back as May 2000, users of the popular online forum "Strengthening Nation Forum" (Qiangguo Luntan) wanted to discuss the murder of a Peking University student. Netizens soon found that posts containing the characters for Peking University (Beida) were blocked. They got around this by posting messages with such phrases as "Bei.Da" and "Bei2Da."

You could find such coded language on Internet bulletin board systems. These discussion forums were home to essays, comments, and fierce debates. In 1995 China's first BBS was set up by Tsinghua University and called Shuimu Tsinghua (SMTH). Other university sites soon followed. Between 1998 and 2000 several popular BBS systems emerged on the scene, such as Tianya and Xici. Xici is where Anti first made his name. He believes his fame on BBS helped to pave the way for his career in journalism. Because of his writing on BBS, editors already knew who he was.

"If one wants to understand the latest change in Chinese

politics, you don't need to read a newspaper or watch TV, just go directly to some of the most famous BBS," Anti once wrote.

BBS discussion conversations had *banzhu*, or section administrators, who moderated discussions and promoted posts within a specific topic area. Group leaders could propose topics for discussion and also curate comments. Being a *banzhu*, Anti said, was like "having my own newspaper." And even then, he relied on his keen perception of the government's bottom line. "Most of the time I decided myself what to delete," Anti told me. "When I finish deleting, the website did not delete anything." He said that he deleted less material than other *banzhu*, though there were certain lines that were uncrossable. Anti said, "We delete almost everything about Falun Gong, even jokes."

He understood that if he didn't censor sensitive content, his "discussion would be deleted, I would be punished." Anti told me his role as *banzhu* was an early lesson that in China, "if you want to be a public opinion leader, self-censorship is part of your job."

"PUT ANY GOOD GUY IN A BAD SYSTEM, AND HE WILL ACT VERY BAD"

After he graduated from college, Anti found a job in a hotel in Wuxi. He thought about applying to graduate school, and he reviewed classical Chinese texts during his free time. During that period, he felt that nothing would make him happier than "swimming freely in the ocean of knowledge." He added, "This fantasyland was shattered by the Internet."

In 1999 Anti downloaded a newsletter from Da Cankao, a website founded by an overseas dissident. Da Cankao had located Anti on BBS sites and begun "spamming" him with email messages that included links and other information. Although some might question the verity of Da Cankao's materials, Anti's worst suspicions about 1989 were confirmed. He had spent his childhood vehemently defending the Party against vicious "rumors," and now he felt betrayed. The deception may have been more devastating than the actual events of 1989. "The scary thing was not that we lived in a tragic era; the scary thing was that we lived in a tragic era and knew nothing at all," he wrote.

Anti didn't want to float through life. He needed a mission. When online images of the Tiananmen dead destroyed his belief in communism, he yearned for something to fill the void. He decided that you couldn't trust human beings. Tiananmen's lesson was clear: "Put any good guy in a bad system, and he will act very bad." So Anti turned to God.

His initial interest in Christianity predated that dramatic night in Wuxi. In high school he had discovered a Christian radio show that was broadcast from Hong Kong. He listened to the program in bed, using headphones so that his sister, with whom he shared a room, couldn't hear. Anti, spellbound, would try to imitate the announcer. He particularly liked such phrases as "brothers and sisters," "grace and salvation," and "put your wealth in heaven, come follow me."

The language of religion was so soft, Anti remembered fondly. He had never heard anything like it. It was completely different from such triumphalist Communist phrases as "We are surely on the march to victory!" Communist rhetoric made him feel like a tiny speck in "a historic, decisive moment already set by Marx and Mao Zedong." The language of religion, on the other hand, had "heart." It made him feel that he mattered.

The language of religion began to shape Anti's own manner

of expression. He admits that his language developed a "preaching style," which is evident in both his online commentary and his manner of speaking. He talks with soaring turns of phrase and an impatient gleam in his eye. Casual conversations about the Web are punctuated with such proclamations as "Now, the whole world is connected!"

Anti's path to Christianity had several phases. At Nanjing Normal University, where he majored in industrial electrical automation, he began exploring areas outside of the hard sciences. He dabbled in philosophy and psychology. He became interested in dreams and started to analyze his own and those of his friends. He describes those university years as somewhat fraught. He went through many girlfriends, trying in vain to "save his soul with love." He hadn't fully abandoned communism, but he still found himself grappling for some higher truth.

When his beloved grandfather died in 1994, Anti felt his world collapse. His grandfather, he said, was his only "psychological authority." He even thought about killing himself, but he was too scared of death. On October 4, 1994, he wrote in his diary, "I always want to have an answer but this time there is never an answer, God bless me!"

That was when he first heard the voice of God. Anti went to sleep feeling released from the burdens of sin, and he slept soundly until the next day, when he felt a true happiness at the bottom of his heart. "Since then, my personality began to rebuild, welcoming in the inner sunlight," he said. Though at that moment he was not yet Christian, emotionally he had entered religion's embrace.

What made Anti finally become Christian was learning about what happened in 1989. "The atrocities and the lies were so rampant, my personality almost collapsed again. How terrible are the human beings who lost nobility," he wrote in a later BBS post. "I began to understand my mission, and my mission is to stop the madness and the pride." He now identifies as a Protestant, though he doesn't go to church frequently.

Although China officially guarantees freedom of religious belief, it is run by the atheistic Communist Party and has regularly banned or limited religious activities. The state officially recognizes five religions: Buddhism, Islam, Taoism, and two branches of Christianity: Protestantism and Catholicism. In the seventh century, Christianity first came to China via Nestorian missionaries, and then later in the sixteenth century with Jesuit scholars. But it gained a permanent foothold only in the nineteenth century, when the country was forced to open its doors to foreign missionaries in the wake of the Opium Wars. After 1949, the Communist Party united various denominations, including Presbyterians, Methodists, and Anglicans under the umbrella of a state-controlled Protestant church. The Party also established a Chinese Catholic church that was not approved by the Pope, which led to battles with the Vatican. Partly as a result, Protestantism in China has expanded much faster than Catholicism.

All of China's religions have centralized governing bodies that are staffed by officials who are loyal to the Party. Worship is supposed to take place at state-sanctioned churches, mosques, or temples, but there are many nonofficial houses of worship, often in people's homes. By 2010 there were an estimated 23 million Christians in China, although if you count all the unregistered Christians, the number is likely to be several times higher. The government has cracked down on unofficial churches and banned Christian radio shows. It is illegal to sell Bibles in bookstores or hand them out on the street, though of course Bible sales do occur.

Anti's first time in church was in 1999. He went to a Nanjing church that was officially approved by the state, but the church's link to the Party didn't bother him at all. It was a church, and that's all that mattered. Or, as he told me, there is "a separation of church and state in my heart."

Anti wanted others to acknowledge this separation, so he took his argument to the Internet. Two of his main opponents were netizens named Wang Yi and Chen Yongmiao, who wrote winding BBS posts that assumed a linkage between Christianity and democracy. Chen, for example, would make arguments along the lines of "constitutionalism must be established on the basis of divine justice."

But Anti didn't believe that Christianity would make China a more liberal or democratic state. Liberalism protects people's personal weaknesses from public persecution, he explained. A liberal society doesn't punish individuals for such behavior as promiscuity. In a series of passionate BBS posts, he argued that liberalism and Christianity were fundamentally different. "Liberal constitutionalism protects the human's right to sin to the greatest extent, but Christianity requires everyone to repent for their sins," he wrote. Furthermore, Christianity demands that you believe in only one God. "It is the opposite of religious freedom!"

He also wrote that the argument that religion will "save" China is not good for Christianity: "If we tell people Christianity is good for democratization, it will at most make more people empathize or like Christianity, but will not make more people become Christians. Because the people who worship the kingdom of God can't become Christian just for the sake of utopia on the earth . . . Christianity is to save human beings, it is not to save the country."

For Anti, this debate was a turning point in his BBS career. He claimed that he unequivocally "won" the argument. "I have the most powerful argument," he said simply. He also had a secret weapon. "I get political knowledge from the Western world," he explained. "Most people don't read English." He said that his views about Christianity and liberalism were heavily influenced by the ideas of the contemporary Slovenian philosopher Slavoj Zizek.

Yet while Anti did not believe that Christianity would bring democracy to China, his own writing reveals a link between his religious beliefs and his political crusade. Learning about Tiananmen compelled him to "become a Christian, to follow the Lord Jesus, to show the world the will of God, and embark on lifelong struggle against authoritarianism."

Anti called Tiananmen "a baseline for comrades." What he meant was that he was not the only pro-democracy activist whose political identity was shaped by a sense of betrayal and deception.

The Chinese novelist Ha Jin told me that the Tiananmen crackdown also upended his belief system. From the ages of fourteen to nineteen, Xuefei Jin (Ha Jin is a pen name) was a volunteer soldier in the People's Liberation Army. In 1985, when he left China to pursue an American literature Ph.D. at Brandeis University, he fully intended to return to China. In 1989 Ha Jin was in Massachusetts, watching media reports that described Chinese soldiers firing on unarmed pro-democracy protesters. Meanwhile, his son was in China, telling his father about an "uprising" in which People's Liberation Army "uncles" were being killed by "hooligans."

"It changed my view of the world," Ha Jin said of Tiananmen. "I had served in the Chinese army. We had been taught you are from the people, serve the people, protect the people. But now everything was reversed."

Shortly after his final exodus from communism, Anti expressed his grief over Tiananmen in a willfully oblique post. It was 1999. Instead of discussing the significance of June 4, the anniversary of the 1989 crackdown, he wrote an entire post about June 1: International Children's Day. When he was growing up, he wrote, Children's Day was like a carnival. Children banged drums and marched through the streets. Shop owners would come out and watch. Anti, a member of the Communist Young Pioneers organization, was dressed neatly in a suit. He was so cute that he looked like a little girl, and some of the other boys teased him. Older kids would play with younger kids, competing for prizes.

The days flew by until Anti turned fourteen (which was in 1989, though the essay does not say the date). That year, everything changed. "There was no children's day," Anti wrote in his post. "Some of the older brothers and sisters disappeared."

Now Children's Day will come again, Anti continued, but there won't be any parade. This year, "while persuading other children from the neighborhood not to go outside, I will stay in the house, commemorating the older kids who died early." He told himself that one day "someone will be on trial" because history will not let him escape. He added that he also believed that the day would come when the children of the peers of those older kids who disappeared can "easily attend the June 1 parade to express their happiness and joy." By that time, Anti wrote, he might have a daughter of his own. And "I will tell her that because of our cowardice, China hasn't had a happy June 1 in over a decade."

The meaning of this essay would have been immediately obvious to Anti's online comrades. But there were no sensitive key words. The sentences were poetic and vague, and even so, it took a few paragraphs to get to the point. So despite the third-rail subject matter, the post wasn't removed and the police didn't invite Anti to tea. This was probably because, as he recounted to me years later with a blend of satisfaction and disgust, "some stupid guy thinks I'm really talking about Children's Day."

"NOTHING IS IMPOSSIBLE TO A WILLING HEART"

As Anti gained confidence and prominence on the Web, he decided that he was done with such opaque commentary as his "Children's Day" post. He wanted to be a journalist, and good journalists speak truthfully and directly to their readers. This would be difficult, even dangerous, but that was part of the appeal. He understood that assets are most valuable in environments where their availability is constrained. He saw an opportunity to set himself apart. "I only do real journalism when people don't do real journalism," he once explained to me.

In 2002 Anti devised a road map for others who aspired to do real journalism in China. His *Manual for New Journalists*, written in several installments, became one of the most important pieces of writing in Anti's early career. As one netizen wrote years later, the manual "has become a must read for many new journalists." The manual is both a detailed blueprint and a cri de coeur, based on Anti's own loss of faith in the official press.

Anti opened the manual by telling the story of the night when he learned about the Tiananmen crackdown. From that moment on, he was no longer interested in the official side of the story: "I no longer believe the propaganda, it is dog shit; I no longer believe any Chinese journalism textbooks, they are garbage." But this was more than a frustrated rant. If you don't like the domestic media, Anti told his readers, then let's try to create something new.

He made his case with a unique combination of profanity and quasi-religious language. "After we've said 'F**ck' to the giant media system," he wrote, "we can begin our individual journeys through the desert to become new journalists. Maybe we won't successfully reach the Holy Land of freedom of the press, but at least we will leave the enslavement of truth." Anti didn't want to encourage reckless behavior, however. Before making this "exodus," he continued, journalists first needed to take stock of their personal situation. "We cannot starve to death," he wrote. If you need your journalism job to survive, it's better not to lose your livelihood in pursuit of the ideal of free press.

Anti's next piece of advice to China's "new journalists" was to master English. In English, he wrote, "Lies can't exist." Wire services such as the Associated Press can be checked against Reuters and Agence France-Press. There is so much competition that fake news cannot persist for too long.

Third, Anti told his readers, you must use the Internet. Online, news is relatively fast and accurate. For Chinese people, this includes learning how to set up a proxy server that lets you jump over the Great Firewall. Furthermore, a good journalist must participate in BBS. Any reporter who does not attend these forums, unless he has considerable rhetorical powers, "will be eliminated from mainstream society." Reporters must have a network of resources, the ability to verify information, and an understanding of political science, economics, and international affairs. The completeness of knowledge determines what kind of reporter you will be.

With these instructions, he was just getting started. In part two of the manual, he compiled a list of the best Chinese-language news materials available from mainland China, along with their Web addresses. He included the wire service Chinanews.com, adding curtly that this inclusion was an act of desperation. At least it was better than the state-run Xinhua.

Anti also posted a list of foreign Chinese-language news sites. The United States State Department website and Japan's Kyodo News could at least provide some insight into the official stances of those countries. He also included the "rigorous" and "passionless" German Deutsche Welle, which "didn't even get excited when the Berlin Wall fell." He listed North Korea's official site, "the world's most nonsensical website." He noted websites from Taiwan, Hong Kong, and Iran. Many of these recommendations came with disclaimers that the sources may not be the most accurate or fair, but at least they weren't blocked by the Great Firewall.

In section three of the manual, Anti listed the English-language sites that were available from the mainland. Number one on the list was *The Economist*. Anti lamented that *The Economist* required readers to pay for articles, which made it tough for Chinese citizens who didn't have foreign-currency credit cards. But Anti, who studied computer science, found a work-around. He told his readers that he spent hours decoding the passwords needed to access *The Economist* for free, and then he posted them in an online forum. Feel free to check out the passwords, he instructed, but please don't repost them. "I know what I'm doing is immoral," Anti said. "But I trust that our friends at the Economist would understand our situation."

Anti went on to recommend the Associated Press; *The New York Times*, whose "history is the history of freedom of the press in the United States"; MSNBC; Hong Kong's *South China Morning Post*; and *The Wall Street Journal*'s editorial page, which reflects the "standard, right-wing point of view."

When it came to accessing websites that were banned in China, Anti treaded more carefully. Although in the first part of the manual he instructed readers to set up a proxy server, in one of the later sections—perhaps in response to requests for specific instructions on how to set up a proxy—he backtracked. First of all, if he publicized a specific proxy address, that address would be censored immediately. More generally, the Great Firewall's technology had been improving every day, Anti noted, so a proxy that worked one day could be rendered useless the next.

So in the second section of the manual he called on Chinese

journalists to be patient: "I have two pieces of advice for all of you so you won't be as pissed off when you see the 'website can't be accessed.' First, happiness lies in contentment. Second, nothing is impossible to a willing heart. We must try to train ourselves to obtain and integrate information in an environment that lacks it. Otherwise, how can we call ourselves journalists?" The fourth section of the manual offered more links to journalism resources.

In one of the appendixes to his manual (yes, there were appendixes) the religious language returned. Anti reeled off the "seven deadly sins" of Chinese reporters: ignorance, cowardice, thirst for power, naïveté, pride, low self-esteem, and, finally, despair. Of the last category, he wrote, "Whenever a ban comes down from above, in every reporter's heart flashes a desperate idea; so many extremely passionate college graduates abandoned their ideals after so many years of torture. I won't be able to convince everyone, I just know that those who persevere will all be repaid in the end."

"THE PEOPLE WON'T FORGET YOU, HISTORY WON'T FORGET YOU!"

From 2004 to 2006, when I was writing my Chinese Internet column, I saw Anti fairly regularly. He always decided our activities. Once, we went to the local Beijing version of *Body Worlds*, a traveling exhibition of preserved human bodies, without their skin, playing sports or the Chinese game of *goh*. Gunther von Hagens, the German anatomist behind the original *Body Worlds*, expressed consternation that the Chinese show had used the Body Worlds brand without his agreement. He also wondered, somewhat unnervingly, where the Beijing exhibition got the bodies. Another time, Anti and I went to a local movie theater and watched *The Lion, the Witch and the Wardrobe*, dubbed in Chinese. We would eat Japanese ramen in brightly colored booths. At the end of the day Anti would abruptly chirp "Bye!" and then vanish into the subway or the stream of Beijing pedestrians, never once glancing behind him.

My *Wall Street Journal* column explored how ordinary Chinese found ways to read and discuss censored information. My inaugural column, in April 2004, was about Vice President Dick Cheney's trip to China. Cheney made it clear that he wanted to speak live and uncensored to the people. After weeks of negotiations, Chinese authorities granted this privilege, or at least so it seemed. The vice president gave a speech at Fudan University in Shanghai. A State Department translator simultaneously interpreted the speech, which was broadcast on CCTV-4, China's major state-television news channel.

But when Chinese state media provided the text of Cheney's speech, serious omissions became apparent. When the vice president talked about "rising prosperity and expanding political freedom" across Asia, the Chinese version mentioned only "rising prosperity." The phrases "the desire for freedom is universal" and "freedom is indivisible" were omitted, and other cuts were made as well.

I set out to find a discussion of Cheney's original speech on BBS. Initially, I searched for the two characters in Cheney's name, *Qieni*, but found nothing. Then suddenly I found a post that explained the difference between the official version of the speech and Cheney's actual words. In my original search I had been looking for *Qieni*, but the post I found replaced the character *qie* with a character that is pronounced the same way but has a different spelling. In English, this would be like writing the word "seen" when you mean to say "scene." In the correct context, the misspelled "*Qieni*" was easy for a Chinese speaker to understand. But an automatic filter wouldn't necessarily pick it up.

I soon found an even longer and more detailed account of the censorship on another Chinese website, and this version had the correct spelling of Cheney's name. The report explained how Cheney's phrases had been changed or deleted in the official state-media version. Beneath the essay there was a forum for discussion. "I just have two words, shameless and deceitful," said one. Another said, "China's news media is just a propaganda tool of the Communist Party!" In this phrase, the characters for "Communist Party" were mixed in with Roman letters—again, likely to throw automatic censors off track. Another said, "We all should have known that words like 'political freedom' couldn't possibly exist in the Communist Party dictionary!" Yet another referenced a well-known point of discord between the United States and China: "This is an infringement of Cheney's intellectual property rights." One comment expressed gratitude for receiving access to uncensored information. "I deeply thank [the person who posted this] for providing us with these valuable extracts."

Of course, the vast majority of Chinese were not accessing this kind of information. Maybe they didn't know how to look for it; maybe they had no interest. But those netizens determined to break through the official silence managed to find a way. This is what happened in early 2005, when Zhao Ziyang died. On January 17, 2005, Chinese state media Xinhua made a terse announcement that read in its entirety: "Comrade Zhao Ziyang died of illness in a Beijing hospital Monday. He was 85. Comrade Zhao had long suffered from multiple diseases affecting his respiratory and cardiovascular systems, and had been hospitalized for medical treatment several times. His conditions worsened recently, and he passed away Monday after failing to respond to all emergency treatment." The announcement left out the rather important detail that he had once been a leader of China, holding the same position that would later be occupied by Jiang Zemin and Hu Jintao.

From 1980 to 1987 Zhao served as premier of the People's Republic of China, and from 1987 to 1989 he was general secretary of the Communist Party. During the 1989 protests Zhao broke from such Party hard-liners as Deng Xiaoping and Li Peng by showing too much sympathy for the students. In the early morning of May 19, 1989, Zhao paid a visit to the square. Surrounded by students, holding a bullhorn, he spoke the chilling words: "We have come too late. We are sorry." He pleaded with the students to stop their hunger strike and urged them not to sacrifice their future. It was the last time that Zhao appeared in public, and he died under house arrest. On January 29, 2005, Xinhua announced that Zhao had been cremated. This article, unlike his death announcement, mentioned that Zhao had held various leadership positions. It included the line: "In the political turbulence which took place in the late spring and early summer of 1989, Comrade Zhao committed serious mistakes."

For young Chinese, the Party had effectively turned Zhao into a historical footnote. A young Chinese woman I know was born in 1989 in Xi'an. Until she was fifteen, Zhao Ziyang was a name that appeared briefly in a middle-school history book. In January 2005 she was studying abroad in the Netherlands. One of her professors showed her a newspaper and asked her if she knew that the former Chinese premier and Communist Party general secretary had just died. She looked at the big portrait in the newspaper and saw a man who was not Deng Xiaoping, Jiang Zemin, or any other familiar leader. She then saw the same face on the front page of other major Dutch newspapers. "That was the first time I realized this man might be much more influential than I was told, or was probably deliberately being forgotten," she recalled.

For the young Chinese who couldn't travel abroad, the government blackout was pierced by the Internet. In January 2005, comments on online discussion forums reflected a combination of sadness, confusion, and anger. One revealing message, posted on a Chinese-language website shortly after Zhao's death, read:

> In 1989 I was only seven years old, I only have a fuzzy impression of what happened that year, as for Zhao, I don't have a very detailed understanding . . . But today, while I was eating, my grandmother said, "Zhao Ziyang died, why isn't the news or the papers reporting it?" I was curious, so I went searching on the Internet, but I found that I couldn't open many websites, which made me think something was strange. It was extremely difficult to even find this website, but after reading it, I was shocked . . . I now can't help but feel worried about the future of our country.

Another message said, "I'm too young, I don't understand the reasons or the results, I pay a silent tribute. This morning I couldn't connect to any overseas websites, and I realized that something had happened. What I really don't understand is . . . [why it's necessary to put so much effort into] blocking all overseas websites, it's as though they have a guilty conscience." Yet another said, "I live in Guangzhou, and that night I wasn't able to access two Hong Kong TV stations, so I realized immediately that something major had happened, it turns out that general secretary Zhao had died! . . . In this era, how much longer can you block information?" Another wrote, "Putting aside Zhao's merits and faults for the time being, we have already completely lost the right to speak, and to hear about him! What kind of world is this?"

These discussions helped link people who needed information with those who were happy to provide it. One person would appeal to other netizens to uncover the truth: "I still don't really understand, because in '89 I was only four years old, can someone senior to me please let me know what happened in that year? What is the truth? Thank you." Someone else would ask, "Is there anywhere that has a detailed report [on Zhao]? A lot of websites are blocked!" and others would post Web addresses or links to accessible sites along with pointers about which were the most valuable. Someone wrote, "Thank you, Internet, for giving us one last place to speak!" Some comments were in reference to a discussion thread that disappeared soon afterward.

But then other sites likely appeared in its place, populated by Chinese who were determined to preserve Zhao's memory. As one person wrote, "Under Communist Party tutelage, there aren't many young people who remember Zhao. Please allow me to represent young people by saying: . . . 'The people won't forget you, history won't forget you!'"

"WHO ARE OUR ENEMIES? WHO ARE OUR FRIENDS?"

The genesis of Anti's pen name came from a story that he wrote for Cissie, the woman who would eventually become his wife. Anti and Cissie met in an English-language study group in Wuxi. At the time, Anti was twenty-one, but Cissie was sixteen and still in high school. They dated on and off, and Anti had various other girlfriends, some of whom, he told me, he can "hardly remember." Before Anti went to pursue a Nieman Fellowship at Harvard in 2007, he and Cissie decided to get married.

In the early phase of their courtship Anti wrote a love letter to Cissie that took the form of a story. The protagonists of the story were a shepherd boy named Michael and a cat named Anti, who always opposed everything. On the Internet, the real-life Anti learned that he had power not only to oppose, but to persuade. "I found I had an ability to do that. Convince people. That's the beginning of my career," he said. "You should have the ability to convince the uncertain majority."

Although China's political system does have non-Communist parties, at least nominally, it is generally considered to be a one-party state. Anti's online universe, in contrast, was a complex map of political identities. There was a split between the leftists who support communism and the rightists who do not. But it didn't end there. Within the rightists there is a crucial division between the *minzhupai* (the democrats) and the *ziyoupai* (the liberals). The democrats, of which Anti is a proud member, believe that China needs a new, democratic system. The liberals prefer to reform the current system.

These differences manifested themselves in debates over the Chinese Constitution, for example. When some netizens advocated reforming the Constitution, Anti argued that this would not address the lack of basic justice. "Over the long run, if we lack justice, a bigger volcano will just erupt," he wrote. In 2011 Han Han, an enormously popular blogger, author, and race car driver, wrote "On Democracy," "On Revolution," and "On Freedom," in which he made clear that he was in favor of working within the current system rather than overthrowing it. "There is no point in frustrating oneself by dreaming about democracy and freedom in our study rooms. Reform is the best answer," Han Han wrote. For Anti, this placed Han Han firmly in the liberal camp.

Anti loved a good debate, but he found that some arguments were pointless. He didn't want to argue with the leftists, for example, who still extolled the Communist system. "I really only argue very seriously with liberal comrades," he told me. "I don't give a shit about leftists. They are on the losing side. I don't want to waste my time."

Sometimes I challenged Anti by assuming the position of someone who disagreed with him. When he seemed confused by this approach, I taught him the English term "devil's advocate." The concept was utterly novel to him. He immediately translated the phrase into Chinese, delighting in the absurd-sounding *mogui de lüshi*, or devil's lawyer. Yet when I actually played devil's advocate, Anti would grow uneasy and suspicious. It didn't make sense: Why would I ask a question if I didn't believe its premise to be true?

If I opened questions with such statements as "Some argue that the Internet is not going to transform China" or "Well, the Communist Party's argument would be . . . ," Anti would stiffen, and his eyes would narrow. Other journalists don't ask those kinds of questions, he would warn me. That's when I knew that hovering above us was the threat of ultimate condemnation: You don't understand China. I eventually learned that there was no place for a devilish lawyer in Anti's rhetorical universe. You were either his comrade or you were not.

It might seem strange that such a zealous democrat would embrace a word like "*tongzhi*," or comrade, which has such a Communist flavor (in recent years, "*tongzhi*" has also been used to describe homosexuals). When I mentioned the term's Communist connotations to Anti, he shrugged and said it was the only word that came to mind. In fact, Anti's declaration "Now I know who my comrades are" was bizarrely reminiscent of Mao Zedong's own words: "Who are our enemies? Who are our friends? This is a question of the first importance for the revolution." I gingerly

pointed this out to Anti, expecting him to explode at being compared to Mao. But to my surprise, Anti said that this was one
thing Mao got right. This is the "most important thing if you really
practice politics," Anti told me—"who is your enemy and who is
your friend. That's the reason I am so against the Party. I will
never compromise with them."

"I TRIED TO ORGANIZE"

Anti's catapult to world fame began in late 2005, when his
Microsoft-hosted blog was closed down. Although he was still
relatively unknown outside China, he was already beginning to
establish himself as a journalist. Anti was also stirring up trouble
on the Web. He started blogging on Microsoft's MSN Spaces
platform only after his previous blog was blocked in China. What
made international headlines was the fact that his blog was shut
down not by the Chinese government, but by Microsoft itself.

Anti, then thirty-one, had been writing on the Internet since
1998. Sure, he had been censored in the past, but he had no intention of getting arrested. Self-censorship, he once told me, was
in his blood. He could intuitively find the Party's bottom line.
What he hadn't realized was that Microsoft had a bottom line as
well. As he explained to me, "I had no idea that an American
company would remove my entire blog."

But it did. And so in 2005 Anti was thrust into the center of
an increasingly heated conversation about the conduct of foreign
Internet companies in China. In theory, Western technology
companies were supposed to be transforming China by providing

greater access to information. In practice, it appeared to be the other way around. China was influencing Western companies by compelling them to play by local censorship rules.

Microsoft shut down Anti's blog in response to a request by Chinese authorities to the company's Shanghai-based affiliate. This was most likely related to Anti's heated blog post about a journalist strike at the *Beijing News*. That December, one hundred journalists from the *Beijing News* went on strike to protest the firing of the paper's editor in chief, Yang Bin, and two of his deputies. Replacements for the fired editors were to be decided by the *Guangming Daily*, the more straitlaced parent of the *Beijing News*.

The *Beijing News* had been pushing the envelope. Earlier that year it reported on the violent suppression of protests against the construction of a power plant in the southern Hebei Province. In general, 2005 was not a good year for freedom of expression in China. Many feared that President Hu Jintao, who replaced Jiang Zemin as president in 2003, was tightening his grip over the media. Just a few days before the journalists' strike, Zhao Yan, a Chinese researcher for *The New York Times*, was indicted for disclosing "state secrets," an accusation that was related to a 2004 *Times* report about Jiang's decision to give up the country's top military position. That same month, an editor at the *Southern Metropolis Daily* lost his job because of a report about a Chinese official who had been punished for a deadly coal mine accident.

Anti, a journalist himself, took all this rather personally. He had reported for the *Huaxia Times* and another southern newspaper called the *21st Century World Herald*, which sent him to Baghdad for a week to report on the Iraq War. In 2003 Chinese officials shut down the *21st Century World Herald* after it published politically sensitive content. Anti then went to work as a researcher at *The New York Times* in Beijing.

He didn't think that Chinese readers should just sit around and watch their media get reined in, so when the *Beijing News* journalists decided to protest the firings by going on strike, Anti called on his blog readers to support them.

On December 29, 2005, he reminded his readers that the new year would arrive in two days' time. Subscribers to the *Beijing News* had already paid for the following year, but they would not be getting the product they had ordered. Instead, the original *Beijing News* editors were to be replaced by people from the more conservative *Guangming Daily*. Anti made it very clear how he felt about this development. "To be honest, I'd rather eat shit than subscribe to the *Guangming Daily* or any of its variants," he wrote on his blog. He proceeded to call on people to telephone the *Beijing News* and cancel their subscriptions. He even included a phone number: 63190000.

In the same blog post Anti called on advertisers, who would ostensibly lose the quality readers of the *Beijing News*, to phone the paper and demand to be paid for their losses. He asked lawyers to help readers file a class action suit against the newspaper for its deceptive practices.

Anti made it clear that this was not only about the *Beijing News*. Citizens had to stand up for their rights. Taking action would "prove we are not pigs to be slaughtered," he wrote. He then appealed to his more pragmatic Chinese readers: "This is a market society, and we have an inherent constitutional right to defend our wallets."

In the post, Anti did not hurl direct insults at the Chinese leadership. He didn't necessarily provide new or secret information. Instead, he did something far more dangerous: he called for collective action. "I called on people to cancel their subscriptions to the *Beijing News*. I tried to organize" was how he explained his blog's shutdown to me. Anti's blog post concluded with words that—to a state terrified of calls to coordinated action—were among the most sensitive in the entire text: "Please repost this. Please call 63190000."

Anti's post was greeted by a variety of reader comments. There were expressions of sympathy with his position: "Defending the freedom of speech is the life of a journalist. If we just watch the enemy occupation of *Beijing News* without doing anything, soon this enemy occupation will turn to you." Some expressed their willingness to take a stand: "I never subscribed to *Beijing News*, but now I will never read this newspaper." Another reader announced plans to unsubscribe, saying that if the *Beijing News* didn't offer a refund, "I will tell the newspaper delivery person to just skip my house and deliver the paper directly to the recycling station." One reader expressed bewilderment: "I am a senior in high school, my family has subscribed to *Beijing News* since 2003, I don't understand why they are dismissing the editor in chief? Is it because *Beijing News* didn't flatter the Communist Party? Or did it report something it shouldn't be reporting?" Not everyone was comfortable with Anti's aggressive style. One commenter asked, "I can understand your rage, but is it necessary to be this extreme?" Among the commenters was a self-described staff member of the *Beijing News* who did not appreciate the suggestion that continuing to work at the paper was equivalent to being a *Guangming* lackey. Nor did this staff member support Anti's appeal for everyone to unsubscribe. "I very much respect your personal right to unsubscribe, but I hope you can have at least a little respect for other people's rights to choose," the commenter wrote.

In any event, the conversation on Anti's blog soon came to an abrupt end. On December 30, the day after he posted his call for action, he found that he couldn't access his own blog. He later learned that without warning, his blog had been deleted. Because he had so completely trusted Microsoft, which stored his blog on servers based in the United States, he hadn't bothered to back up any of the files.

Anti had moved to Microsoft after his previous blog was blocked in China. That blog was hosted on Blog-City, which was also hosted in the United States. The difference is that Blog-City was blocked by the Great Firewall, not deleted by the company itself. Anti's previous blog was apparently blocked after he posted an open letter by a journalist named Li Datong. Li, the managing editor of Freezing Point, a section of the *China Youth Daily*, lost his job after publishing a letter condemning Chinese media censorship. After Anti posted the letter, all of Blog-City became inaccessible in China. Anti wrote on his new Microsoft blog, "Here I apologize to all Blog-City users, but of course it is the China Youth Daily and CCP who are responsible."

An interview in early 2005 sheds light on Anti's faith in Microsoft as a trusted resort if other blogging platforms fell through: "If they ban Blog-City, there is still MSN," Anti told Deutsche Welle, a German broadcaster. "Many friends have left blogcn and blogchina to go to MSN. The world is not far away."

Microsoft's move shouldn't have been so surprising. Foreign companies need to tread carefully in China if they wish to survive. In 2002 more than a hundred companies signed a pact to promote "self-discipline" in China's Internet industry. Microsoft in particular had already been criticized for filtering such sensitive words as "democracy" and "human rights" in its Chinese blog posts. Microsoft argued that this was the price of doing business on the mainland. "While this is a complex and difficult issue," Brooke Richardson, a group product manager for MSN in Seattle, told *The New York Times*, "we remain convinced it is better for Microsoft and other multinational companies to be in these markets with our services and communications tools, as opposed to not being there."

This line of argument was familiar. Western companies were

increasingly under fire for cooperating with Chinese censorship. The most egregious example took place in 2005, when a thirty-seven-year-old journalist and democracy advocate named Shi Tao received a ten-year prison sentence for posting an anonymous message to Democracy Forum, a Chinese-language website based in the United States. According to Chinese authorities, the post contained information that fell under the broadly defined category of "state secrets."

Shi sent this message from a computer at his workplace, using his Yahoo! email account. Yahoo! would have seemed safer than a domestic Chinese email service. In theory, Chinese state security would not have been able to identify the writer of an anonymous post on a foreign website. Yahoo! assisted with this task, claiming the company could not ask local employees to resist lawful demands, even if Yahoo! didn't necessarily agree with the law. The American company provided records that detailed when and from where Shi sent the post. This information helped pave the way for his conviction.

Then, in 2006, less than a month after Anti's MSN blog disappeared, Google launched a search engine, Google.cn, that was custom-made for mainland China. This meant that if you were inside China and searched for news about such banned terms as Falun Gong or the 1989 crackdown on student protesters at Tiananmen Square, not all links would come up. The links would be removed by Google itself, whose local staff reportedly worked with Chinese officials to ensure that search results would not deliver information that would be offensive to Beijing. In an attempt at transparency, Google posted a disclaimer indicating that the search results users were receiving were not complete.

Google, which conducted business under a "don't be evil" mantra, was particularly vulnerable to charges of hypocrisy. On January 27, 2006, Andrew McLaughlin, the company's senior policy counsel, wrote in a blog post, "Launching a Google domain that restricts information in any way isn't a step we took lightly. For several years, we've debated whether entering the Chinese market at this point in history could be consistent with our mission and values."

Google decided to take this controversial step, McLaughlin explained, because their previous service in China had been so poor. Google.com, which was hosted on servers abroad, would often be either shut down or painfully slow to access. The only way to solve this bad service problem, Google argued, was to create a local presence. And creating a Chinese presence meant following Chinese rules. McLaughlin wrote, "Our continued engagement with China is the best (perhaps only) way for Google to help bring the tremendous benefits of universal information access to all our users there."

In February 2006 Yahoo!, Microsoft, Google, and Cisco were the subjects of lawmakers' wrath at a U.S. congressional hearing. Representative Christopher Smith of New Jersey, a Republican, slammed the companies for their "sickening collaboration" with the Chinese government. Representative Tom Lantos, a California Democrat, added, "I do not understand how your corporate leadership sleeps at night." In 2010 Google, apparently fed up with censorship and hacking, shut down its Chinese search service and redirected users to its uncensored Hong Kong–based site. Yahoo! and Microsoft have also experienced setbacks in China, yet none of these companies has been willing to abandon such an important market.

Even Anti ultimately expressed sympathy with Microsoft. Microsoft, after all, had contributed to the explosion of voices on the Chinese Internet. As of early 2006, Microsoft had an estimated 3.3 million blogs in China. In 2008 Anti acknowledged that at the time, he was angry with Microsoft for taking down his blog. He added, "But still, I will appreciate everything Microsoft did [for] the Chinese people."

"I SPEAK IN COMPLICATED SENTENCES THAT
MY COMRADES CAN UNDERSTAND"

Anti believed that journalists should try to speak directly to the public. But among his comrades he preferred to communicate in a kind of code. "I speak in complicated sentences that my comrades can understand, but my enemies cannot," he once told me. This language was based on a shared set of references, both literary and historical, much of it shaped by the ideas of Western thinkers whom Anti would invoke to support his arguments. In one online post he wrote, "Now when we look back at [Friedrich] Hayek and Karl Popper's warning about socialist sentiments in the old days, we have no choice but to bitterly smile." He also wrote, "I still want to remind the faithful of Hayek's original intention: he spent his whole life resisting the power of authorities who want to control everything."

Unless you read Friedrich Hayek, Anti told me, "you don't fulfill the common criteria for being a democrat." Comrades needed to know the history of Nelson Mandela and South African democracy as well as the works of the Czech dissident turned president Václav Havel, such as *Living in Truth*, and the human rights document Charter 77. And of course there were Orwell's *Animal Farm* and *1984*.

But Anti said some of the most important literature for China's pro-democracy netizens is the work of a Chinese couple known as Lin Da, who spent years living in the rural United States. In a breezy, conversational style, Lin Da explains the American political system to Chinese readers.

Anti wrote in a BBS post that *The President Is Unreliable*, the title of one of Lin Da's books, have become key words for Chinese people to understand American democracy. "Whenever we talk about America, we talk in terms of the picture this book gave us," Anti said.

The President Is Unreliable is written in the form of a letter from a Chinese person living in the United States to his friend in China. It focuses on the U.S. Constitution and the checks and balances between the three branches of government. Unlike in China, where the leadership is essentially above reproach, Lin Da describes how the U.S. Congress would express different opinions from the president: "The same 'government' is almost simultaneously delivering different information. This behavior of not caring about the government's external image is very confusing, especially for those from the East who care the most about 'face.'" Lin Da also marveled at how the U.S. president was "dancing on a grassland filled with landmines" in that he is even more vulnerable to lawsuits than the average citizen.

In Anti's view, literary references become a coded language among the online dissident class. One example is a phrase from Hu Feng's poem "Shijian kaishi le" ("Time Has Begun"). The first installation of the poem was published in the official *People's Daily* shortly after the founding of the People's Republic of China. Hu Feng eventually fell out of favor with the leadership, but his poem was not originally a message of dissent, as it was actually written in praise of Mao Zedong, the people of the revolution, and the bright new era that was about to begin. When Hu Feng said "time has begun," he was championing the arrival of the new regime. When the opposition to China's Communist Party used the same phrase, they might also have been calling for a new regime.

If you read the right materials, Anti declared, "you can speak Democrat." Furthermore, the specific titles were far less important than the fact that his comrades were reading them together. Anti pointed to Leo Strauss, who talked about how philosophical texts can be read in multiple ways. Anti explained, "Every book is not revolutionary, but if you keep reading it in a certain way, it will become revolutionary."

"I EXPRESS WHAT THEY WANT TO SAY BUT CANNOT WRITE DOWN"

If Anti was the preacher of the Chinese Internet, using soaring rhetoric to extol the virtues of free speech and democracy, He Caitou was the storyteller. His blog posts were laced with metaphor, emotion, and literary detail—in which an ordinary bathtub is as clean and white as jade, and the hot water that pours out of the faucet sounds like thunder.

Anti introduced me to He Caitou (pronounced "huh sigh-toe") in 2009. They seemed nothing alike. While Anti was jumpy and lean, He Caitou was pudgy and balding, with glasses, thick lips, and a baby face. Anti spoke in sharp angles and soaring prose, while He Caitou chose his words carefully. When we first met, He Caitou worked as an editor at the blogging site of Tencent, which in 2013 was China's biggest publicly listed Internet company by market capitalization. When he came to meet me at a Beijing Starbucks, he was wearing a company ID around his neck.

He Caitou first struck me as pleasant and mild, two qualities I didn't associate with star Chinese bloggers. The Chinese Internet story was blowing up, and so were local egos. Western journalists were enchanted by the idea of courageous, envelope-pushing

Chinese bloggers, and the bloggers knew it. So by 2009 I came to expect a few things from a meeting with an influential Chinese netizen. In winter, he would wear a puffy coat with a fur-trim hood. He spent most of our time staring at his smartphone or his laptop. If I challenged his assertions or asked questions whose answers seemed too obvious, he would imply that I didn't understand China. He would complain about other Chinese bloggers, saying things like "he's a bad writer," "he's arrogant," "he'll inform on you to the police," or some version of "he doesn't understand China." And yes, he would most likely be male. This was apparently because, as Anti breezily explained, "women don't understand technology."

He Caitou, aside from his puffy jacket and furry hood, seemed different. Most netizens I met in Beijing had little interest in Internet dissidents outside China. He Caitou, on the other hand, appeared to be sincerely fascinated by this phenomenon. At our first meeting, he took a piece of paper and drew a map of the world dotted by candles, representing the voices of freedom.

This is not to say that He Caitou would call himself a dissident. With his Tencent ID around his neck, he looked more like a corporate employee than an online provocateur. And when we did discuss matters like freedom of speech, He Caitou certainly didn't sound like Anti. "Chinese people don't care about freedom," he said plainly. Then he added, "But they do care about justice. And justice needs true words."

He Caitou and Anti had been reading each other on BBS for years, and He Caitou later told me that he was deeply impressed by Anti's attempt to create a new kind of journalist. "Both he and I knew that there was no such thing as 'news' in China," He Caitou said. He read Anti's journalism manual and thought, "Somebody is doing something obviously impossible." Such a person deserved respect.

By 2009 He Caitou was already a popular blogger. He said he

had 350,000 email subscribers and 15,000 visitors every day. He actually had three blogs, all with the same content. Two were hosted on servers in the United States and one in China. This meant that two of his blogs were based outside China and weren't subject to Chinese law. The one inside China was actually hosted by his friend, who had registered as an Internet content provider.

He Caitou was careful to maintain a certain level of balance on his blog so that he would not be branded as politically radio-active. "If I write that something is unfair, like tearing down houses, I post ten articles about entertainment," he said. None-theless, popularity had its price. Over the years He Caitou has heard that his former BBS activity and the fact that he has tens of thousands of Twitter followers got him on the official radar. In late 2009 his two U.S.-based blogs were blocked by the Great Firewall. When I asked him why, he simply responded, "I will never think about it." He explained that the thought process would just lead to self-censorship.

As we were getting to know each other, He Caitou didn't make any particularly controversial statements. Rather, he enthused about his iPhone, which he liked to use to access the Internet. So I didn't understand why other Chinese netizens kept issuing cryptic warnings. One bitterly referred to him as "a tyrant who didn't happen to be in power." When I asked what he meant, he turned his head and snapped, "I don't want to talk about it." I also heard, "Be very careful, He Caitou is a master of the Chinese language" and, even more enigmatic, "he's not capable of telling the truth."

I only later understood that this was probably a reference to censorship. He Caitou may have been a provocative blogger in his free time, but he also worked for a major Chinese Internet com-pany. And everyone knows that working within the system means playing by the system's rules. Which meant that one of China's more popular bloggers was also a censor.

"I'VE BEEN SCARED ALL MY LIFE"

"I've been scared all my life," He Caitou once told me. "We always have all kinds of things to be scared about. Don't say sensitive words. Do not criticize."

He Caitou, born as He Jian, uses his pen name on the Internet. He kept "He," his real surname. "Caitou" is a pickled vegetable dish that he ate while growing up in Yunnan Province.

"I will use this fake name my whole life," he said. "It makes me feel safe." I pointed out that it only takes a brief online search to find his real identity. He didn't flinch. "I take a piece of paper in front of my face and pretend people can't see me," he explained. "But still, you feel better with this piece of paper. Now it's hard to tell if there is a difference between my real name and my fake one."

He Caitou learned the art of caution from his parents, who still bore the scars of the Cultural Revolution. His father was the first in his family to go to university. He dreamed of becoming a physicist. But in Mao's China, ordinary people didn't dream for themselves. And so it was decided: his father would build nuclear weapons. He watched scientists fight each other in an attempt to demonstrate who had a better understanding of Mao Zedong's thought. He also saw great thinkers betray each other to prove their loyalty to Mao. When farmers fight each other, "they just use their fists," He Caitou said, "but intelligent people set traps."

He Caitou's mother, however, admired Mao. She was one of ten children, but only four of them survived. She was the only girl left, and her family did not have money to support her. She quit high school and became a farmer, and this turned into an opportunity. Mao scoured the farms looking for a new generation of leaders. He Caitou's mother was a chosen one. She was sent to become a construction worker in Dongchuan city in Yunnan Province, and later to Kunming, where she would study Maoist theory and train to be a future leader. She felt indebted to Mao. If it were not for him, she would still be a farmer and never would have had a chance to live in Kunming, the capital of Yunnan.

He Caitou's father went to Kunming for the spring festival and met He Caitou's mother at a party. She was a healthy, red-cheeked girl with long black hair. They married, but spent only one month of the year together in Kunming. When He Caitou was a year old, his father was sent to make nuclear weapons in the far western province of Xinjiang. He took his son with him because He Caitou's mother was one of the youngest in her family and had no experience looking after babies.

His father felt that he could handle it because "he was a man," He Caitou explained. So the young He Caitou went off to Xinjiang, an isolated military place, and he and his father had a lot of time to talk. He remembers a river surrounded by small mountains. One of the mountains was made of red rocks. One day his father took him to view a test of a nuclear bomb. They watched from the balcony of his father's Soviet-style gray office building. He Caitou still remembers the view of the bomb. "We were far away from the test ground, and black smoke rose up," he said, his voice tinged with awe.

The majority of Chinese are Han ethnicity, but He Caitou's father is Bai, one of the fifty-six ethnic groups recognized by the Chinese government. In 2000 the Bai population of China was less than 2 million, and they generally lived in the Yunnan area. "Bai" is Chinese for "white," as the Bai people were traditionally known to favor white clothing and decorations. He Caitou described his father as a tall, thin man who was strong and fast. Once, he was amazed to see his father catch a small brown bird with his bare hands. His father, not realizing his own strength, accidentally killed the bird with his grasp.

In the 1980s He Caitou and his father returned to Kunming, which was still a very traditional place. As a teenager, He Caitou had a sense that he thought differently from his peers. He felt displaced, as if he were the last "dinosaur on earth."

When he was around fifteen, he went on a class trip to visit the tomb of Nie Er, composer of "March of the Volunteers," the national anthem of the People's Republic of China. He Caitou was annoyed that China still honored this man, and he didn't hesitate to say so to his classmates. "We should pay more attention to the great generals who suffered at the hands of the Japanese. We always forget them," he informed the class. Nie Er, He Caitou pointed out, didn't even die in a particularly honorable way. "This guy just drowned," he said. His classmates were shocked.

He Caitou won a reputation as "cynical," but he still managed to be popular. "To be popular is a very easy thing," he said. "You talk about beer, gambling, girls." When he was younger, he used his influence to shake things up. In China, from primary school right up to high school, one student is named *ganbu*, which is a kind of class leader. That person is supposed to keep an eye on the other classmates. If he sees someone cheating in school, for example, he writes down that person's name and informs the teacher. Then the teacher, as He Caitou put it, does not hesitate to "beat your ass."

At one of his class meetings He Caitou declared to his teacher that the *ganbu* system was unfair. He thought the *ganbu* should be democratically elected rather than appointed by the teacher. It was 1991. The teacher was stunned, but felt that the request was reasonable. The election was held, and He Caitou became *ganbu*. Suddenly, he said, informing on other students ceased. The balance of power between the students and the teacher shifted. The teacher slowly improved. The class, in turn, behaved and even surpassed other classes in the grade. People did their best because "it was a question of honor," He Caitou said. "It gave me a deep impression that people can manage themselves."

But He Caitou didn't have political ambitions. Ever since he was a boy, his father had driven home the following messages: Believe in science and technology. Stay away from politics. Keep your hands clean. This is similar to what Anti grew up believing: Literature is dangerous. Science is safe. Ironically, the result of these lessons was the creation of two computer geeks whose technological skills helped them become China's earliest active netizens.

Anti described China's late-1990s Internet scene as a very small group of *wangmin*, most of whom were "close to IT technology. Otherwise you have no chance at all." Like Anti, He Caitou also bought individual parts and got someone to assemble his first computer. It was a plain white box, with a 16-bit color screen that was just "a little better than black and white." His Internet life began in 1997, when he and his friends would break into the university lab at night and play the Internet game Diablo with people from other countries. It was especially fun to battle with the Japanese. "We were so young, stupid, and patriotic," he said.

He Caitou eventually bought his parents two computers. His parents worried about his online writing, in particular a blog post in which he criticized those who are starry-eyed about Communist ideals. The post's language was often indirect, but the general message was clear. He Caitou referred to the founding of the People's Republic of China: "In 1949 someone wrote a check to the people." Many years later, he wrote, most people have given up hope that this check will be honored. "The promise is one thing, the reality is another."

His parents said, "Your blog is too critical. This is not a game you can play." He Caitou's parents' fears were largely rooted in the past. They didn't discuss the Cultural Revolution in detail, "they just say it is tragedy," He Caitou said. They avoided direct persecution by trying not to get involved. One main lesson, which they passed on to their son, was that you should never forget that you are alone in the world. You may think you know a person's face or his heart, but you don't. The whole world wants to hurt you.

In Mao's China, friends hesitated to share information that could eventually be used against them. Such details as house furnishings or eating habits could suggest that someone was not truly a member of the proletariat. "They have seen the worst of human beings," He Caitou said of his parents. "I grew up with this kind of lesson. The world is full of taboos. Do not touch this, do not touch that."

But, he said, his parents have nothing to worry about. "I'm not a protester. I have no organization." As for politics, he added, "I never think it's a game I can play. I'm trying my best not to get involved."

"JUST LIKE IN A JAILBREAK, THERE'S A HOLE IN THE WALL"

On the Internet, He Caitou found a reprieve from the tedium and solitude of daily life. In 1997 he graduated from Nanjing University. He studied meteorology, a decision that was made by his university, not him. "I don't believe we can forecast the weather," he said plainly. Nevertheless, for the next two years he worked as a weather forecaster for Yunnan Airlines in Kunming. He would periodically step out of his office to record details about the temperature, precipitation, and air pressure. He would put this information into a message that the pilot received in his cabin. "Nobody knows who you are. Nobody cares about you," He Caitou said.

By the end of 1999 he was transferred to Shangri-La, a county in Yunnan Province. He was still at Yunnan Airlines, working on technical support and weather forecasting. In 2002 Yunnan Airlines became part of China Eastern Airlines, and He Caitou came back to Kunming to work as a flight dispatcher. He stayed there until 2006, and in 2008 he moved to Lijiang, also in Yunnan Province.

Eager for a break from the tedium of everyday life, in 2000 he discovered BBS sites. He particularly liked CYOL.net, the BBS of the *China Youth Daily* newspaper. He got into all sorts of debates with other netizens, including about whether the Chinese were capable of choosing their own government. Remembering his experience with *ganbu* elections in high school, He Caitou vigorously argued that they were.

"We would write thousands of words a night, debating each other," he said of his early online experiences. "We tried our best to express ourselves. If we got into a fight, and I could not beat you down and you could not beat me down, we became good friends. It is a shortcut to getting to know who someone really is." In the beginning He Caitou and other netizens would sometimes chat in English because "language would become a filter for the most qualified people." Besides, English felt safer than Chinese.

Thanks to the Internet, he found himself leading two lives, one far superior to the other. "One life is doing a fucking boring job, day after day, year after year." In the other life, which he found online, "I met a lot of interesting people, we argued, we shared opinions, we made friends, we traveled together."

The camaraderie He Caitou found online didn't extend to real life. In Beijing, when we were out in public, sometimes he suddenly switched from Chinese to English. "Your Chinese is good, you understand," he would explain, his eyes quickly scanning the room. "But you never know." Another time, when we were talking about his friends in Beijing, He Caitou said, "I could take you to a party, but maybe it wouldn't be so good for you." I asked him why. "Because no one would say anything," he said. "We don't trust each other." I eventually learned that I too had passed a basic screening before he started talking to me. First of all, I had come to him via Anti. He also knew I was a friend of Yu Hua, a novelist he admires.

Real-life friends, he said, may not have the opportunity to get close. They may go to a bar together, but after they turn thirty, they go home to their families and their separate lives. Netizen relationships are far more resilient. "I spend years observing them, what they say, what they do," He Caitou said. "We know each other better than friends you know in real life."

"The Internet rebuilds the ability to trust other people," he once told me. "That's why I love the Internet." He explained: "Just like in a jailbreak, there's a hole in the wall. When you go through the hole to the other side and you find people, you tend to trust them because you know they have been in the same place. We have made the same attempt to escape."

"Why is my blog so popular? Not because I'm so good at writing," He Caitou said. "People think I am because I express what they want to say but cannot write down."

In a 2008 blog post called "The Endless Road," He Caitou describes his momentous decision to leave Kunming. He was thirty-three. He should have been settled down with a family by then. Instead, he left a secure job at a state-owned airline and took off for Beijing. He wasn't sure what he would do when he got there. He knew he was sacrificing a stable, predictable future.

He wrote on his blog that if he stayed, he would lead a life of "paying taxes, patriotism and learning Chinese chess for the father-in-law." He would read the newspaper and feel as if his little town weren't so far from the rest of the world. Eventually he would replace his television with a bigger one, and he would put a nicer speaker in his car. He would go fishing and pick fruit. And when he got old, he would walk into town like a retired king.

It may sound pleasant enough. And yet, He Caitou wrote, some people cannot resign themselves to this kind of life. The unknown is scary, but stasis is terrifying. Or, in his words, "even if the ocean swallowed countless people, and everyone was aware of this, there would be no smaller number of sailors and pirates." After spending more than a decade pretending that he was just a "normal person," he realized he was more like a sailor or a pirate.

So, eleven years after graduation, he wrote on his blog, he cast aside his career, his experience, and his professional contacts. In the post he evoked the American prison film *The Shawshank Redemption*, which also inspired Anti. Andy spent years digging through the wall of his prison, He Caitou wrote, "I spent 11 years and two months." Furthermore, his wall was at least half of his own building. He concluded the post, "In front of me is an unpredictable, endless road. I didn't know which direction it would lead me. But I already felt the winds of freedom, I saw the unfathomable blue."

Hundreds of readers responded to "The Endless Road." Many expressed fervent support. They congratulated He Caitou for his move and said "*jiayou!*" a Chinese expression of encouragement. One reader wrote, "Call me stupid because after I read this I wanted to cry." He Caitou believes that such readers may have harbored the same dream but were to afraid to take the first step.

Some commenters admitted that they had grappled with similar thoughts. One wrote, "I also quit, for the same reasons as He Caitou. If there is a path and you don't follow it once, you will always feel regret." One woman described how her husband quit his job at a bank to pursue a Ph.D., even though he was already thirty-one and the couple had a three-year-old child at the time. Now "all three of us are living happily in the Netherlands," she wrote. Not everyone was so lucky, of course, to be able to leave their stable lives behind. Some reacted to He Caitou's post with longing. One commenter wrote, "I'm also 33 years old, I have the same feeling, thank you for your truthful confession, but I can't be so free, I can give up my life, but my wife and son can not."

"WE ARE LIKE PLANTS WITHOUT ROOTS"

"I hate the past," Anti once told me. China had changed too much, too fast. Rather than trying to make sense of it, it was easier to just move on. "I choose to forget; otherwise I have no time to deal with the new thing," he explained.

Generally speaking, modern China is not terribly sentimental about the past. Mao famously destroyed historical and cultural artifacts in his attempt to rid the nation of bourgeois traditions. In the post-Mao era, historic architecture has been destroyed to make way for new real estate. People have been evicted from their homes so that the government can build development projects. Winding *hutongs*, or alleys, have been razed. The 2008 Beijing Olympics spurred even more frantic development. Since 2001 Beijing has funneled billions of dollars into infrastructure projects and Olympics venues while renovating entire neighborhoods.

By 2010 Anti and I no longer went to Houhai Lake. Instead, we would meet at a Starbucks in a brightly lit shopping mall, surrounded by Louis Vuitton and Cartier stores and well-dressed consumers drifting across the glossy floors. "It's more convenient," Anti explained. And he was right. But Beijing no longer felt familiar, and I constantly got lost, wandering halfheartedly through subway tunnels or mazelike shopping centers.

In 2013 I went to visit the campus where I lived in the 1990s. I walked down the path to my old dormitory. Yet instead of the little brick dorms, I found myself facing a slate-colored building. I went in and asked a friendly old guard if he had any idea what happened to my school. "Those little houses?" he said cheerfully. "*Dou chai le!*" All torn down!

He Caitou openly grieved for the past. He felt that China's modernization left people feeling like "plants without roots. It makes everyone feel homeless." He felt this dislocation acutely upon returning to the city of Kunming, where he grew up. He told me that as a boy, he would walk under the big leaves of *wutong* trees, also known as parasol trees. Even when it rained, He Caitou recalled, those trees would keep you dry. On Jingxing Street people sold birds, goldfish, and puppies. He remembered the sound of shoes clicking down the stone streets.

Now trees have been cut down, streets rebuilt, and houses demolished. The new city looks like "a woman who injected some Botox on her face," He Caitou said with disgust. The streets were also populated by new faces. He Caitou used to hear local dialects spoken on the street; now it seemed to be all Mandarin, the standard language of China.

"Things change too fast. Even my hometown. I came back after half a year, and things are torn down," He Caitou said. He no longer has anything in common with his old friends. They have all gone their separate ways, chasing their own ambitions. "It's getting harder to find common things to discuss. You come to your hometown to cure homesickness. There's no such thing here. So I'd rather stay in Beijing."

One of He Caitou's blog posts explores his feelings of alienation upon returning to Kunming for the mid-autumn festival. He starts the post by remembering his university days. He would take a long train ride to Kunming. When he got home, he would throw his luggage down and call friends to get together and drink or listen to music. Now he takes a short plane ride from Beijing. When he gets home, he plops down on the bed. He doesn't feel like seeing anyone or eating or drinking. He just wants to keep lying there, alone.

Finally, he ventures outside. The shops he used to know have turned into other shops or have disappeared entirely. The wide noodles taste the same, but he doesn't have the appetite he once had. He describes a street his friend had worked to build. Once you saw the stones in that street, you would immediately know that this friend was a true Kunming person. Each stone was carefully selected, and he spent countless hours making complex and exquisite patterns. He Caitou writes that the newly built street has become "coarse and vulgar."

He Caitou returns to his house, where he sweeps up some dust, takes off his shoes, and opens a window. There's a telephone, but nobody he wants to call. Outside the window there are no clouds, and the sky is almost "dripping with blue." Yet even in a densely populated city he is overwhelmed by a feeling of isolation. "This city has millions of doors, tens of millions of windows," he wrote on his blog. "A few days out of every year, I need to open one of these doors, sit beneath a window. Even if this city is filled with strangers, I will still come back and look for my door and window."

Like so many other Chinese, he left his hometown to pursue his dreams. He acknowledged in his blog that if he hadn't done so, he and his city could have changed together and "grown old together." But his nostalgia stops short of regret.

The blog post concludes with a reference to the 1994 Luc Besson film, *Léon: The Professional*, in which Léon, an assassin, takes the teenage Mathilda under his wing after her parents are killed. He Caitou's post includes a Chinese translation of dialogue from the movie. Mathilda asks, "Is life always this hard, or just when you are a kid?" Léon responds, "Always like this."

He Caitou couldn't stop his hometown from changing, but at least he could preserve its memory on his blog. I once asked him, who so often said that he didn't trust anyone, why he told me his story. He explained that things in China moved so fast, he didn't want his own life to disappear. "I try to tell someone. I try to prove that I'm existing in this world," he said. "I do exist in this world, because other people know my story."

"I CAUSED A LOT OF FIGHTS ON THE INTERNET"

He Caitou may have tried to avoid confrontation with the Chinese authorities, but he loved to provoke his fellow netizens. "Some people don't like me," he admitted. "Because my tongue is horrible. I hurt a lot of people. I caused a lot of fights on the Internet." In that sense, he didn't listen to his father's advice about keeping his head down. "I like fights," he said. "I like destroying taboos. I must make him very disappointed."

Nor did he subscribe to Western notions of political correctness. In 2009 he posted a cartoon on his blog depicting "evolution" in various countries. The cartoon was based on the "ape-to-man" illustration of evolution. In Africa, the ape evolved to become a larger ape. When this post was criticized by Charlie Custer, an American who at the time was teaching English in China, He Caitou went on the offensive, calling political correctness a "made in the USA" taboo. He wrote on his blog, "None of my race ever caught and shipped any single black man from Africa to China as [a] slave. So I can make fun of them, just as they can make fun of me."

An even bigger fight took place in September 2005, when He Caitou decided to take a stand against the dangerous mob mentality that was poisoning Internet life. The incident was sparked by a 2005 post on the popular BBS site Tianya Club. The author of the post claimed to be a twenty-year-old college student in Chongqing. Her father had died years earlier, and now her mother was dying of liver disease and desperately needed a liver transplant. Panicking over the high costs of surgery and follow-up treatment, the girl wrote on the Internet, "How I hope some good-hearted people will save my mom!!!" In exchange for kindness from strangers, she wrote, "I would sell myself in any manner or I'm willing to work for him/her unconditionally after I graduate." She included her phone number and email address in the post.

The post was greeted with a torrent of sympathy and support. Several people asked Chen Yi, the author of the post, to provide bank account information so that people could send donations. Once she did, donations started to come in. Local newspapers in Chongqing reported the story. By November she had received donations of more than 114,000 yuan.

But soon after the first post appeared, this seemingly heart-warming story took a drastic turn. A netizen named Lan Lian'er chimed in on the BBS discussion, claiming to know Chen Yi personally. Lan accused Chen Yi of being far from the impoverished student she appeared to be. She owned the latest models of Nike and Adidas shoes and even had expensive contact lenses. Readers sprang to attention. Was this girl abusing the trust of the netizen community?

Onto the scene came a netizen called Ba Fen Zhai. He demanded that Chen Yi publish her bank account and allow her donations to be managed by a charity organization. When she didn't reply, he decided to travel to Chongqing to undertake his own "independent investigation." He wrote, "Goodwill must not be allowed to be trampled upon."

So on October 9 Ba Fen Zhai flew to Chongqing. Several members of the Tianya online community met him there. They interviewed Chen Yi and her mother. They visited Chen Yi's dorm and her family's apartment. They studied her bank account. Ba Fen Zhai's report, which he called "the first independent investigation on the Chinese Internet" and was published in nine installments on Tianya during the month of October, claimed that there were problems with Chen Yi's original story.

Meanwhile, Ba Fen Zhai and his coinvestigator Jin Guanren became Internet heroes. They were praised online as "men who have the courage to do what they want to do." The Chinese Internet expert Yang Guobin observed that each new installment of Ba Fen Zhai's investigative report generated an outpouring of praise: "Many commentators said they saw hope in a corrupt world because there were still brave people fighting for justice."

He Caitou was horrified. He saw Ba Fen Zhai as an opportunist and a phony. In a series of scathing BBS posts, he ripped into Ba Fen Zhai and his admirers. He believed that after making donations to Chen Yi, netizens relinquished the right to ask how she spent this money. In one of his posts He Caitou spelled out the perverse logic of Chen Yi's investigators: "Because you received my kindness, therefore you must be subject to my malicious requirements. You must be ethically perfect, unable to tolerate even the most minor flaws. Otherwise, you are a liar. I gave you money, thus I have the right to judge you, and to occupy the moral high ground."

In one post He Caitou claimed to have read Ba Fen Zhai's "independent investigation." He commented that the report imparted crucial information—the weather is cold in Chongqing and people eat a lot of rice. What the report failed to illustrate were the basic facts about Chen Yi's mother's condition and whether she really needed donations. He Caitou wrote that he took away one message from Ba Fen Zhai's report: "This is the Chinese Internet's first independent examination!" He Caitou's post then proceeded, mockingly, to repeat that sentence dozens of times. "This is the Chinese Internet's first independent investigation!"

He Caitou didn't always take the high ground. In one post he wrote, "Brother Ba Fen has a very kind heart, but he looks like a pig butcher." In another instance he wrote, "This mother is dying! Someone is dying! . . . Where is the kindness? Where is the so-called dog shit morality?" Some of his criticisms of Ba Fen Zhai were laced with profanity and crude sexual references.

This incident highlighted a much larger issue. In a country with little faith in the rule of law, hordes of netizens often seek justice on their own. This allows those who are denied justice through the legal system to call attention to their plight. The downside is that those accused of a crime, whether wrongfully or not, end up defending themselves in the court of online opinion. This is what happened to Sun Wei, the main suspect in the poisoning of Zhu Ling, the poisoning victim mentioned earlier. Nobody had been convicted, but many netizens decided that Sun Wei, Zhu's roommate, was clearly guilty. Sun Wei reportedly had access to thallium and had undergone questioning by the police. Some believed she was driven by jealousy. The Internet teemed with rumors, accusations, and even efforts to hunt down Sun Wei. People believed that she escaped prosecution because her relatives were powerful government officials.

The online pressure became so fierce that in 2005 Sun Wei felt compelled to post a statement on the Tianya BBS site. "I am innocent," she wrote. "I am also a victim of the Zhu Ling case." Sun Wei compared Chinese netizens to the mobs of the past: "The unthinking and gullible blind obedience reached a peak during the Cultural Revolution, and resulted in a huge national disaster! On the Internet, even though everyone is just a virtual ID, one should still be rational and objective, and responsible for his own behavior."

———

When members of the Chinese online community decide that someone has violated their moral code, they will sometimes find that person and make sure he or she pays. This phenomenon is known by the creepy name of "human flesh searches," or *renrou sousuo*. In 2006 one famous case was sparked by a video of a stiletto-heeled woman stomping a brown-and-white kitten to death. Netizens asked one another if anyone recognized the woman or the background of the video. Newspapers and television picked up the story, and less than a week after the search began, someone wrote on an online forum that the woman lived in her small town. The cat stomper's name, Wang Jiao, became public, as did her phone number and employer. Wang, a nurse, was promptly fired from her job.

In 2007 Chinese Internet vigilantes struck again after a woman committed suicide and her sister made the dead woman's diary public on the Internet. The diary revealed that her husband had been unfaithful. Enraged netizens decided to hunt down the husband and his mistress. The husband's personal details were swiftly located and revealed, and he received harassing phone calls and even death threats. He and his girlfriend, coworkers at an advertising agency, ended up leaving their jobs.

In the case of the sick woman's daughter, Chen Yi, which made He Caitou so angry, the situation also spun out of control. It became a morality crusade. How could Chen Yi have lied to the online community? In their search for the truth, netizens hacked her personal email and IM records. One of these hackers wrote about breaking into Chen Yi's email in the middle of the night: "I know I shouldn't have done this, but I did it anyway." After reading four hundred emails in her account, the hacker discovered a few basic truths: Chen Yi's naïveté was real, the mother's illness was real, and so was the kindness of the netizens who donated.

While some netizens hailed the hackers as heroes, others were growing uneasy. Meanwhile, Chen Yi's mother died in surgery.

It appeared as if her decision to have this surgery, rather than wait for a liver transplant, was an attempt to clear her daughter's name. Moreover, Chen Yi turned out not to be the swindler people thought her to be. In November someone posted a message on the Tianya BBS site providing a detailed account of all the donations to Chen Yi. Of the 114,550 yuan she received, more than 40,000 yuan were spent on the surgery. The remainder was donated to a foundation for children with leukemia.

Years later, He Caitou was still furious about the whole fiasco. "The so-called investigation made no conclusion, but the mother was pushed to operate under the 'network of public opinion,'" he told me. The online community crossed a line, and He Caitou did not hesitate to let his fellow netizens know. "Now someone is dead, this isn't a procedural failure, it's murder," he wrote at the time, adding that Chen Yi's mother's death was "caused by a spectators' carnival, caused by Chinese-style crazed morality fans."

Anti says that on the Internet, "morality becomes a kind of currency" for judging people's worth. In a country whose courts are not guaranteed to deliver a fair result, netizens try to right the balance themselves. And when that fails, "you can only chase morality, which is most close to justice."

"THEY WANT TO KNOW THEY ARE NOT SO LONELY ON THIS PLANET"

He Caitou saw the Internet as the place where individuals could seek the sympathy and encouragement they couldn't find in real life. He may not have been a dissident, but he was a democrat in the sense that he believed that everyone should have a voice. With this in mind, in 2008 he created "tree hole," an anonymous online confessional for ordinary Chinese.

The name "tree hole," or *shudong*, is inspired by the tale of King Midas, who according to myth had a pair of donkey ears. The king was able to hide his donkey ears from everyone in the world, with the exception of his barber. In the version of the story that He Caitou knows, the barber understands that he should keep his mouth shut, but he ultimately finds that the secret is too much to bear, and he needs to relieve himself of the burden. So he tells the secret to a hole in a tree. Then the truth comes trumpeting out of the tree's branches, blasting "The king has donkey ears!" throughout the land.

He Caitou decided to create his own tree hole on the Internet. He asked people to email him their stories, and he posted them online, anonymously, on a website called *shudong*. He used his blog to promote the site.

He Caitou wanted to create a forum to discuss the problems that would not be aired by state media. In 2008, he said, "Lots of people lost their jobs, but no media would report their suffering." He created tree hole for those who had nowhere else to turn. This included people who were unable to get help from official channels, and also those with secrets they couldn't share with relatives, friends, or colleagues. People could cry into tree hole, He Caitou wrote on his blog, so that the next day they wouldn't "jump off a building."

The problems expressed on the tree hole site were all over the map. In one post a man talks about how he dropped out of high school and then found that he couldn't get a good job. So he bought a university diploma for 80 yuan. His wife believes that he has a real degree. He feels so bad about this deception that he tries to be extremely conscientious toward his family, even doing extra housework and putting in special effort at work. But when he was praised for being an excellent employee, he wrote, "This additional reward further increases the pain in my heart." He has trouble sleeping. In his dreams, he is called a liar. He has one source of solace: "When I tearfully speak into the tree hole, the feeling in my heart is a kind of personal salvation."

The anguished post was greeted with empathy. Netizens told him to stop beating himself up, especially as he was already working so hard. They encouraged him to come clean to his wife. "I feel your wife will understand you, she didn't marry you for a piece of paper," one commenter said. Another wrote, "You are a truly good person. Let your wife read this tree hole, she will love you even more."

One commenter wrote, "I have the same experience as you, I started to work when I was 18, now I am 28, I went through life with a fake diploma . . . My wife often comforts me and tells me not to feel pressured, these are just survival skills . . . maybe she is right." Another wrote, "In a society ruled by liars, one shouldn't live being overly critical of one's own behavior." Another advised him not to overstate the importance of a status symbol such as a diploma. "A Coca-Cola costs 3 yuan in a supermarket, but 5 yuan in a hotel. You are still the same you."

Tree hole was home to stories about economic pressures, suicide, and homosexuality. One person felt a lack of confidence stemming from a physical handicap. In one particularly scandalous post, a girl claimed to have had an affair with her biological father. In another entry, an employee complained that he couldn't live off his wages alone. So he, like many others, took kickbacks.

As editor of the site, He Caitou maintained control over its content. Letters from young men suffering from puppy love, for example, wouldn't make the cut. "This is not real pain, real suffering. So I just ignore these emails." He also avoided overtly political complaints, explaining that he was unable to confirm their veracity.

The tree hole community enjoyed a sense of solidarity. As one commentator said, "Half of the stories are about ordinary people: we all encounter small bitterness, it makes us feel that we ourselves are not alone." He Caitou wrote on his blog that tree hole allowed him to see "a hundred phases of life" and "the greatness of ordinary people."

He spoke of tree hole with great pride. "This is my second successful project on the Internet," he told me. "The first is my blog. I think I understand people and know what they want. They want to express themselves. They want someone to hear them. They want to know that they are not so lonely on this planet."

"THIS IS HOW I IMAGINE THE FEELINGS OF THE GUARDS"

In 2010 I went to Beijing for a U.S.-China economics conference. This got me a room in a fancy hotel, with chandeliers and the faint scent of flowers in the lobby. There were yoga classes and a breakfast buffet with sushi, stuffed buns, and bright pink dragon fruit. This pleasant dream was interrupted when I tried to connect to the Internet in my room and the following message flashed onto my laptop's screen:

> You are reminded to comply with all local laws, rules and regulations in connection with your Internet access, and you will be solely responsible for any breaches of the same. Please also be informed that your online activities (e.g. sites visited) may be required to be logged by local authorities. Further, some web

sites may be unavailable pursuant to local laws, rules and/or regulations.

We hope you enjoy the complimentary use of the service.

As intimidating as these messages can seem, in reality China is a blend of suffocating restrictions and countless loopholes. Earlier that week, when I went to China Mobile to buy a local SIM card for my mobile phone, a severe-looking woman intercepted me at the door.

"You'll need to show your passport," she said.

"I didn't have to do that last time," I responded, sounding more panicked than I would have liked. I would have remembered surrendering my U.S. passport to the country's state-owned telecommunication company.

"The rules have changed," she retorted. I had no illusion of phone security, but this seemed like going too far. While I was hesitating, the lady at the door suddenly softened, as sometimes happens in China, for no apparent reason.

"If you don't want to register, you can just go across the street and get the same SIM card from that *xiaomaibu*," she said, pointing out the window. I thanked her and went to the bodega, where I found a shy and shifty-eyed shopkeeper surrounded by magazines. He looked startled, as if I was disturbing a private moment. Then he pulled a China Mobile SIM card from a drawer. It was pretty much the same price as in the store. The card had some residue from where a sticker had been removed, but it worked fine.

I found it no more difficult to jump over the Great Firewall. I just asked Anti, who recommended buying a virtual private network (VPN). Fifteen minutes and $40 on my credit card later, I had my own virtual private network that allowed me to browse the Chinese Internet as if I were outside of China. I logged on to Twitter, and my feed lit up with Chinese tweets.

After I had secured a SIM card and a VPN, I went to meet He Caitou. I waited for more than an hour in my hotel lobby while his taxi muddled through Beijing traffic. When he finally arrived, he was dressed in all black, with a hooded sweatshirt under the usual down jacket with a fur-trim hood. He took me to a lush, dark bar where we sat on red velvet couches in our own spacious booth. A chandelier bled red glass droplets, and there was a big window frame lined with red-and-gold curtains. The window looked out onto a stone wall.

At first He Caitou spoke quickly, in Chinese. His stories snaked through the air and didn't always have a clear beginning or end. He spoke in a slow baritone, with the hint of a smile on his thick lips. He would occasionally scroll through the steady feed of emails and tweets on his mobile phone.

He Caitou had a dreamy, sentimental quality. His phone's dial tone was a version of "La Vie en Rose." He would order a bottle of red wine in the middle of the day. He also had ideas about how men and women should behave. He ordered beer for himself and some lemonade-type drink for me. Rather than offer me his Chinese cigarettes, which were apparently too harsh, he bought me a pastel-and-white box of the skinniest cigarettes I had ever seen.

Although he wrote poetic blog posts during his free time, his day job was in the heart of China's Internet machine. In 2008 he had joined Tencent—founded in 1998 by Ma Huateng, better known by the more colorful name of Pony Ma. Tencent is celebrated for its instant-messaging service, QQ. As of December 2012, Tencent had close to 800 million active instant-messaging user accounts. QQ also had a blogging platform, of which He Caitou was an editor. He decided the headline of the day and recommended Tencent blog posts to his readers. There were four major portals in China: Sina, Sohu, Netease, and Tencent. He Caitou said that finding the best user-generated content was key to beating the competition. His job was to choose "unique content from millions of blogs."

By lunch, He Caitou said, he had read hundreds of blogs. "People always feel that they are choked by countless news, so I have to be the filter of information and choose real news or good stories." He told me proudly that hundreds of millions of subscribers read his selections via RSS feeds over the course of a day, and tens of thousands would go directly to the QQ site. "They can share different points of view in comments; then they can get their topics for the dinner table conservation," he said.

He had more than a dozen members on his team. They all helped choose blog posts, edit reader comments, and decide the next day's hot topic. On Mondays, He Caitou said, when everyone was "full of energy," they would choose a social problem. One example of such a problem was the case of a female university student known by the name "Chanel." In 2009 Chanel, a student at Beijing Foreign Studies University, wrote a series of posts on her personal blog complaining that the national education system forced her to study a foreign language. She wrote, for example, "Foreign languages influence and decide the lives of Chinese citizens."

She then claimed that as a result of these complaints, the university forced her to withdraw. (The university denied this.) When QQ recommended her post on its blog home page, it caused a small uproar. I asked He Caitou why her writing caused such a commotion, and he said it was unusual to see a student at a top university challenge the education system. In describing the reaction to the piece, he said that he was "astonished" to discover that so many Chinese people didn't like the higher education system.

On Tuesdays, he said, he would try to choose a relationship problem. This could be, for example, tensions that stem from the one-child policy the government employed to control population growth. When two single children get married, and each set of parents lives in a different city, a horrible conflict can erupt over where to spend Chinese New Year. Wednesday and Thursday topics would depend on current events. Friday would be something lighter, like entertainment. Of course, nothing was static. He Caitou would watch the number of clicks on a particular article, and if there weren't enough, "we have to change right away."

It all sounded pleasantly apolitical. But it was no secret that someone in his position would likely have some hand in censorship or, as the Chinese euphemism puts it, "harmonizing" of content. Tencent's own mission statement says that the company "strives to help build a harmonious society." Chinese Internet users are bound to step over the line. And when that happens, editors will be told to delete sensitive comments or close down entire discussions.

It was in that same silly bar, amid the red velvet and the chandeliers, that I carefully asked He Caitou about his own role in censorship. "How does it make you feel?" I asked. The question sounded ridiculously American, even to me, but he answered right away.

"I feel horrible," he said. Then he said something that sounded like a clash of vowels. It was a foreign word, neither English nor Chinese.

"Auschwitz," he repeated. He paused. "This is how I imagine the feelings of the guards."

I was too stunned to respond. He smoked his cigarette quietly, thinking. He obviously understood the difference between Internet censorship and mass murder, and later he admitted that his analogy was somewhat flawed. But he wasn't speaking literally. The link he was trying to draw, at least as I understood it, was the terrible feeling of simply following orders.

Yet ultimately, pragmatism trumped idealism. In that sense

He Caitou was a true child of Deng Xiaoping. It doesn't matter if the cat is black or white, China's former leader famously said, as long as it catches mice.

"Then why do you do it?" I asked. "You don't have to work for a major Internet company."

"I used to work for a state-owned airline," He Caitou replied. "We lost too much money. I want to have my own Internet company one day."

"YOU HAVE TO PLAY BY CERTAIN RULES"

Later that year, He Caitou sent me a text message: "Come see my company." An hour or so cab ride later, we met on a Beijing street corner. He led me into the glossy lobby of what appeared to be a hotel. His office was across from a swimming pool. There were cubicles, some halfhearted plants, and harsh office lighting. We went into the conference room. A girl who worked in the office brought him tea in a plastic cup. She brought me a small paper cup of water, not making eye contact with either of us.

He Caitou was wearing black as usual and had a company ID around his neck, but no longer for Tencent. He was now the head of Fanfou, a Chinese Twitter clone that had been closed down a year earlier. Now Fanfou was back in business, with some twenty employees. I also noticed that He Caitou was wearing a yellow-gold wedding ring.

He told me that his wife was an engineer. "I don't need to fix any electronic devices anymore," he said proudly. "If we discuss the latest Internet products, we fight badly because we both think the other is smartest. She fixes the air conditioner; I tell her why this book is good, why this man is interesting. When she reads a novel, after three pages she will fall asleep."

Fanfou was founded in 2007 by Wang Xing, a young entrepreneur who specializes in the art of cloning. Wang and two friends created Xiaonei, which in 2009 became known as Renren, or the Chinese version of Facebook. Then, in 2010, Wang and his friends launched the popular Meituan, otherwise known as the Groupon of China.

Fanfou was closed down in 2009 following the deadly riots in Xinjiang Province. The riots were sparked when ethnic Uighurs took to the streets to protest social injustices. Nearly two hundred people were killed and more than seventeen hundred were injured. Chinese authorities apparently believed that the riots were fueled by the Internet, text messages, and long-distance phone calls, and that overseas activists used the Internet and mobile phones to stir up unrest. People also used social media to spread graphic photos allegedly from the riots, and, in some cases, calls to violence.

Chinese officials cracked down hard. "We cut Internet connection in some areas of Urumqi in order to quench the riot quickly and prevent violence from spreading to other places," said Li Zhi, the Chinese Communist Party chief of Urumqi. Xinjiang Province essentially lost access to the Internet for ten months until "stability" was restored. Around this time, Twitter, Facebook, and YouTube were blocked. And Fanfou, China's domestic microblogging site, was shut down.

Then, in 2010, Fanfou suddenly reappeared. A group of venture capitalists apparently wanted to restart the business because Sina Weibo, a microblogging site that launched in 2009, was hot and they thought there must be a market for people who didn't want to use Sina. Fanfou had a strong brand and a relatively small but seemingly loyal user base. At the time of its closing, Fanfou had about a million users, and Chinese authorities were apparently able to get over the fact that Fanfou was once regarded as a threat to national security. "This is why I like China," He Caitou said. "Business is business."

In late 2010 Wang Xing, the original founder of Fanfou, became the face of the revived company. But He Caitou was the one running it. "Nobody knows I am CEO of this company. Most of my users don't know. Wang Xing is standing in front of me," He Caitou said. His role at Fanfou was more low profile than top secret. He didn't particularly want to be in the spotlight, and Wang was much better known. Plus, He Caitou said, the "Wang Xing fights back!" story line had more appeal. In many ways, He Caitou was the right man for this job. A year earlier he had helped develop Tencent's own microblogging service.

He Caitou wanted to set Fanfou apart. He found Sina's VIP system, where celebrities and other important people's accounts are tagged with a golden *V*, to be undemocratic. Fanfou tried to cultivate a warmer image. One user wrote that Fanfou had more of a "grassroots" appeal, while "Sina Weibo is cold and lacks humanity." He Caitou tried to make Fanfou home to "the most creative netizens in China." He described a game in which users would try to describe a Chinese classical novel in 140 characters.

Still, leaving a major company like Tencent for such a venture as Fanfou carried its share of risk. He Caitou described his move as "lonely." "When I did this, the fans disappeared. When I asked for some help, people disappeared . . . people came to me and said, I have two choices. Plan A: come to your company and work with you. Plan B: stay, get a promotion and get a salary. So you tell me: What should I do?"

From the window of Fanfou's bland conference room we could

see a Microsoft building, a constant reminder that his company was in the shadow of big players. "People always say they love the free life, love to create something that doesn't exist, to challenge themselves. But if there's a real opportunity, they step back," He Caitou said.

But this wasn't what was keeping him up at night. By October 2010 Sina Weibo had 50 million users. According to Bill Bishop, an Internet analyst in Beijing, Weibo would have killed Fanfou eventually even if Fanfou had never been shut down. Sina had a better product, Bishop said, not to mention the celebrity contributors who migrated to Weibo from Sina's massive blog platform.

He Caitou agonized over how to attract new users. Once the users were there, you could sell them virtual products, direct them to other websites, or offer them promotions. He Caitou said that he was following the traditional strategy of Chinese Internet companies: "We burn money. Burn until the day we have enough customers."

Fanfou once had somewhat of a freewheeling reputation, which explains why it got shut down in the first place. The new Fanfou would have to be a lot more careful about keeping sensitive material off-line.

In China, small to midsize Internet companies would have "hosts," in the form of Internet data centers. Officials would likely inform the host of sensitive words that need to be deleted. The host would then inform the company's owner, who could either delete the material in-house or hire an outside company to do it. If a user crossed the line too far, the police would come to the host, who would ask the website owner for the offender's IP address.

One could argue that someone in He Caitou's position had more control than an employee at Tencent, who would just be "following orders." A person in charge would have the power to delete explosive content before it got a user into serious trouble.

He could also make strategic calculations about the length of time a certain post stays afloat. One enormously popular microblogger told me that he was out and about when he received a call from Tencent saying that his posts would be taken down. He negotiated with the company to keep his doomed posts alive for a couple more hours so he would have a chance to go home, copy them, and save them. Of course, other activist bloggers would scoff at the argument that company employees were doing a service for their users. "I could never do what he does," another blogger said of He Caitou.

He knew his job was controversial. "I do not need any sex life," he told me. "Because netizens fuck me every day. They say, Fuck you. You cooperate with the Great Firewall. You delete my words."

But he was far from apologetic. "It is not our responsibility to try and change the rules," he said. "We are a commercial company, not a human rights foundation. It's not just about me. This involves the company, the venture capitalists, and hundreds of thousands of users."

As Fanfou had directly experienced, if a Chinese Internet company can't keep its users in line, it will be shut down. And what good would that do? He Caitou believed that the closure of Fanfou would ultimately obstruct the flow of information rather than facilitate it. In truth, his argument wasn't all that different from Western companies' attempts to justify their cooperation with Chinese censorship.

"When you are running a company, your point of view of censorship changes," He Caitou said. "In a mainland-based company, you have to follow the rules of the state. When you are a user, you just think censorship is a bother. Now it decides whether your service lives or dies."

He Caitou was also a man of ambition. "I have been a player on the Internet for more than ten years," he said. "I don't want to be a player all my life. I want to create something all by myself.

But if I want to create something new, I can't do it all by myself. I need a company, I need a team, I need partners. So you have to play by certain rules." He said that if he followed in the footsteps of the popular blogger and author Han Han, for example, he wouldn't have these troubles. "A car racer and independent author is not burdened by these kind of things," He Caitou said. "Somebody should do the dirty job."

"I love the Internet," he said. "I want my own company. I want to try to prove that what I think is right. I don't want to give a VIP blog to a celebrity. All tweets are equal. All people are equal."

"I'M A JOURNALIST AND I KNOW NOT TO CALL FOR ACTION"

The first and only time I ever saw Michael Anti look shaken was in 2011. I was visiting Beijing, and we met at our usual Starbucks. Anti was almost unrecognizably subdued. He had been trying to avoid writing about China, and he was working on a long article about Iraq. He showed up in a striped blazer. "You look professional," I commented. "It's not a suit!" he said defensively.

Anti said he hardly saw his friends anymore. When I asked why he agreed to meet me, an American no less, he responded plainly, "Because you are a girl." Female friends were less likely to be viewed as political comrades.

Anti had once again been invited to drink tea, and this time it was dead serious. Before, he had been called in by relatively low-ranking public security officials. Now the invitation came from the National Security Bureau. Anti said his interlocutor was a man in his thirties. His demeanor was polite, as usual, but the content of the conversation "wasn't friendly at all." He wanted to know about Anti's connection to the U.S. embassy. Anti said he had only participated in one recent blogger event that had already been made public online.

Only a year earlier, the Chinese dissident community had seemed more energetic than ever. On December 25, 2009, the Chinese activist Liu Xiaobo, who later went on to win the Nobel Peace Prize, was sentenced to eleven years in jail. When I visited Beijing in early 2010, I heard Liu described as a Mandela-like symbolic leader of the Chinese opposition. Once he was released, some believed, a new era would begin. I heard stories of opposition-minded Chinese organizing meetings in expensive restaurants because the people ordered to follow them would not have the budget to eat there.

But by 2011 all this seemed to have ground to a halt. Chinese authorities, shaken by the Arab Spring earlier that year, embarked on a feverish crackdown. In February, anonymous calls for a Chinese "Jasmine Revolution"—a reference to Tunisia's successful overthrow of its government—began to appear online. They surfaced on an overseas website and also on Twitter. The call was for protests in major Chinese cities, including Beijing and Shanghai. Even though large-scale protests ultimately never took place, the call for physical assembly unequivocally crossed the line.

Authorities reacted swiftly by preemptively rounding up journalists, activists, and dissidents. Dozens were detained, and some were charged with "inciting state subversion." There were reports of foreign journalists being beaten by authorities. The Chinese word for jasmine, "*molihua*," was censored online and blocked in text messages. Officials even declared war on the actual flower. At Beijing's Sunhe Beidong flower market, several people said that local police had forced vendors to sign pledges to not carry jasmine.

In April 2011 Ai Weiwei was detained at Beijing International Airport as he attempted to depart for Hong Kong. The well-known artist and dissident had long been a troublemaker. Ai had been the author of a popular blog, and was a vocal critic on Twitter. He had also embarked on a long campaign to publicize the deaths that resulted from the 2008 Sichuan earthquake, which he accused the Party of trying to cover up. He went on a mission to collect the names of all of the young earthquake victims, and had a show in Munich, "So Sorry," which featured thousands of backpacks to honor the students who died after poorly constructed schools collapsed.

In 2009 Ai went to Chengdu, the capital of Sichuan Province, in an attempt to testify at the trial of another political activist, Tan Zuoren, who was also investigating the Sichuan earthquake. According to Ai, he woke up to police banging on his door in Chengdu. He said a policeman punched him in the forehead. A month later in Munich, where he was preparing his exhibition, Ai went into surgery after being diagnosed with a brain hemorrhage.

Chinese monitoring can be sleek and whisper-soft, except in the case of high-profile dissidents like Ai, who are subject to a theatrical level of surveillance. When I went to visit Ai at his studio in Beijing, he walked me to the front gate and cheerfully pointed out two cameras nearby. One was attached to a pole, and I felt it leaning in toward us, a dissident and a foreigner chatting in the doorway. "There used to be security guys outside, or in the bushes, but maybe it's too cold now," Ai said. "I would try to talk to them, to be friendly, but they wouldn't respond. These cameras are more polite." He waved sarcastically at the cameras. "Hi!" he called out.

In 2011 Ai was arrested for "economic crimes," but many suspected that he was another casualty in China's war on jasmine. Given the intensity of Beijing's paranoia, Ai's mocking Twitter post in February certainly didn't help his case: "I didn't care about jasmine at first, but people who are scared by jasmine sent out information about how harmful jasmine is often, which makes me realize that jasmine is what scares them the most. What a jasmine!"

Ai's arrest sent an effective message to the dissident community that anyone could be next. Not only was the artist well known all over the world, but his late father, Ai Qing, was a celebrated poet. "He's so famous. He has Ai Qing," Anti said in disbelief. Anti had always been so proud of his survival skills. Even his wife, Cissie, a journalist for CCTV, had been arrested for working on an independent documentary related to the Sichuan earthquake. Anti said that Cissie was so politically inexperienced she didn't realize the danger of the situation. Anti never would have made such a serious miscalculation. But during the Jasmine crackdown he saw "no clear line between safety and non-safety."

Even so, Anti's political instincts were keen. He was at his friend's house when he saw a tweet, which he believed was from an overseas dissident, talking about a jasmine gathering in Beijing. Anti remembered that when he called for action on his Microsoft blog, his blog disappeared. The stakes were infinitely higher now. "I'm a journalist and I know not to call for action," Anti told me. So he did not retweet the message. And once again, he survived.

"TWITTER IS EVERYTHING ABOUT ME"

"Twitter is everything about me," Anti told me in 2012. "First, it's my existence on cyberspace. It's the way I get information." He used it to spread the word: "I recommend to Chinese followers which information they should know." But perhaps most important, Twitter was a direct line to the outside world. In the complex map of the opposition, Anti was perfectly clear about his personal role. He wasn't interested in rallying the Chinese masses. Rather, he would work with a small group of comrades to communicate their goals and concerns to the world. Any democratic change, Anti believed, would need the help and support of the foreign media.

When the Western media reference social media in China, they are often talking about Weibo, Sina's domestic microblogging service. It's not hard to see why. Twitter has an estimated tens of thousands of mainland Chinese users, and Weibo has hundreds of millions. And although Weibo is heavily censored in China, Twitter is completely blocked by the Great Firewall. Because Twitter is beyond the wall, it is inaccessible to the majority of Chinese, but this also means that Twitter is not subject to Chinese censorship.

Chinese netizens access Twitter via such tools as proxy servers or virtual private networks. Around 2010, netizens told me that sometimes they didn't even need these tools, thanks to an aspect of Twitter's design. Twitter has an open application programming interface (API). This API allows people to send and receive tweets on sites other than Twitter.

"Coders in China can still find wholesale access to twitter.com blocked," Jonathan Zittrain, codirector of Harvard's Berkman Center for Internet and Society, explained to me in 2010. "The idea is that coders elsewhere get to Twitter and offer up feeds at their own URLs—which the government has to chase down one by one." Facebook, also blocked by the firewall, was harder to access. Furthermore, unlike Twitter, Facebook required real-name registration. Anti's Facebook page was deleted when the company decided that a page registered under Michael Anti and not Zhao Jing violated its "real name" policy.

Twitter has thus become a magnet for activists like Ai Weiwei, whose accounts were not welcome on Sina Weibo. Ai Weiwei was so passionate about Twitter that in 2010 he flew to New York and confronted Jack Dorsey, the cofounder of the company. He called Twitter the one place where Chinese people could express themselves frankly, "a ray of light" in a very dark room. I moderated this surreal conversation, which took place at New York City's Paley Center in the form of a dialogue between Ai, Dorsey, and Rick MacManus, then the editor of a tech website called ReadWriteWeb.

"The Chinese people think you are some kind of God," Ai told Dorsey. But the obsession was not mutual. Dorsey, speaking via teleconference, casually admitted that he hadn't even known that Twitter was blocked in China until I had informed him by phone shortly before the event.

Some will argue that Twitter is irrelevant in China, largely because it has relatively few users. But China's twitterati weren't addressing the general population, they were speaking to one another. When I pushed Ai Weiwei on the significance of Twitter, he put it this way: "For any change, you always need leaders. Unfortunately, I am one of the leaders." That conversation was in 2010, in Ai's Beijing studio. A year later, he was arrested.

"Twitter can create a faster information flow than any official agency," Anti told me in 2010. "That means people would get information faster than the government." Weibo couldn't accomplish this, he argued, largely because its servers are in Beijing, giving the central government control over its content. "Twitter, whose servers are in a country with free speech and a rule of law, is a tool for revolution," he wrote. "But Weibo, whose servers are in an undemocratic country, is '1984' in action for the first time."

Anti had an account on Weibo but never trusted the service. Sure, Weibo hosted a volcano of anger and opinions, but if the dissent wasn't organized, he figured, what was the point? Weibo was better suited to the *ziyoupai*, or liberals, who wrote in clever code to avoid censors. "People who get information this way are also cynical, smart, and will not sacrifice themselves," Anti said.

In April 2012 Chinese Twitter users demonstrated their capacity to impact world events. The story began after Chen Guangcheng took refuge in the U.S. embassy. Chen is a blind human rights lawyer who had tried to fight against forced late-term abortions and the sterilization of women who violated China's one-child policy. In August 2006, in a trial that lasted two hours, Chen was sentenced to more than four years in jail for "damaging property and organizing a mob to disturb traffic." Amnesty International, however, stated that Chen was "jailed solely for his peaceful activities in defense of human rights." After being released from prison in 2010, Chen was put under house arrest in Shandong, where he was closely monitored by authorities. In the weeks leading up to Chen's 2012 escape, he convinced his captors that he was ill in bed. On the night of April 22, with the help of his wife, he managed to climb over a wall around his house, breaking his foot along the way. With the aid of a network of activists and even a car lift from U.S. officials, he made it safely to the U.S. embassy.

Chen's stay at the embassy threatened to be a disaster for both Washington and Beijing. The United States didn't want a conflict with China, and the Chinese certainly didn't need such a high-profile embarrassment. It was difficult to imagine how a solution could be reached without either the Chinese losing face and giving in to the United States, or the Obama administration appearing to be "soft" on China. Meanwhile, Chinese censors sprang into action. On the day of Chen's escape, domestic newspapers went silent. Within twenty-four hours, Chen's name, the initials CGC, and even "the blind man" were purged from the Internet.

Then it suddenly appeared as if a diplomatic solution had been reached. On May 2 Chen left the embassy, apparently of his own free will. He would be freed from house arrest and proceed to study law in China. A major collision between the United States and China was avoided. Chinese state media claimed that Chen left of his own "volition," while Secretary of State Hillary Clinton said that the outcome was in line with American "values." Not long after, the embassy released photos of Chen, seemingly overcome with gratitude, grasping the hand of a U.S. official. Media reported Chen was so happy that he wanted to "kiss" Secretary Clinton.

Once upon a time, official statements from the United States and China would have been enough to shape the public narrative of Chen's departure from the embassy, at least temporarily. Now it was only a matter of hours before tweets from China turned the story upside down. The celebratory mood of Chen's release halted when Chen's friend, the activist Zeng Jinyan, tweeted the urgent English-language message: "GUANGCHENG TALKED TO ME. WHAT MEDIA REPORTED IS WRONG."

This was followed by a torrent of Chinese-language tweets suggesting that the public had been duped. Chen apparently didn't ask to "kiss" Secretary Clinton but rather to "see" her. Zeng went on to say that Chen's embassy departure wasn't so voluntary. He had been told that if he didn't leave, his wife would be sent back to Shandong, where Chen had been living under house arrest. As Zeng's tweets were retweeted, people asked her for more information. Other commenters further fanned the flames of doubt.

Another friend of Chen's, a lawyer named Teng Biao, tweeted that Chen had been threatened into leaving the embassy. Foreign reporters, many of whom are on Twitter, scrambled to catch up with these pronouncements. Some spoke to Zeng to confirm that her tweets were real. Things turned even more grim once Chen himself finally managed to talk to the media. Washington, so recently celebrating its victory, was suddenly on the defensive.

Zeng made a calculated decision to make her announcement on Twitter and not Weibo. Rather than go directly to the media, she tested the waters on Twitter, where there were people she knew and trusted. The support she found there encouraged her to say more. "She leaked more and more with the twittersphere's responses," said the blogger Isaac Mao. He added that such a chain reaction couldn't have had the same impact on the heavily censored Weibo.

It soon emerged that the dark version of events portrayed on Twitter wasn't entirely accurate either. Later reports indicated that Chen did leave the embassy of his own volition but had a change of heart after arriving at a hospital. The issue was ultimately resolved with the United States and China agreeing to send Chen and his family to New York, where he would study at New York University.

But for the Chinese twittersphere, this was a landmark event. A few tweets not only overturned the official narratives of two powerful countries, they may have altered the course of diplomacy.

"IF I DON'T STAND UP FOR ZHU LING, WHO WILL STAND UP FOR ME?"

Kai-Fu Lee, the former head of Google China, has said that if you have ten thousand fans (or followers) on Weibo, it is as if you have created a magazine. If you have a hundred thousand, every Weibo you post will get as much attention as if it appeared in the local newspaper. When you reach a million fans, your voice will be as powerful as the headline of a national newspaper. "If you have ten million followers, then, wouldn't you feel like the host of a TV program, in that you could easily let all the people in the country hear your voice?"

As Lee illustrates, in a country with strict limits on free expression, the Weibo era creates the possibility for an individual to communicate directly with the public. The two major Weibos, or microblogs, were run by Sina and Tencent. Both are tightly monitored, of course, but the sheer volume and speed of messages present a serious challenge for Chinese censors. One famous example took place in 2011, when a train crashed outside Wenzhou. The railways ministry was quiet, but more than 20 million messages appeared on microblogs. Then, in 2012, rumors of political intrigue surrounding the downfall of the Communist official Bo Xilai spread like wildfire. Around that same time, rumors of a coup in Beijing got so out of control that both Sina Weibo and Tencent Weibo temporarily shut down their commenting function.

Anti did have at least one comrade on Weibo: Murong Xuecun, a popular novelist and outspoken online critic. Murong, whose real name is Hao Qun, published his first novel directly on a BBS site. The book, whose English name is *Leave Me Alone: A Novel of Chengdu*, is a raunchy tale of sex and corruption in China's southwestern Sichuan Province. He published the text online, one increment at a time. Although the novel is a tale of prostitution and misogyny, in real life Murong is gentle, with a boyish face and a happy laugh.

In 2012 Murong told me that he didn't really use Twitter, largely because he doesn't want to deal with the *mafan*, or trouble, of getting over the Great Firewall. Besides, he was happy with Weibo, as imperfect as it was. He had millions of followers and a big *V* for "verified," or VIP. He posted about everything—from freedom of speech to the Great Famine to dirty jokes about Mao Zedong.

Murong, too, occasionally crossed the line. He told me that he once got a phone call from a Sina employee informing him that his account would be suspended. "We received an order to ban you," Murong was told. The employee didn't say how long the ban would be in effect, nor did the person mention the specific post that overstepped the line. Some two weeks later, Murong got another call telling him that he could post again. He believed that his popularity made him a valuable asset to the company. "I'm good friends with people at Sina. They support my opinions. They just have no choice." In 2013 Murong had his account shut down completely, possibly for speaking on behalf of a professor whose own account had been silenced.

It was ironic to see this harsh punishment doled out to one of Weibo's more adamant defenders. Murong believed that Weibo was helping Chinese people evolve from "*renmin*," the general term for "the people," to "*gongmin*," or citizens. On Weibo, people were starting to wake up. They recognized that the Communist Party had problems, and they liked the abstract concept of democracy, but they had no idea how to realize it. They were recognizing that they were individuals first, Chinese second, and that they had rights. They were no longer "bricks in a revolution or screws in a machine," Murong explained. He said, "If I am beaten, I am going to go online and tell you about it." Because, the thinking goes, if I don't speak up for you, who will speak on behalf of me? And sometimes, people found justice that was denied by the legal system.

One such case took place in 2010, in Jiangxi Province's Yihuang County. Members of the Zhong family faced the forced destruction of their home to make way for a transport redevelopment program. They posted requests for help on the Internet. Three members of the family set themselves on fire, and one of them died from the burns. The incident soon disappeared from major media outlets and Internet portals.

Then, Zhong Rucui and Zhong Rujiu, two female members of the family, headed to Beijing to petition their case to the government. They were chased by police and government officials. They locked themselves in the bathroom of the Nanchang airport and sent mobile phone text messages to reporters. The story exploded on microblogging sites, with many expressing sympathy for the family. As a result of the public attention, the house wasn't torn down. Furthermore, eight officials in Yihuang County were removed from their posts.

There have been other Weibo victories as well, especially in the area of environmental protection. In 2013 an entrepeneur named Jin Zengmin, from Zhejiang Province, announced on Weibo that he would offer a $32,000 reward to a local environmental-protection chief should he be brave enough to swim in a nearby river for twenty minutes. The offer was declined, but the post went viral. Also in 2013, a well-known activist and journalist named Deng Fei posted a provocative proposal on Weibo: "How is the river in your hometown? While you're home for the holidays, take a photo of the river or stream in your hometown and upload it to Weibo for us to see." Thousands responded to his call, with some netizens sending photos of rivers clogged with trash, and the post became a trending topic on Sina Weibo. Such Weibo campaigns attracted widespread attention from even the state media and occasionally officials. Following Deng's campaign, for example, the Shandong government offered a reward for proof that companies were pumping waste water underground.

Chinese netizens also waged a battle against official handling of air pollution. Even as residents braved dangerous smog, Chinese authorities measured pollution particles only over 2.5 micrometers in diameter. The U.S. embassy in Beijing, however, also tracked the counts of particles below 2.5 micrometers, or PM 2.5, a level that can be more damaging to lungs. Much to the authorities' annoyance, the embassy announced its readings on Twitter, which only highlighted the contrast with Chinese figures. In 2011 Chinese activists purchased their own air-quality monitor and publicized its readings online. Pan Shiyi, a Chinese property developer with millions of followers, also launched a vote on Sina Weibo, asking if China should adopt stricter measurement standards. Almost everyone agreed that the answer was yes. In a move that was likely a response to these online pressures, in 2012 Beijing finally released hourly PM 2.5 data.

Despite these success stories, it's easy to be skeptical about Weibo's overall influence. Some argue that by letting citizens air their grievances, Weibo actually strengthens Communist Party rule. People blow off steam and thus are less likely to protest in the streets. Weibo's army of censors will head off any nascent revolution, the theory goes. But these arguments put too much emphasis on the censorship of information and not nearly enough on the psychological change taking place among citizens of the Web. People are not only defending their individual rights, they are joining forces to defend those of others as well.

This attitude was apparent in the spring of 2013, when interest in Zhu Ling's poisoning case was reignited by an unrelated story at Shanghai's Fudan University, where a postgraduate was poisoned, also allegedly by his roommate. Many netizens remained convinced that Zhu Ling's former roommate Sun Wei was guilty of Zhu's poisoning but was protected by her official family connections. As long as the truth hasn't come to light, nobody has been brought to justice, one netizen wrote, "the Chinese dream can only be the powerful officials' dream."

So nearly two decades after Zhu Ling's life was saved by the Internet, Chinese netizens once again leaped to her defense. So much anger exploded on Weibo that the censors got nervous. On Saturday, May 4, the characters for "Zhu Ling" were censored in search results, but netizens quickly got around it by writing the words in roman letters. The censorship only made people more furious. The popular Chinese actress Yao Chen wrote to her 45 million followers: "Nineteen years ago, the young Zhu Ling was poisoned. Nineteen years later, this name has again been poisoned." Others suspected a cover-up. One netizen wrote, "A lot of information about Zhu Ling has been censored. So we can then see that Sun Wei is the [attempted] murderer."

By Monday, Zhu Ling's name was once again searchable, perhaps because someone realized that censorship was making the situation more volatile. I wrote a *New Republic* article about the case, and a Weibo user named @saysayjiajia quickly translated it into Chinese and posted it on Weibo, where it was retweeted more than 120,000 times. Commenters seized on a line in the piece, which was repeated over and over in English and Chinese: "If I don't stand up for Zhu Ling, who will stand up for me?"

Other netizens chimed in with similar sentiments. "Caring about Zhu Ling is caring about ourselves," one person wrote. "If power can manipulate the truth, then every one of us is in danger." Another wrote, "The cry for Zhu Ling is the cry for the absolute majority of us, because every one of us could fall to the situation of Zhu Ling and her family." Yet another said, "Every time I see the persistence of the netizens on Zhu Ling's case, I see a little bit of hope and feel that all the impossibilities will be possible."

Bei Zhicheng perhaps put it best when I asked him why people were still so fascinated by Zhu Ling's case. First, he said, the case involved attempted murder and the offspring of a senior official. Then he added, "Many of our generation have successful careers and comfortable lives. Zhu Ling should have been one of us."

Weibo's censors could remove the two characters for Zhu Ling. But this explosion of empathy, particularly in a country whose social fabric had been torn apart by politics, would be difficult to erase.

"NOBODY KNOWS THE WHOLE PICTURE"

In the winter of 2013 Beijing was still reeling from a particularly bad bout of air pollution, largely owing to emissions. January was the worst, but when I arrived in March, the city was still slightly out of focus, the bare trees like gray charcoal strokes on a white sheet of paper. People checked their smartphones for PM 2.5 data to see if it was safe to take their kids outside.

Anti and I met for dinner in a spacious, immaculate restaurant. The tables were pale wood and the lighting bright white. Around us were men in button-down shirts and eyeglasses, one customer chatted on his cell phone. Anti hardly resembled the skinny, excitable kid I first met in 2004. Back then, he spoke only Chinese. Now he had studied at both Cambridge and Harvard and spoke English confidently.

That very day, Anti had returned from a trip to Europe. He was wearing a black blazer and was carrying an iPad mini in a brown leather case. His face looked fuller and softer. He glanced at the menu. "The prices have gone up so much!" he exclaimed. I asked the waitress if I could have mapo tofu without the meat. She agreed, but Anti was annoyed. "That's not mapo tofu," he informed me.

He told me he was looking for a fellowship abroad so that he and his wife could have a baby who breathed clean air. He wasn't worried about spending some time away from Beijing. His Communist education had emphasized the struggle toward a brighter tomorrow. Anti had abandoned communism, but he was still betting on the future. If decades passed and China still had the same form of government, then all his efforts would have been in vain. Or as he told me with just the faintest thread of uncertainty in his voice, "If history is messy, without direction, then what am I doing now?"

On that same trip I saw He Caitou, who had left Fanfou to start a company that developed iPhone apps. He spent most of his time in Shenzhen, but I caught him in Beijing. He said he had five employees, and they had made six applications in ten months. We met in a coffee shop that had plush booths, reddish walls, and glittery beaded curtains. He Caitou always seemed to find these kinds of places. He was wearing his usual black hooded sweatshirt and seemed a little balder than before. He now had three iPhones and a little weight-loss gadget that monitored how many steps he took. He said that "another fat guy" had given it to him. He had almost totally abandoned Twitter and now used only Weibo.

He said he used to be more active, but now he was a "pure bystander." People had been complaining about the same issues for years, and there was so little progress. He preferred to focus on what he could control, like creating a good environment inside his company. At least among his employees, he said, "everyone can express their opinions clearly and directly."

Anti had told me that he saw He Caitou as a friend, but not as a comrade. And He Caitou preferred it that way. He thought the word "comrade" was harmful and drew overly clear battle lines. In He Caitou's world, an enemy one day could be a friend the next. But despite their different rhetoric, He Caitou and Anti understood each other. They both wanted a more open China, even if they disagreed about how to get there. More important, they were both true devotees of the Internet, which freed them from their isolation and made them the men they are today.

"We know we can trust each other," He Caitou said. "We don't blame each other: 'Why don't you be a braver fighter?' We would never ask that kind of question. Bravery is not necessary in China. Patience is more important."

When I asked Anti about He Caitou, he said, his voice soft with admiration, "His writing is so good. So funny and so good."

They had, after all, been reading each other for years. "The Internet has many opinion leaders. We watch each other. We support each other. But we don't belong to each other. It's a very good example of decentralized, real politics," Anti said.

And no one can reveal the road map, because there isn't one. "Nobody knows the whole picture of the comrades," Anti once told me. But "years later you will see the results: everyone with the same purpose."

PART TWO

CUBA (FEAR)

"YOU NEVER KNOW WHO IS WHO"

Nunca sabe quién es quién, you never know who is who. I heard this warning often in Cuba. I hadn't been with Laritza Diversent for fifteen minutes when a man sat down nearby. He was wearing sunglasses, cotton pants, and a polo shirt. He looked to be in his forties. He made himself comfortable in his seat and then proceeded to do precisely nothing.

We were at a nearly empty café at the Hotel Nacional in Havana, surrounded by palm trees and sand-colored stone archways. Laritza was describing the challenges of being a lawyer and a critical blogger in one of the most repressive countries in the world. I nervously speared my fork into soggy pizza and shifted my gaze toward the man at the next table, but Laritza didn't seem to notice him. After her name first appeared on the Web, she told me later, Cuban authorities began studying her as if she were a laboratory rat. "When I made the decision to write, I was aware that they would rummage around in my past, particularly for 'personal secrets' that I might have. There is really no way to know how and when they search for and obtain information about you."

I asked her if she wanted to order something, but she had no interest in eating. Instead, she launched into an animated description of how her blog, *Laritza's Laws*, tried to educate people about the rights that Cuban authorities trampled upon every day.

The man shifted in his chair. Laritza was born in 1980. When we first met, in 2009, she was wearing a long black skirt and a conservative button-down shirt, and she had her hair tightly pulled back. Stud earrings glinted in her ears. "I'm black," she had informed me on the phone so that I would be able to recognize her, though I knew this from the photo she posted on her blog. She had a pretty face, with a straight nose and expressive eyes. She was calm, poised, and extremely aware. She spoke in rapid-fire Spanish and didn't lower her voice.

I envied Laritza's composure. I was an American in Havana, spending the day with a known dissident under constant police surveillance. I was already picturing myself being hauled to the airport, another unwanted journalist deported to the United States.

"Let's go," I told Laritza, who shrugged in agreement. I went inside the restaurant and hastily paid the bill. "Who was that guy?" I asked her once we had left the café.

"I think he was just a foreigner," she said.

"Really? Are you sure?"

"No."

I had read Laritza's blog in the United States, but setting up a meeting with her had not been easy. She had only intermittent Internet access, and our phone connections were fuzzy, if the calls got through at all. Not helping matters was Laritza's reluctance to commit to a specific time and place. "Call me an hour or an hour and a half before," she instructed me by email, and "and I will receive you with pleasure." So when I finally managed to have a short conversation with her from a pay phone in a Mexican airport, I told her to meet me the next day at the fountain in back of the Hotel Nacional.

Laritza and I left the café and strolled on the grass behind the hotel. We sat down on a bench that was far away from the building, and I was relieved to see grass on all sides. Facing us was Havana's Malecón, the promenade along the wall that blocks off the Atlantic Ocean. Sometimes the waves broke over the wall and crashed down on anyone who happened to be passing by.

Children would shriek happily and young couples would continue walking, their clothes drying in the sun. The wind was loud, and I had to lean in to hear Laritza.

After about ten minutes I noticed a young man in athletic clothes pacing the rear grounds of the hotel. He was lean and muscular, and carrying either a cell phone or a walkie-talkie. He began walking in our general direction, staying about thirty feet away. He gave us a sideways glance, then turned on his heel and headed back toward the hotel.

"Now, that guy," Laritza said, "he's definitely security." She told me he was going to the hotel to report what he had seen.

"What is he going to say?"

"He'll say that there is a Cuban talking to a foreigner."

Whenever I went out with Laritza, we were never quite alone. A man would sit down at a nearby table and stare straight ahead or thumb listlessly through a newspaper. Someone would come over to our table and ask for the time, or perhaps a cigarette. Who were these people? Were they threatening or just chatty and a little bored? The answer wasn't black and white. In Cuba the line between state informer and ordinary neighbor is razor thin—if it exists at all.

The Nacional is one of the most majestic buildings in Cuba. The long pathway to the hotel entrance is lined with palm trees. The lobby is airy and expansive, with Spanish-style tiling on the walls. The hotel hints at some half-forgotten dream of warm Havana nights, songs like "Chan Chan" wafting through the leaves. Inside the imposing ivory-colored building, your guest room may smell vaguely of mold.

The weekend I met Laritza, Havana was hosting a meeting of nonaligned nations—whose membership boasts North Korea, Iran, Syria, and Burma—so the hotel guards seemed jumpier than usual. For the most part, however, the Nacional created an alternative reality for the tourists drinking mojitos on the veranda. They could pay to drive colorful old-style cars from a company whose logo was literally "rent a fantasy." The Nacional's dining room had buffet tables piled high with meat, fruit, glazed pastries, and other treats that were generally unavailable to the average Cuban.

During my first trip in 2008 I took a banana from the buffet and later gave it to María, a university student I'd befriended in Havana. She shook her head in disbelief, saying, "I can't remember the last time I saw one of these." In 2008 hurricane damage apparently made bananas hard to find.

Before 2008, Cubans weren't allowed to stay at tourist hotels. The ban had been lifted, but for many people hotels remain prohibitively expensive. Cuba has a dual currency system, and tourist goods and services—as well as many other products—are priced in convertible pesos, whose value is pegged to the dollar. Most state workers are paid in Cuban pesos, which are worth about one-twenty-fifth of a convertible peso and generally purchase less desirable goods. I passed a store whose goods were sold in Cuban pesos. Its largely empty window display boasted pencils and plastic knives.

Raúl Castro has tried to spur private sector activity and has allowed a limited degree of nonstate business and farming. In 2009 the private sector had around six hundred thousand workers or farmers. By 2013 that number had reached around a million, but still paled in contrast to the roughly 4 million Cubans who worked for the state, where the average salary was less than $20 a month. People do receive health care and food rations, yet many still struggle to fulfill basic needs. To get by, some people make purchases on the black market or even resort to prostitution or petty crime.

A typical Cuban day is a day full of risks, Laritza wrote. "The danger lies in the necessity to resort to illegality in order to survive." In another post she wrote about the seventy-two-year-old Julia, who receives a pension of $6 a month. After 5:00 p.m. she would park herself on a street corner and sit on a small bench with a piece of board over her lap. On the board would be a bar of soap, a tube of toothpaste, lollipops, her ration of cigarettes, and a few other goodies. It is illegal to trade without a license, and Julia has already been warned by the neighborhood "chief." "Her 'commercial activity' is economically insignificant," Laritza wrote on her blog. "Selling on the street will never cause her to end up in court. However, it constitutes a crime, subject to fines." The post is titled "Laws Made to Be Broken."

It wasn't simply economics that drove Laritza into the world of dissent. It was the fact that she couldn't express herself. She felt suffocated by the lies and hypocrisy she saw all around her. Heroic portraits of Che Guevara and such slogans as "All for the Revolution!" were splashed across city walls, often in bold primary colors. But the darker corners of the Cuban Revolution did not appear in Cuba's national dailies, *Granma* and *Juventud Rebelde*, because the government owns and controls these and all other sanctioned media outlets.

"I write a blog because I can't access my country's media," Laritza wrote in 2009.

> It is the only way that I have to detail Sonia's life. She is a 20-year-old woman who prostitutes herself in the capital's streets. It's about explaining why she abandoned her studies and the motivations she has for her tomorrow. It's about communicating the anxieties that plague Roberto, a young man who does not work for the state but spends his days sitting on a park bench. Why there are thousands of workers who steal from their jobs. Why there is so much delinquency and alcoholism. This is a reality that the official media tries to conquer because they are forbidden to explain why. This is a truth the government hides.

Laritza's decision to become an independent journalist—which can serve as a euphemism for "dissident"—radically changed her relationship with the state. She wasn't revealing state secrets or even telling people what they did not already know. She was doing something far more threatening. Fear was the Cuban authorities' most powerful weapon, and Laritza had declared herself immune.

She was also attempting, in her own modest way, to rewrite the story of her nation. Words like "Cuba" and "Revolution" had become propagandistic abstractions that had little to do with the actual people of the country. Laritza described blogs as "the place where we give life to our land, where it stops being Cuba and it becomes the Cuban people—flesh and blood people with their own existence." She said she started her blog in an attempt to "show my country as I see it and feel it."

"RESIGNATION BECAME MY ONLY COMRADE"

Laritza Diversent was born in 1980. Her father, Claro Diversent, is of Haitian descent and was a true Cuban revolutionary. In the late 1950s he fought as a guerrilla in the Sierra Maestra mountain range in Cuba's Oriente Province. Laritza's mother, who was handicapped in one leg owing to a childhood accident, fell in love with the uniformed warrior. Laritza still speaks affectionately about her father, even though he was a womanizer who was not cut out for family life. When Laritza was very young, he separated from her mother, giving her a tiny monthly sum to take care of her daughter. In an admiring blog post about his friend Laritza, the blogger Iván García wrote that she defied the odds by not becoming an inmate or a prostitute.

Laritza grew up during what was officially called the "Special Period in Times of Peace," and unofficially known as economic disaster, spurred by the collapse of the Soviet Union. In 1991 Gorbachev announced that the Soviet Union would no longer provide its $4–5 billion annual subsidy to Cuba. In the early 1990s the Cuban economy contracted by 34 percent. Laritza described a childhood in which apples, loaves of bread, and even paper bags disappeared. Neglected dogs were taken to the butcher. Adolescence was no easier. When Laritza got her period, she wore uncomfortable, folded-up rags. She polished her shoes with toothpaste from the ration book.

Yet even this dark period had moments of hope. The best movies on television were shown on Saturdays. She would watch legal dramas, often from the United States, on a black-and-white television. She no longer remembers the names of the exact films, but she told me they were comparable to the television series *Boston Legal*. She loved the idea of lawyers doing everything in their power to defend their client. "I liked all the effort, all the ecstasy and the passion of the people you saw in the movies," Laritza told me. And she didn't want to be just an ordinary lawyer, she wanted to rise to the top of her field. "One always dreams, when one studies, of being one of the best in what you do."

Laritza dedicated herself to her studies, landing in the elite Vladimir Ilich Lenin high school. She became pregnant with her son at age eighteen, but managed to graduate. She then studied law at the University of Havana. But even after she graduated with a degree in law, Laritza's future looked bleak. She realized that the wages offered to a lawyer would not be enough to provide a decent life for her family. She worried that survival would demand some form of self-corruption, either by taking kickbacks or pursuing unseemly work on the side.

"Today I have a degree in Legal Studies, period. I can't aspire to work for a salary that would allow me to have a house, if not one of my own at least a dignified place where I can live with my son and my husband. I don't have the opportunity to realize my potential either as a person or as a professional," she wrote on her blog in 2009. But she was not willing to sacrifice her principles. "I will not sell my body to the first foreigner who passes down Fifth Avenue in order to achieve my goals. That was and still is the easiest, though risky, way for Havana girls to leave behind the needs of themselves and their family." When I first met Laritza, in 2009, she was fulfilling her three years of postgraduation "social service" by working in a property registry. The job was fairly mundane and repetitive, and basically entailed keeping a list of Cubans who had rights to property. Her starting salary was less than $10 a month.

On his blog, Iván García described how she lived in a run-down wooden shack with no running water and an outhouse for a bathroom. "That is Laritza Diversent, lawyer and journalist, as poor as any inhabitant of a remote African village, a Brazilian favela or a shantytown in Argentina," Iván wrote.

Laritza started writing online in 2007 for the Miami-based website Cubanet, whose purpose is to provide a platform for independent voices inside Cuba. In 2008 she began blogging for another website, called the Asociación Pro Libertad de Prensa, which published various independent journalists. This led to invitations to write on other sites and to form group blogs with various Cuban journalists. Later that year she started blogging on a group site, Desde La Habana, with writers like Iván García and Luis Cino. That blog was administered by Iván's mother, Tania Quintero, a journalist who lived in Switzerland.

Laritza told me that the simple experience of writing the truth had a transformative effect on her psyche. She used to be constantly depressed. She would cry all the time, sometimes feeling that death would be the only relief. Most unbearable was the overwhelming feeling of impotence. Rather than thinking about how to change her bleak reality, it was easier to just accept it. "Resignation became my only comrade," she said.

Laritza saw the same frustration all around her. She felt that "studying and becoming a professional is not enough to achieve your personal aspirations. Nor is it enough to have an eight-hour workday and a monthly salary." She added that in one year, ten people in her neighborhood took their own lives and others made suicide attempts. They included men and women between the ages of twenty-three and forty-five, and even an eleven-year-old boy. She knew someone who killed himself after his bicycle had been stolen for the fifth time.

Furthermore, complaining too loudly would just get you in trouble. The citizen informer system was a pillar of revolutionary society, established by Fidel Castro himself. In 1960 he created the Committee for the Defense of the Revolution, or CDR. Each block has its own CDR that keeps files on residents. "In the face of the imperialist aggression, we're going to implement a system of collective vigilance," Castro said of the CDR, "so that everybody knows who lives on the block, what they do, and what relations they have with the tyranny, and with whom they meet." As recently as 2012, I spotted a huge CDR propaganda sign on the road from the airport with the slogan DEFENDING SOCIALISM FROM THE BARRIO!

The CDRs were supposed to monitor the activities of individuals in their respective housing blocks and keep files on residents. While the CDRs are involved in such activities as disaster relief, they are also constantly on the lookout for any "suspicious" political behavior. As of 2010, more than 8 million of Cuba's 11 million population were registered CDR members. But CDRs are only part of a much larger phenomenon. Ordinary people will also act as informers, Laritza wrote, in an attempt to save themselves. The thinking, she said, goes something like this: "I take part in denunciations and snitching on what others do, so that I am allowed to continue my own illegal activities." Others might inform on neighbors because of envy or personal grudges.

"Keep your position at the Committee for the Defense of the Revolution meetings, or walk at the square with the crowds. Watch, listen, and inform your superiors whenever you are ordered to," Laritza wrote in a 2009 blog post. Most important, she said, remain silent and submissive. "That is why there are no voices, just murmurs. You can yell, but then you'll have to accept the consequences."

Laritza said that her personal anguish stopped only when she started writing the truth. "It's incredible, the inner peace and spiritual tranquility that I have now," she said in 2009. "It doesn't matter that I haven't yet achieved my dreams and goals . . . expressing myself freely has been an unsurpassable experience. For that reason I am working hard to get Cuba to respect fundamental human rights, in particular the freedom of expression."

"THE WORLD KNOWS THE NAME AND FACE OF DISSIDENCE"

Laritza was one of a number of Cubans who wrote blog entries on makeshift home computers—sometimes assembled from spare parts purchased on the black market—and saved their writing on CDs or flash drives. When they did find Internet access, perhaps in a hotel or an embassy, they would post these entries on the Web or email them to friends abroad who could do it for them. Laritza's first computer was a donation from an overseas NGO.

In today's interconnected world, Cuba's Internet penetration is stunningly low. According to some 2012 estimates, only about 5 percent of Cubans periodically have access to the World Wide Web (official figures are higher). Many Internet users can only connect to a national "intranet," which limits politically objectionable content. Most Cubans are not allowed to have Internet access at home. Mobile phones generally cannot access the Internet. In 2013 the Cuban government announced the arrival of 118 public venues where the public could use the Internet, although activists assumed that Internet use there would be tightly monitored.

Another major obstacle is cost: computers are prohibitively expensive, and an hour of Internet access in a hotel can be around $8. Even the new cybersalons cost $4.50 an hour, amounting to nearly a week's salary for the average Cuban state worker. Hotel Internet cards can be the best gift a foreign visitor can bestow upon a Cuban blogger.

Laritza couldn't afford to waste precious minutes of hotel connectivity time composing the text of her blog. She would begin her work on her home computer, write her blog in Word, and then save the text on a flash drive. She eventually learned to use a template that allowed her to transfer the text directly to her blog once she had an Internet connection.

The causes of Cuba's low connectivity remain somewhat mysterious. A much-anticipated Venezuelan cable that was supposed to dramatically increase the island's connectivity somehow failed to do so. At one point it looked as if the U.S. embargo was part of the problem. But in 2009, when President Obama loosened regulations to enable U.S. telecommunications providers to do business with Cuba, the overall landscape didn't really change. In part, some American companies probably didn't see Cuba as a profitable market. But the larger issue may be that the Cuban government was not terribly enthusiastic about ordinary citizens being online.

Generally speaking, Cuba remained impressively disconnected from the rest of the world. I personally have never stumbled upon a foreign newspaper in Havana. The U.S. government–funded Radio Martí is largely blocked in the capital. For years, the U.S. Interests Section in Havana, which exists in place of a U.S. embassy, tried to broadcast pieces of news via a red-lettered Spanish-language electronic billboard that could be seen in the building's upper windows. Aside from selected news items, the billboard posted such provocative messages as "In a free country you don't need permission to leave the country. Is Cuba a free country?"

The Cuban government fought back by putting more than 100 tall flagpoles in front of the building, each with a black flag with a white star. In December 2008 I was near the Malecón with María, trying hard to read the billboard's red messages behind the sea of black flags. I thought I saw something about O. J. Simpson, who I later learned was sentenced to jail that month. María looked at me blankly. "Who's O. J. Simpson?" she asked. A year later, the U.S. Interests Section finally took down the billboard.

The problem is bigger than getting news into Cuba, however. Bloggers worry that if they don't speak up, everyone will think the island is full of happy campers celebrating free health care and education, high literacy rates, and other triumphs of the revolution. Cuba's independent journalism movement almost screeched to a halt during the infamous Black Spring of 2003, when plainclothes police banged on doors and detained seventy-five Cubans, including more than two dozen journalists.

In 2009 there were at least twenty-five independent, journalistic, and regularly updated blogs produced by Cuban writers, according to the Committee to Protect Journalists. Most bloggers were based in Havana. The most famous of these bloggers was Yoani Sánchez, who started her own blog in 2007. Owing to the lack of connectivity on the island, the readership of Cuban bloggers has been primarily overseas. According to 2012 statistics for Laritza's most recent blog, *Jurisconsulto*, the majority of readers were from Mexico. In second place was the United States, and then Spain.

A key audience for Cuban bloggers is the vast network of Cuban exiles. Another well-known blogger, Miriam Celaya, told me that her readers were largely Cubans outside the country. Her blog helped establish bridges between the Cubans outside the country and those within it, two groups that were dramatically ripped apart by the 1959 revolution and its aftermath. Blogging helped Miriam reconnect with her own family. Her cousin was living in the United States when he spotted her name online. He wrote to her and then printed material from her blog and mailed it to her uncle in Miami.

Miriam said that many Cubans abroad read her blog and then email it to their friends and family in Cuba. Given the high cost of Internet access, bloggers wanting to get their texts to other Cubans have to save them on flash drives or CDs and deliver them manually. Sometimes they print blog texts and pass them out as flyers.

Laritza didn't foresee a Black Spring for bloggers. Their international visibility played a pivotal role in helping them avoid the fates of *desaparecidos*, or those who have disappeared. This is precisely why some Cubans posted their real names and photos on their blogs. "The fact that the world knows the name and face of dissidence, people of flesh and blood with their own existence, gives us a little bit of protection," Laritza said. "But the subtle methods of repression continue and sometimes are much more effective, because they affect an individual's psyche."

If the government can't throw the bloggers behind bars, it will just wage psychological warfare on them. When she began writing on the Internet, Laritza became an object of that warfare.

"YOU SEE AGENTS OR INFORMERS EVERYWHERE"

Nunca sabe quién es quién. I once asked María about this phrase. It was evening, and we were sitting along the Malecón. "You see that couple over there?" she said, pointing to a pair of lovebirds embracing on the other side of the street. "They could easily be state security who know that you are here to research Cuban bloggers." María was not a dissident, or even particularly politically engaged. Paranoia extended to every level of society.

Surveillance is part of Cuban life, but Laritza considerably raised the stakes when she started blogging under her own name and became known as a "counterrevolutionary." She believes that state security has made contact with her friends, former classmates, neighbors, and family. "It's difficult to know who might betray you," she said. "Anyone who I've had a relationship with could give information about me, even without knowing it. This creates a kind of paranoia that makes you distrust everyone around you. You see agents or informers everywhere."

Her trials began with a series of state security "interviews," or regular meetings with officials who tried to pull her back from the brink. At first the language was plaintive, almost protective: this is a world that you don't know, and it's our duty to warn you. It's as if "dissidence is something dirty and impure, and they are Christ the Savior," Laritza explained.

She was assigned her very own security agent, "Ricardo," whose main purpose, she said, was to "let you know that they know everyone you meet, everywhere you go. That you know that they are controlling you, following your every step. No matter what you do or where you are, they are omnipresent." She added, "To confront this situation in my psyche, I repeated to myself one and a thousand times: 'My life is public, I have nothing to hide, nothing that they search for or find is going to affect me.' That is how I overcame those first challenges." However, it was more difficult to ensure that what she did wouldn't affect her family.

State security first confronted Laritza's father. They told him that his daughter was meeting with "worms" and that she was writing for a counterrevolutionary website. If she didn't stop, they warned, she would go to prison. Ricardo, the young agent assigned to Laritza, then tried to make her husband jealous by telling him that Laritza went out alone and met with other men. "Cuban men are very macho in this way," Laritza explained. The authorities even tried to convince her husband to forbid his wife from going to certain locations. Ricardo essentially tried to turn Laritza's husband into a collaborator.

This was not the sole attempt to create trouble in her marriage. For Laritza's son, getting to school required crossing a dangerous intersection. So her husband would go and pick him up. Several times her husband noticed an attractive, well-dressed woman lingering nearby. There was something strange about her. One day Laritza's husband arrived early and noticed the woman talking to someone in a car, and he looked like a security agent. Laritza wondered if the goal was to lure her husband into an affair and then blackmail him for information about his wife.

Although Laritza's marriage has thus far survived these intrusions, she remained concerned about her son. When he was around ten years old, one incident put her on alert. At home Laritza kept a little box with some colorful rubber bracelets with the single word "*cambio*," or change. In the United States, people wear similar bracelets to promote a brand or such causes as breast cancer awareness. In Cuba, the rubber bracelets are a quiet act of defiance. I had noticed another blogger wearing a *cambio* bracelet, and he told me that an overseas Cuban had given it to him.

Laritza told her son that under no circumstances should he bring these bracelets to school, but, she said, "you know how little boys are." He brought one to school and, in true Cuban fashion, traded it for two marbles. When his teacher spotted the bracelet, she demanded to know who brought it in. Laritza was then urgently called to the school. "They asked me if I knew what the word on the bracelet meant. For them it was counter-revolutionary, and they feared that someone was using the child to introduce enemy propaganda into the school. I had to lie and say that it had been given to me by a stranger in the street and I hadn't the slightest idea what it represented."

Making matters worse, her son had proudly announced at school that his mother was a journalist who wrote for an "Internet magazine." When school authorities asked Laritza what she did, she neither affirmed nor denied her son's declaration and simply said that she was working as a lawyer for a state institution. Not long after this incident Laritza noticed that her son began having problems at school, so much so that he eventually had to transfer. "Whether or not this was caused by my activities, I just don't know," she said.

Laritza believed that the ultimate point of these authoritarian mind games was to transform her into an informer who would turn fellow dissidents over to the state. "To do this, they search for dark secrets, they scrutinize the most intimate of your relations: lovers, family, sexual preferences, anything they can use to black-mail you. When they discover something, they are unscrupulous in using it to make you do what they want."

The blogosphere was one area where people like Laritza enjoyed a rare feeling of support and trust. But the national motto of "you never know who is who" applied to the Internet as well. Before arriving in Cuba, I contacted one of the women who was generally acknowledged to be part of the island's blogger movement. I noticed that her site appeared on the blogroll of a respected Cuban blogger, and her name also came up in conversations with U.S.-based press freedom advocates.

I sent her an email saying that I had read her blog and would like to meet her in Havana. I was surprised when she responded immediately, saying she would be delighted to meet. Most other bloggers took days, if not longer, to respond. It seemed as if she had an unusual degree of Internet connectivity. She asked me to send a photo of myself so she would be able to recognize me. None of the other Cuban bloggers had asked me to do this, and something instinctively stopped me. I told her I'd be wearing a bright orange blouse.

I also asked her to meet me at the fountain at the Hotel Nacional immediately after I planned to meet with Laritza. Grasping for a thread of discretion, Laritza and I didn't wait by the fountain. We kept watch from a short distance away, but the blogger never arrived. I called and left several messages with a woman who answered her phone. I never heard from her again.

The incident left me uneasy. We had set a fixed time and place, and she struck me as organized and competent. Soon afterward I had coffee with other bloggers, and I casually asked about her. They matter-of-factly told me that she was "*oficialista*," meaning that she worked for the state. This didn't necessarily mean that her opinions weren't authentic or that she was some sort of spy; it just meant, well, that you never know.

When you are constantly meeting with dissidents in Havana, it can be difficult to decide where to spend the night. Checking into a place such as the Hotel Nacional can feel like turning your-self in to the police. The other option is the *casa particular*, which is where you can stay in a home with a Cuban family for about $30 a night. All these casas, of course, are registered with the government.

There was one apartment close to the Hotel Nacional that had been recommended to me by another journalist. It was run by a woman named Rosa, a garrulous Cuban with dyed blondish hair who was completely over the moon about the election of Barack Obama. The apartment was clean and comfortable, decorated with framed photos, glass animals, and other contemporary Cuban kitsch.

Unfortunately, Rosa knew that I had worked as a journalist, as María had foolishly come to the apartment asking for Emily "*la periodista.*" I said I wasn't in Cuba to write an article (which was true) and that I wrote books. She didn't question me further, al-though her husband seemed to be taking an extremely long time copying the details of my passport into their official guestbook. I reminded myself that I was staying there only one night.

At one point I noticed that Rosa was wearing a little gold owl around her neck. "Owl jewelry is very stylish in New York right now!" I exclaimed, which also had the benefit of being true. "Oh, this thing?" Rosa said, touching the chain. "My friend has them. I can get you one." I smiled and put my bag into the room, then went out.

I didn't get back to the house until late that night. The house was dark, but the kitchen light was on. Rosa's bedroom door was closed, and I couldn't tell if she was sleeping or out. My flight to Mexico was scheduled for early the next morning. I had paid the bill when I checked in, but it seemed rude to leave without saying goodbye. I was pacing around the kitchen uncertainly when I heard the front door open. Rosa didn't seem surprised to see me. "I have something for you," she said. She handed me a small owl charm, gold-colored but not actually gold. I held the owl in my palm and thanked her a bit too enthusiastically.

Rosa stared at me. "Has nobody given you a gift before?" she asked. Not in Cuba, I wanted to say. The house was silent. "Emily," Rosa said. She stepped in closer, studying my face. Her voice was like a hand, reaching out to stroke my arm. But there was something unfamiliar in her eyes. "Which publication do you write for? Why did you come to Cuba for such a short time?"

"*Vacaciones*," I stammered. I had not set foot on a single Cuban beach. Rosa continued to gaze at me, smiling vaguely. A long moment passed, and then pragmatism prevailed. "Well, make sure to tell all your friends to stay here." She handed me some cards with her address and phone number. Then she wished me a good trip and went to bed.

I went to my own bedroom. It was tidy, with a white dresser and a mirror above it. On the bed was a faded pink quilt. I lay down fully clothed and set both the alarm clock on the dresser and my cell phone alarm to make sure I wouldn't miss my painfully early flight to Mexico. I was still wide awake when the alarms went off, one right after the other. I had spent the past five hours in a not entirely rational panic, terrified that something would prevent me from leaving the island. Images flickered through my head, newsreel-style. Emily, which publication do you write for? Rosa's husband meticulously recording the details in my passport. *Nadie sabe nada*, nobody knows anything. In Cuba, my American credit and ATM cards were useless pieces of plastic, and I was burning through my pesos convertibles. If I couldn't fly to Mexico the next day, what would I do when I ran out of cash?

I got up and went to the bathroom several times; a night-light led the way through the living room. Across the living room was another guest room, with a closed door. I thought Rosa had mentioned that a Japanese girl was staying there, but I hadn't seen anyone else that evening. On my way back and forth to my bedroom I kept passing a ceramic dog. It was roughly the size of a real dog, and it cast a lifelike shadow on the wall. Its white back glimmered in the light. Even though I knew it would be there when I entered the room, it never failed to give me a start. It was both harmless and strangely menacing. I've come to think of that dog as emblematic of my whole Cuban experience.

Like most people I met, I felt scared all the time, but it wasn't always clear why. Nobody confronted me directly, and even after that last sleepless night I made it safely to Mexico with my passport clenched in my palm. True, Rosa's questions were both a warning and a reminder that my leaving the next morning was for the best. But even if I had been cornered by authorities, I probably would have just been sent home.

An American friend once came back from a trip to Cuba bewildered by the paranoia that has infested the island. "I don't get it. What are they all so afraid of?" she asked. The answer is not simply the government, Fidel, or Raúl. Rather, Cubans are afraid of one another. A long tradition of citizen informers has broken down the social fabric. This decentralized paranoia is what makes coordinated rebellion so difficult, and the government knows it. You never know whom to fear, so you fear everyone.

The Cuban novelist Jose Manuel Prieto eloquently described the phenomenon: "The whole country is permeated with it, this fear that fatally manifests itself in lack of initiative, dark uncertainty." This feeling returned to him when he wrote critically about Cuba, even though he was no longer living in his homeland. "Some will argue with me on this, some will say, No, there is no fear. And I can present no counterargument, no 'data.' I will only add, in bewilderment: but if I myself, if I myself, still now, as I write this, am full of fear?"

Prieto, born in 1962, represents an older generation of writers.

But Cuba's new bloggers are another story. Laritza says that she is a completely different person since she began blogging. On the Internet she is part of a larger group, one that is composed of different viewpoints and opinions. It is different from the streets of Havana, where everyone has been taught to think before they speak. Laritza no longer cares if she is being filmed or photographed, or if her conversations are recorded. She still worries about the safety of her family, but the impotence she felt before she started blogging was much stronger than these fears. In the hall of mirrors of daily Cuban life, bloggers like Laritza have found something that feels real. After she started blogging, she stopped going to parades to celebrate the successes of the Cuban Revolution. She didn't bother to participate in the "pathetic" meetings of the Committee for the Defense of the Revolution. "I comport and project myself as I am, without hypocrisy," she said. Even as she maneuvered her way through constant surveillance and quiet intimidation, Laritza described herself as "free."

"I COMPORT MYSELF LIKE A FREE MAN"

I called Reinaldo Escobar from a pay phone in Havana. To my astonishment, he answered right away. Phone service was always sketchy in Cuba, and dissident bloggers seemed to have the most dropped calls of all. It was December 2011. Reinaldo and I hadn't spoken for almost two years, and I wasn't sure if he would remember me. "I have an excellent memory," he assured me over the phone. We made a plan to meet the next afternoon in front of a movie theater. "I am very punctual," he said.

A few minutes before our scheduled meeting I spotted him coming down the street. I recognized his weathered face, thick black hair, and broad grin. Reinaldo, well into his sixties, was wearing a backpack, like a giant schoolboy.

We went to a café near La Rampa cinema. We sat down at a table with red-and-white-checkered tablecloths. Ceiling fans whirred unenthusiastically. There was no one next to us, just some green leaves erupting from a planter. Behind the bar were brightly colored signs for Lucky Strike and Havana Club rum.

A tired-looking waitress appeared. "We'd like some coffee," Reinaldo said. His voice was cheerful and bright, as if he were inviting her to a party.

"No more," the waitress responded. This often happened in the afternoon.

"Carbonated water?" I suggested.

"No."

I could see a refrigerator behind her. There were juice boxes behind a glass door.

"How about orange juice?" I asked.

"We have guava juice," said the waitress.

I ordered the guava juice and turned back to Reinaldo. Suddenly he was distracted. He grabbed his phone and pointed it like a camera. He aimed it at two teenage girls at a nearby table.

"If they are going to photograph me, I will photograph them back," he explained. "It's only fair."

I looked over at the girls. They were holding a digital camera, and the lens was facing in our direction. But they looked completely harmless, like two teenagers having coffee. They seemed to be happily perusing photos, perhaps of them and their friends, on the camera's screen. Sure, it's possible that they were subtly pointing the camera at us. But it seemed highly unlikely.

Reinaldo didn't wait to find out. He pointed his phone and shot, and the girls shrank into miniature on his screen. I took a mental photograph, just in case. The girls were both wearing tank tops. One wore dark blue, and bright silver chains gleamed against her dark skin. They didn't seem to be paying us the least bit of attention.

Reinaldo insisted on paying for my juice, which was extremely unusual in a country where foreign visitors have such disproportionate economic power. Aside from blogging, Reinaldo wrote for overseas publications, which paid him for his articles. But he was also asserting the dignity of a man who can invite a guest to a drink in his own country. He joked, "Next time you will pay, and it will be champagne!"

Later, when we had left the café and were out on the street, I mentioned that it seemed as if the girls were looking at their own photos, not taking pictures of us. Reinaldo shrugged. "Maybe."

"Would political police look . . . like that?" I asked.

"They could be anyone," he said, echoing the unofficial motto of Cuba: *Nunca sabe quién es quién.* "Anyone! If they all had the same face, it would be much easier."

Perhaps, he said, they were trying to take photos of him having coffee with a woman. Then they could try to blackmail him for information about the world-famous dissident blogger Yoani Sánchez, Reinaldo's partner. "Anyway, Yoani knows where I am," he said. "She knows I'm with you."

To those who hadn't spent time in Cuba, Reinaldo's behavior would seem overly paranoid, even eccentric. But in Havana, cameras of any kind were not to be trusted, especially by such a high-profile dissident as Reinaldo. Photographs can be used against you later, evidence waiting for a crime. Once, I asked María if she would ever have coffee with someone like Reinaldo. She immediately refused. By way of explanation, she darted her eyes and made a vague gesture with her hands, as if she were typing something. Her point was that information is always being filed away, so your voice and image can come back to haunt you at a later date. And although there's a good chance that this will never occur, you can be sure that the mere possibility will alter a person's behavior. It will cause her to lower her voice in public, to shrink away from cameras, and to avoid having a cup of coffee with someone like Reinaldo.

But Reinaldo didn't dodge cameras or modify his words. When he sensed that he was being watched, he didn't suggest moving to another café. Instead, he took out his phone and turned his lens on his suspected photographer. In a simple but powerful act of defiance, he refused to be a passive object of surveillance.

He walked boldly through the streets of Havana, breezing through the doors of hotels as if he had every right to be there. He was aware of everyone around him, always, but he didn't care what they thought.

Reinaldo told me that his fellow countrymen had started mistaking him for a foreigner. They thought he was Colombian, or maybe Mexican. His appearance lacked a fundamental Cuban feature: fear. Or, as Reinaldo explained it, "It's because I comport myself like a free man."

My first meeting with Reinaldo was kind of an accident. When I made my inaugural visit to Cuba in 2008, I was trying to meet Yoani Sánchez, Cuba's most famous blogger. The media refers to Yoani as Reinaldo's wife, although he tells me that they were never formally married. "We don't know each other well enough yet," he said jokingly of his partner of around two decades. The spotlight on Yoani was so bright that it was easy to overlook Reinaldo's intelligence and talent as a blogger and general observer of Cuban life.

Reinaldo, who had been married several times, is also old enough to be Yoani's father. When the couple first met, she was eighteen and he was forty-six. Yoani was looking for a copy of *The War of the End of the World*, a book by the Peruvian novelist Mario Vargas Llosa, whose work is banned in Cuba. A mutual friend told Yoani that Reinaldo had a copy. Reinaldo thinks that the mutual friend wanted to show off his own literary connections. "It was a serious error," Reinaldo said happily of his friend's decision to introduce him to Yoani.

Yoani began writing for the Internet magazine Consenso in 2004, but her rise to fame began in 2007, when she launched her own blog, *Generación Y*. The blog, administered by her supporters abroad, covered food shortages, banned books, and her young son's early experiences with Cuban paranoia. By 2009 her blog was attracting more than 14 million monthly page views. Not only is she the most famous blogger in Cuba, but she even made *Time* magazine's list of the hundred most influential people in the world. She has been extensively profiled by foreign media and has received a number of foreign prizes. Her blog is now translated into more than a dozen languages. Yoani told me that when she began writing her blog, expressing herself in the virtual world was a kind of "practice" for exercising her voice offline.

This fame has propelled Yoani from an ordinary blogger to a kind of diplomat. In 2009 she sent questions to President Obama about the state of U.S.-Cuba relations. They included: Did Obama consider Cuba to be a foreign policy issue or a domestic one? Would he ever consider Raúl Castro as a legitimate interlocutor? And who is to blame for the lack of connectivity on the island, the Cuban government or the U.S. embargo? What's more, Obama actually responded.

Yoani is also one of the very few Cubans who tweets on a regular basis. She has hundreds of thousands of followers on Twitter, which she mainly accesses via her mobile phone. She sends text messages to a special phone number, and the tweets appear from her account. It costs more than $1 per message, which is rather expensive by Cuban standards. In most countries Twitter is a conversation, but in Cuba it is more of a broadcast mechanism. Cubans simply don't have the kind of connectivity that allows for Twitter's real-time exchanges. People like Yoani can't always access the Internet to see tweets or direct messages as they come in, but supporters all over the world send them text messages to inform them of what is being said on Twitter.

Yet even while tweeting blind, Yoani learned that Mariela Castro Espin, the daughter of Raúl Castro, had started a Twitter feed. Yoani immediately provoked her. "Welcome to the plurality of Twitter," she wrote, "here no one can shut me up, deny me permission to travel, or block entrances." Castro fought back, telling Yoani that her rhetoric resembled the "old mechanisms of power" and that she needed to study. When people pummeled Castro with abuse, she called them parasites who were being ordered by their employers.

Before 2013, Yoani made more than a dozen attempts to travel overseas, and all were consistently denied by Cuban authorities. She has been painted as a CIA operative and a "mercenary" funded by the U.S. government to undermine the Cuban regime. And, of course, as a liar. At a Washington think tank seminar about the Internet in Cuba, I heard a Cuban official spit out Yoani's name with almost theatrical derision.

But the Cuban government's repression only bolstered Yoani's international appeal. She wrote for *The Huffington Post* and for *El País* in Spain. She was embraced by some in the Miami community as well as by freedom of speech activists. It didn't hurt that she was the master of press-perfect sound bites about the lack of freedom in Cuba and the role of the Internet as the great liberator of the Cuban people. She also became an effective advocate for a major Cuban government goal: the lifting of the embargo. In 2013

Raúl Castro lifted travel restrictions for Cubans to leave the island. Yoani thus embarked on an eighty-day voyage to three continents. She gave speeches, received awards, and tried to convince hard-liners in Miami that the embargo was doing more harm than good by giving the Cuban government an easy excuse for the problems on the island.

Yoani was such a poster child for Internet dissent that I was initially a bit skeptical. It didn't make sense to me that Cuba would allow an ordinary citizen to continually air the country's dirty laundry online. Reinaldo later opined that the Cuban leadership was macho and senile. They underestimated the young woman and the power of technology. By the time they caught on, Yoani had such an enormous international following that they couldn't suppress her without causing an uproar.

Still, in those early years, Yoani seemed too good to be true. These suspicions were hardly abated in 2008, on my first trip to Cuba, when she failed to show up for our scheduled appointment. Reinaldo came in her place, saying that she couldn't make it. Reinaldo, an influential blogger in his own right, seemed sincere enough. His comments about Cuban life were subtle and trenchant. Nevertheless, when he asked me if he could take a photo of me "to show Yoani," the Cuban paranoia kicked in and I immediately declined.

Less than a year later, I learned that Yoani indeed existed. I had coffee with her and Reinaldo at a generic café in Havana. She looked exactly like the photo on her blog, with a pretty face and dark hair that streamed down her back. I asked her about other dissident bloggers on the island. After our coffee she hailed a taxi, jumped in with me, and took me to the home of Miriam Celaya. Once we had safely arrived at Miriam's apartment, Yoani quietly took off.

Yoani exuded a cool, calm intelligence, but despite her bold rhetoric and high-profile status, in person she was rather mild. Reinaldo said he had a similar impression when he first met her in the early 1990s. He saw a timid woman with a "gift of invisibility" that allowed her to fade into the walls.

"I KNEW EVERYTHING WAS BAD, BUT I HAD TO WRITE THAT EVERYTHING WAS GOOD"

Reinaldo was born in 1947, in the province of Camagüey. He studied journalism at the University of Havana, finishing in 1971. He was once a true believer in the Cuban Revolution. At fourteen, he went to the countryside to teach people to read. At sixteen, he joined the army to learn how to handle the modern weapons that were being supplied by the Soviet Union.

But by the time he got to university, Reinaldo was starting to question things. "Communist Party militants in the university—students and professors—would use the following phrase: 'He has opinions,'" Reinaldo said. He expressed these opinions to none other than Castro himself. One day the Cuban leader came to visit the University of Havana, where he took questions from students. A student asked the Comandante why *Granma*, the official newspaper of the Cuban Communist Party, was not reflecting the problems inside the country. Castro breezily responded that *Granma* had only a few pages.

Reinaldo couldn't help but jump in. "I don't agree with what you are saying," he told Castro. Castro asked why. "Because if a newspaper only has a few pages, it should publish what is most important," Reinaldo replied. "And what is the most important?" Castro inquired. Reinaldo responded, "The most important is what you said. You said yourself that the country's problems are the fault of the leaders. And *Granma* doesn't talk about this."

Reinaldo said that Castro grew "furious." The famous beard hovered in front of Reinaldo's face. "And what is it that you want me to say?" Castro asked him. "That I don't know how to govern? Fine," he said, "then I'll say it. *Yo no sé gobernar! Yo no sé gobernar!*" And Reinaldo, terrified at this point, still managed to respond that it wasn't an issue of Castro saying it right there, but of *Granma* actually explaining it.

Reinaldo said that his outburst shouldn't be interpreted as bravery. He trusted Castro, and "when you trust a person, you can be sincere with that person," he said. "Only when you are full of faith can you do something like this." And he thinks Castro understood this.

Back then Reinaldo still identified as a revolutionary. "I felt like a married man who was cheating on his spouse," he said of his creeping doubts. "I was in love with the revolution, but I was cheating." People would say, okay, you are criticizing inefficiency and opportunism, but you are still a revolutionary, right? And Reinaldo would answer yes. He described that "yes" as the final hurdle a person needs to leap over. He doesn't know exactly when he finally fell out of love with the revolution. "It's like a person who stops believing in God. You don't know which day it happened."

Reinaldo became keenly aware of the chasm between the reports in the official press and the realities on the ground. In the 1980s he worked for a magazine called *Cuba Internacional*, where his job was to explain Cuban realities to the outside world, or rather, to show the world that everything in Cuba functioned perfectly. He wrote about Cuba's schools, hospitals, and natural attractions. Or, as he put it, "I knew everything was bad, but I had to write that everything was good."

When perestroika hit the Soviet Union in the 1980s, Cuba seemed to be opening a little as well. Reinaldo decided that he wanted to try to change the country from within. He thought it was possible to have a better form of socialism. So he went to work at the newspaper *Juventud Rebelde*. But it didn't take long for him to come into conflict with the paper. He found himself writing articles that couldn't be published. Even more troublesome were the articles that he did publish, touching on such issues as the dangers of mediocre functionaries and the need to be an opportunist in a totalitarian state.

One offender was an article called "Es Muy Fácil Prohibir" or "It's Very Easy to Prohibit." This article criticized Cuban schools' prohibition of male students wearing long hair. Reinaldo argued that this was an absurd ban, as the way a person thinks is not reflected by the length of his hair. He told me that this article caused a *terremoto*, or earthquake, shaking all the way up to the Ministry of Education.

Reinaldo called the fallout from the article the most "beautiful" experience he has had in journalism. Students posted the article on the walls of their schools. When the papers were taken down, the students wrote entire paragraphs on the street with chalk. He received supportive letters from students, as well as hate mail from school principals.

In late 1988 *Juventud Rebelde* offered him an opportunity to wash himself clean of the scandal. He was asked to write an article celebrating the upcoming thirtieth anniversary of the Cuban Revolution, with the theme of "youth." He happily obliged and turned in an article called "Thirty Years Later, What Are Young People in Cuba Complaining About?"

Reinaldo said that the content of the article wasn't so inflammatory. Sure, he argued that the youth of Cuba wanted more freedom. But what young person in any country doesn't want more freedom? Demanding greater liberty is the anthem of the young! Besides, his main point was that thirty years ago was worse, and thirty years hence will be even brighter. In retrospect, Reinaldo said, the article was actually pro-Castro. *Juventud Rebelde*, however, didn't see it that way. They showed him the door.

Reinaldo did other jobs. He worked in the national library. He was an elevator mechanic. But his calling was journalism. He couldn't write for the state, so he moved to the next logical frontier: foreign media. He became a freelancer for whatever publication would take his work. But, tired of having to adhere to another publication's editorial line, he still wasn't satisfied. In 2004 he started working on an Internet magazine with other critical-minded bloggers. Eventually he moved on to write his own blog, *Desde Aquí*. It wasn't until this point that Reinaldo felt that he was "the absolute owner" of his words.

"THE FEAR OF THOSE WHO LEARN THEIR LESSONS THROUGH THE TRAUMA OF OTHERS"

Cuba breeds a particular kind of fear. Reinaldo uses the term "*pena ajena,*" which another blogger, Miriam Celaya, describes as a feeling that is "provoked by the acts of others and that, involuntarily, moves one to feel a certain mix of compassion and shame for the protagonists." Reinaldo is referring to people whose fear stems from what has happened to those around them rather than from any direct repression. Or, as he put it in a 2008 blog post, "the fear of those who learn their lessons through the trauma of others." Call it secondhand terror.

As Laritza's experience shows, once you are branded a counterrevolutionary, the Cuban authorities will go to great lengths to intimidate you and your family. But most ordinary people never got to this point. In the same blog post Reinaldo plainly admitted, "You can be certain that in Cuba the vast majority of the people living on the island have never suffered on their own flesh direct repression by the government." Sure, some have been taken to prison and others have been issued warnings. Still, he wrote, "the number of people who have been beaten or insulted at a rally is so small, compared to the atrocities in Rwanda, the abuses in the Gaza strip, or the outrages in Iraq, that it's almost painful to denounce it." He continued, "Why then does an index finger cross the lips, eyes widen, or a look of horror reflect on the faces of my friends, when at their houses I commit the indiscretion of making a political comment within earshot of the neighbors?"

In 2011, on my third trip to Cuba, I personally fell victim to this kind of secondhand terror. My stated reason for being in Cuba that year was the International Festival of New Latin American Cinema, which I did in fact attend. But there's no question that the Cuban government would not look kindly on my spending so much time chatting with dissident bloggers—or, in their view, counterrevolutionaries. I had previously worked at the U.S. State Department, as a member of Secretary of State Hillary Clinton's Policy Planning Staff. And although I had formally left government several months earlier, I was concerned that I would be mistaken for some kind of undercover, U.S. government–funded agent.

Still, as on my two previous trips, nobody confronted me. If I was being watched or followed, I didn't know about it. Yet when the people who ran the bed-and-breakfast where I was staying asked to take a photograph of me, most likely to have a picture of another happy tourist in their casa, I felt almost sick with anxiety. This was rather silly, as the couple already had my passport number, which the wife, Elisa, had diligently marched over to the authorities the morning after I arrived. She had also taken the visa out of my passport. I didn't like the idea of being in Cuba without a visa in my possession, but Elisa promised she would bring it back after showing it to the relevant authorities. "It's just about control," she explained. The translucent veil of disapproval around the word "control" made me suspect that she wasn't entirely sympathetic to the Cuban Revolution. Her house was decorated with pictures of her smiling daughter and her family, who were living in Miami.

Two incidents were the source of my secondhand terror. The first was the fate of Alan Gross, who had recently been sentenced to fifteen years in prison for trying to distribute communications equipment to religious groups in Cuba. In 2009 Gross, a sixty-year-old subcontractor for USAID, was arrested at Havana's José Martí International Airport and taken to Villa Marista prison. Development Alternatives Inc., the Maryland firm where Gross worked, had a multimillion dollar government contract for Cuban democracy promotion. Gross had visited Cuba to deliver computer and satellite equipment to members of Jewish groups. On the visit that led to his arrest, he was on a follow-up mission.

In March 2011 Gross was handed his fifteen-year sentence. The case was appealed to the Supreme Court of Cuba, but the sentence was upheld. Gross's health deteriorated, and he lost a hundred pounds while in custody. The U.S. government has been utterly unable to get him released, creating another painful sticking point between the United States and Cuba.

Gross was convicted of participating in a "subversive project of the U.S. government to try to destroy the Revolution, by way of the use of info-communication systems out of the control of the authorities."

I understood perfectly well that Gross and I were not in the same league. There was a vast difference between interviewing bloggers and actually trying to aid in covert communications. And although Gross's punishment was clearly excessive, Cuba's reaction was hardly surprising. The customs form I filled in to enter the country directly asked if I was bringing weapons, live animals, pornography, drugs, commercial samples, satellite communications equipment, or walkie-talkies. It was obvious that in all these cases the only right answer was no.

The greater cause of my secondhand terror involved someone in a situation far more similar to my own. Right before departing for Havana, I had coffee with Ted Henken, an ebullient Cuba specialist and academic at New York's Baruch College. In April, Henken had traveled to Cuba and had interviewed eighteen bloggers as well as micro-entrepreneurs. His trip ended rather badly. As he was preparing to leave the country from Havana's José Martí Airport, he spotted two state security agents scoping him quite openly. He then heard his name called on the loudspeaker, asking him to proceed to immigration.

Upon passing through immigration, he was led into a small interrogation room. "The agents quickly closed the door behind them and begin immediately to ask me very pointed questions, demonstrating that they were perfectly clued in to all of my movements during the previous 12 days," Henken wrote on his blog afterward. The agents were clearly displeased. They told him that someone visiting Cuba on a tourist visa should be sipping mojitos on a beach, not conducting interviews. He was also told, "You met with a bunch of bloggers who are nothing more than counter-revolutionary elements—and you support them."

In fact, Henken had made a point of meeting with bloggers of various political stripes. He aimed to hear the perspectives of such government critics as Laritza as well as those of more conciliatory writers, or "*oficialistas*." It's unclear what made the authorities more angry: Henken's meeting with counterrevolutionaries or his apparent attempt to foster understanding between bloggers on different sides of the political divide. In any event, he was told that this would be his last trip to Cuba.

After hearing Henken's story, I couldn't imagine how I would safely conduct my own interviews. Henken had met, only eight months earlier, with many of the same "counterrevolutionary" bloggers I was planning to see. I ended up keeping a far lower profile, having fewer meetings than Henken, and also abstaining from tweeting or posting any public information during my trip.

Although nobody confronted me, I was haunted by Henken's and Gross's experiences. I was constantly dissembling to the infinite stream of chatty Cubans who crossed my path. I didn't use my real email address. It got comic: for some bizarre reason I told the people I was staying with that I taught Latin American literature. It was the first thing that came to mind. Almost immediately thereafter a white-haired neighbor appeared with a list of other literature "experts" I had to visit in Havana.

I sometimes felt as if I were rising outside of my body and viewing myself through the lens of a camera. There I was, buying ice cream for a Cuban friend, waiting outside a movie theater for Laritza, or lingering a little too long at a café. Even after I left Cuba, I continued to worry about photographs taken of me on the island or information that I may have accidentally given away. In other words, I was acting crazy.

Nor was I the only foreigner behaving this way. One day I was at the film festival headquarters at the Hotel Nacional, waiting on an endless queue to check my email. A frizzy-haired woman, seemingly from North America, was taking her sweet time browsing through photos on one of the few precious computers. She noticed me fidgeting impatiently behind her, and she said in a loud, nervous whisper to her friend beside her, "I really don't like the way people watch me on the computer." She essentially mistook *me* for some kind of Cuban agent.

Reinaldo described this abstract paranoia as a kind of brain damage that has paralyzed three generations of Cubans. One of the results of this *temor paralizante* is widespread docility. In a 2009 blog post Reinaldo wrote about a visit to Santiago de Cuba, known as the cradle of the revolution and the grave site of the revolutionary hero Frank País, who helped launch a rebellion against the Fulgencio Batista regime.

Reinaldo mused in his blog,

At any site in Santiago de Cuba, I ask myself the same question: Was the rebellion a thing of the past? Is it possible that the fear of losing a job or a university career is stronger than the fear of losing a life? Is it easier and less risky to take up arms than to express our ideas? I talked to young and old, men and women, Protestants, [Catholics] and atheists, workers, intellectuals and students. I didn't find a single person who told me they felt happy with their current situation or the conditions the country is living through, but nor did I find anyone (actually I found one) who had publicly expressed their discontent, their dissatisfaction, or even the slightest difference of opinion.

After the Egyptian Revolution in 2011, Laritza wrote on her blog that such an event was unlikely to take place in Cuba, in part because Cubans were too busy making small talk with officials to fight for justice. The Egyptian Revolution made her envious, but also made her see Cuba as a place where "fear, the father of resignation and conformity, immobilizes." She added, "*The Silence of the Lambs* should be the name of the film that Cubans star in every day." This sense of resignation permeated everyday life. I witnessed it even at the film festival, which I first attended in 2008. That year the festival hosted a competition that included more than a hundred recent Latin American films, as well as many others from around the world. Tickets were cheap, theaters were comfortable, and the films were often truly first-rate. Some Cubans took about two weeks of vacation from work, half of their yearly allowance, just to attend the festival. After all, where else would they go? Some people would see up to five films a day.

Jorge Luis, twenty-nine, a vendor in a food market, took two weeks off to attend the festival. He carried a piece of paper on which he marked the films he had seen with initials to distinguish between the good, the bad, and the just okay (*B*, *M*, or *R*—*buena*, *mala*, *regular*). He told me he dreamed of visiting Canada or Puerto Rico, but Cubans, he said, "don't do what they want; they do what they can."

This attitude of calm acceptance permeated the festival. Right in the middle of an entertaining Puerto Rican film, *La Mala*, the screen went blank, likely due to a technical problem. The audience waited, but the movie never came back. After a few noises of protest, the crowd calmly filed out of the theater.

While Cubans would wait on endless lines to see a film, my foreign status afforded me special treatment. Once, I went to see a movie with María, and I balked at the long waits outside the theater. "Come with me," she said, bringing me to the side entrance. "Now, don't speak Spanish," she ordered. There was a woman guarding the door, and as we walked past her, I loudly said a few random phrases in English. María nodded in silent agreement. The woman at the door threw us a brief, disinterested glance as we sailed past her into the theater. María started referring to English as "*el idioma mágico*," or the magic language.

When I was alone, however, I didn't like to use the foreigner trump card. For this reason I was unable to get into a screening of one of the most popular films at the 2011 festival. *Fábula*, which was made in Cuba, had already generated considerable buzz for its harsh look at the country's economic desperation. The line for it stretched into infinity. Without my magic language I had no chance of getting in, so I just watched the crowd from across the street. What I saw was telling.

The line was cordoned off and broken into several sections. Police were letting in only a handful of people at a time, making sure that no one else got anywhere near the theater door. As Cubans clamored to see a movie about the troubles they faced every day, foreigners and other dubious "VIPs" streamed through a roped-off entrance. Most striking was the crowd's total acceptance of this ludicrous reality. Sure, there were occasional flickers of energy in the line. One older woman baldly walked ahead of everyone and tried to enter the theater from the side, and a cop pushed her back.

But the resistance was halfhearted. Nobody really expected to reach the front of the line. The police efforts to control the crowd were equally spiritless. The cops tended to be diminutive men and women with thin arms. There wasn't the slightest threat of escalation. And when the movie finally began, a huge crowd of Cubans was left waiting outside. Soon enough, they placidly retreated. A few cops milled in front of the building. I was almost certain that several rows in the theater remained empty for the entire show, waiting for VIPs who never arrived.

"PEOPLE HAVE TO SEARCH FOR THEIR OWN VOICE
BECAUSE THEY NEVER HAD ONE"

Reinaldo and I arrived at the Malecón. It was growing dark, and we sat on the wall beside the blackening, boatless sea.

"I want to tell you a story," said Reinaldo. He and Yoani had recently left Havana and snuck away to Cienfuegos Bay. They just wanted a bit of fun and relaxation, and they soon came upon a boat that offered a tour of the bay. Immediately, an argument ensued. Yoani guessed that such a decadent-looking boat must be off-limits to Cuban nationals, but Reinaldo wanted to get on board. He was reminded of a boat he had taken in 1975, when he was working for the official publication *Cuba Internacional*. There had been an open bar and an extravagant buffet. But what struck him most was that rare feeling of being one of the chosen ones. For once, he was among the writers and photographers who boarded the boat while everyone else stayed on land. This long-ago boat ride had taken on an almost mystical status, and he wanted Yoani to have a similar experience.

Reinaldo's will prevailed, and the couple went to the marina office and bought two tickets. They didn't bother to hide their Havana accents, and they weren't asked for identification. They boarded the boat, finding themselves surrounded by sunburned French-speaking tourists. They found a choice corner where they could take photos of the expansive bay, and Yoani's doubts momentarily subsided. Were they really going to get away with this?

Reinaldo and Yoani enjoyed the view for a few short moments until a boat captain approached and asked where they were from. "I am from Camagüey, she's from Havana," Reinaldo said proudly. The captain continued to smile and mentioned something about drinks. He left and returned soon after to tell them that no

Cubans were allowed on board. Yoani briefly considered clutching the rails in protest, but then she decided, what's the point? Reinaldo dusted off his French and explained to the bewildered tourists what had just happened. Nobody got off the boat in solidarity. Reinaldo and Yoani disembarked, and the boat pulled away.

Reinaldo finished his story. He was sitting cross-legged on the seawall, still wearing his bulging backpack. He seemed enormously pleased with himself. It all seemed pretty depressing to me.

"We both blogged about the boat, Yoani and I!" he explained. "We have evidence of the apartheid in Cuba for everyone to see!" I must have looked unconvinced. "Okay, imagine this," he said. "I go into an office and ask to have an Internet connection in my house. Now, I know that I don't have the right to this connection, only foreigners do. It's just a fantasy. But I want to put on a performance. So I go to the office and ask for a contract. The employee says, 'Of course, sir, just show me your passport.' So I show her my Cuban identity card."

Unsurprisingly, this hypothetical scenario ends with Reinaldo leaving the office without an Internet connection. Reinaldo beamed. I was confused. "I am happy!" he exclaimed. "I have proof of discrimination against Cubans." In a similar piece of performance art, Yoani posted an audio recording of herself demanding an explanation from Cuban authorities who, yet again, refused her permission to leave the country.

Most Cubans wouldn't dream of pulling off such a public spectacle. You always have to be politically correct in front of others. Reinaldo told me that Yoani's father worked as a train engineer. In the 1980s one of his relatives gave him a pair of blue jeans. He loved them. But wearing the jeans around town would have raised questions about the purity of his ideology. So he only wore his jeans inside the house.

The blogger Iván García once told me about an experience he had in high school that affected him deeply. In 1980 an economic downturn and other problems led ten thousand Cubans to seek asylum in the Peruvian embassy. As a result, Fidel Castro announced that any Cuban who wanted to leave was free to do so. This prompted a mass exodus from Cuba's Mariel Harbor and led to a flood of Cuban immigrants in Miami, some of whom had been released from prisons and mental health facilities.

Cubans who intended to take part in this exodus, widely known as the Mariel boatlift, were subjected to acts of "repudiation" on the island. Iván remembered that his high school literature teacher, whom he deeply admired, planned to participate in the boatlift. The head of the school directed him and other students to go to the teacher's house and throw tomatoes, eggs, and stones at his windows. The order bothered Iván, but what followed disturbed him even more.

He went to talk to his history teacher, whom he trusted. "I don't want to go and throw tomatoes simply because he wants to leave Cuba," he said. His history teacher told him that if he didn't want to participate in the group repudiation, he should tell everyone he was sick. Under no circumstances should he give his real reasons for staying home. Iván was struck by the understanding that he lived in a country where teachers instructed you to lie.

The result of these kinds of pressures, as Reinaldo explained, is "three generations of muzzled Cubans who had no material way to express their ideas." And if someone was accused of being a counterrevolutionary, Reinaldo said, he would scramble to justify his behavior rather than assert his rights. "It's like when a man walks into a room and finds his wife in bed with a lover, and the lover says, 'It's not what you think!'" Hardly anybody, Reinaldo continued, thinks to say, "I want my lawyer, and *nada más!*"

Reinaldo believed that the experience of blogging could liberate people from their submission. In today's Cuba, he said, "People have to search for their own voice because they never had one. And when a person finds his own voice, he starts to know himself better and to like himself more. Because these are people who were speaking with someone else's voice for their entire lives, the voice of *Granma*, the voice of the television news, the voice of Castro. And then they discover that they have their own opinion and their own distinct way to say things; they find themselves."

Reinaldo noted a dividing line between online critics and those who took to the streets. He doubted the effectiveness of those Cuban activists who, carrying signs, yelled "*tiranía!*" "That person's shout is heard by fifty or a hundred people within a thirty-meter radius," he said. "But the voice a person uses in digital space is a message that reaches many more people, and that remains there for all time."

Reinaldo was the "godfather" of several blogs. Some of the bloggers had no experience at all with the Internet. They may have lived outside of Havana, and Reinaldo instructed them on how to find Internet connections in hotels. Sometimes people nervously sent proposed blog texts to him. They asked, "Do you think I can write this? Is it correct?" And he responded, "That's your problem." Reinaldo told me that one blogger tried to cram all his complaints into every post: "When you try to say everything in each text, then each text becomes the same. If you want to talk about the Internet, don't talk about exit visas. If you are going to talk about the ladies [who wear white in a gesture of protest], don't talk about how there's not enough food or how salaries aren't high enough. Each one is a big theme, you have to focus. But I also say, 'It's your blog, and you can do what you want in your blog.'"

Reinaldo noted one of the best things about blogging, after all, is that you can communicate with your audience without the intervention of an editor. Owing to the lack of connectivity on the island, it used to be that bloggers in Cuba communicated primarily with their readers overseas. But Reinaldo said that this is changing. "Every day there is more of an echo because more people have computers."

And sometimes a simple computer is all you need. In 2008 Ricardo Alarcón, then president of the Cuban National Assembly, addressed students at a university for computer science. A student asked about restrictions to Internet access and why workers' salaries are in Cuban pesos when so many basic goods are sold in convertible pesos. "That means a worker has to work two or three days to buy a toothbrush," the student said. Although the video of the speech was never aired publicly in Cuba, Reinaldo said many Cubans got a chance to see it. These viewers did not necessarily have an Internet connection, but they may have had flash drives.

Reinaldo has a saying: "When you leave your house, always bring money, a condom, and a flash drive." He quickly assured me, laughing, that this somewhat macho motto isn't to be taken literally. "Don't worry, I didn't bring a condom." Then he reached into his backpack and pulled out a small flash drive, an essential tool for the Cuban blogger. Although these drives can be rather expensive to buy in Havana, Cubans often receive them as gifts from foreign visitors.

Reinaldo explained it to me this way. Say you have a friend who wants to learn how to play guitar with his toes. One day you are on the Internet and you miraculously find an entire page dedicated to the art of playing guitar with your feet. In America, one would simply copy the Web address and send it by email. In Cuba, you would copy the page onto a flash drive, get on a bus, and deliver the drive to your friend. It takes a little more effort, but the information still gets there. "In the world, information has to compete to attract attention," Reinaldo said. "In Cuba, however, people have to fight for information."

———

It was growing dark along the Malecón. The city lights gleamed off the water. The wind picked up and waves rose and crashed below us. A black man with long braids was approaching. He carried a guitar. He spotted me and Reinaldo sitting on the wall. Would we like to hear a song? Maybe he too mistook Reinaldo for a foreigner. The guitarist had a gentle demeanor. He hardly spoke, just faced us and the water, waiting. I lowered my eyes and smiled apologetically, an approach doomed to fail with any halfway persistent vendor. The man stood and waited.

Reinaldo turned to him and said cheerfully, "We are conspiring here."

The guitarist smiled.

"No, really," Reinaldo said, "we are conspiring together." He gestured vaguely toward the road. "And there are cameras everywhere." The man still smiled, but uncertainty was crawling across his face. I was feeling a little uncomfortable myself, even though I knew this performance was largely for my benefit. Reinaldo was fighting absurd paranoia with absurd bravado. The guitarist slowly puckered his lips, as if to say something, but then he lowered his head and glided away. Reinaldo turned back to me as if to say, Now, where were we?

Reinaldo's ebullience was contagious. Even though I was out in public with one of Cuba's high-profile "counterrevolutionaries," I was breathing more easily than I had since arriving in Havana. Reinaldo openly mocked the virus of fear that had infected his country. For one evening at least, we comported ourselves exactly as we were. He was a critical Cuban blogger, and I was an American writer, and we were two people chatting by the sea. Why be afraid? I realized then that if the Reinaldos of Cuba reached a critical mass, the island would be a radically different place.

Reinaldo seemed to believe this would happen. He said that more people were performing small acts of defiance. He told me about a group of Cubans who protested the double currency system by trying to pay national money in places that accepted only convertible pesos. This would likely end with someone calling the police.

"All your stories have unhappy endings," I said. "What's the point of protest if you never win?"

Reinaldo looked at me. He responded, "What is the difference between us and Rosa Parks, who thought she had the right to sit on that bus?"

"I WANT MY LAWYER, AND *NADA MÁS*!"

In December 2011, two years after we first met, I found myself waiting for Laritza outside a crowded movie theater in Havana. I sat down on a ledge next to a man who was making miniature animals out of string and rolled-up newspaper. Compared with China, where buildings were built or razed in the blink of an eye, Cuba hardly changed from one trip to the next. It felt as if I would arrive in Havana and find people standing exactly where I had left them years earlier.

Laritza was so slow to respond to my emails that I decided it would be more efficient to fly down to Cuba and talk to her directly. I called her soon after I arrived, and she told me to meet her the following day. But just as we were about to nail down a location, her phone went dead. Her phone had been temporarily cut off in the past, likely because of her dissident activity. But this time she just had no more money on her phone. It took another few days before I was able to reach her.

When Laritza finally arrived, her hands were covered in a

thin white powder. "I just ate a churro," she explained. Laritza seemed infinitely more relaxed than she had been two years earlier. The first time we met, she had her hair pulled back and was as focused as an arrow. Now she seemed less earnest, or maybe just more comfortable in her skin. She looked a little plumper and was wearing jeans, a denim jacket, and sneakers.

She also had an apprentice. We were soon joined by Yaremis Flores, who aspired to be a blogger like Laritza. Yaremis was black and in her late twenties, attractive and polished in a slim T-shirt with a light scarf draped around her neck and a professional-looking shoulder bag. The three of us went to a nearly empty café and sat at an outdoor table. We asked for coffee and learned that there was none left. So I ordered a pizza that was unappealing even by Havana standards. It was enormous and covered with thick, greasy cheese.

Laritza and Yaremis communicated in Cuban Spanish, fast and furious like everyone around them, but they also spoke the language of law. This is a highly precise vernacular, dotted with specific rights, crimes, and punishments. The two women quoted from the penal code, the law of civil procedure, and the Cuban Constitution, referring to specific articles by number. They provided these details like students who are too impatient to raise their hands in class.

Laritza and Yaremis met while studying law at the University of Havana, where they discussed Cuba's constitution and compared it with the constitutions of other Latin American countries. In their studies and chats outside of class, they became increasingly aware of their country's limitations. Laritza learned that unlike in the American movies she had watched on TV, Cuban courts didn't have juries. The Cuban Constitution grants some right to assembly, but only provided it is not "exercised against the existence and objectives of the socialist state." Or, as Yaremis put it, "in Cuba, you have the right to associate, but only if it's in favor of the government. You have the right to free expression, but only if you are going to say what the government wants to hear. So in reality, what rights do we have?"

Yaremis's doubts only increased after graduation, when she went on to become a young judge. She certainly wasn't doing it for the money: she told me her starting salary was around $13 a month (it eventually increased to around $40 a month). In that role she not only stared Cuban injustice in the face, she actually participated in it. Instead of by a jury in municipal court, a person's fate would be determined by a panel of three judges, only one of whom had a degree in law. That person was Yaremis. "When the judges sit down to deliberate," she told me, "you realize you have another person's life in your hands . . . I had to explain to the accused and their families why this decision was taken. It is very difficult to explain something of which you are not convinced."

Often the crimes seemed linked to economic desperation. In the café, Yaremis reeled off a string of Cuban economic crimes. *Receptación*: you accept an object, but it turns out it was stolen; you should have known better. *Acaparamiento*: you bought too many things. What are you doing with so many cases of oil, for example? You must be planning to sell them or distribute them illegally. *Incumplimiento del deber de preservar bienes y entidades estatales*: failure to protect the goods of the state. Say you have something that is considered property of the state and you lock that object in a safe. But you entrust the password to someone else and they steal from you. You should have known better. Furthermore, the definition of state property is wide. If you are a storekeeper, the goods and appliances in the store may well fit this definition.

Yaremis was also highly skeptical about the judicial process. Often accusations were based on the reports of some citizen informer. A person could go to jail for three months to a year, she said, "based on the mere suspicion of having done something." It was even worse for political cases. Yaremis told me a story about a sixty-five-year-old man who was accused of having cables in his house to connect to the Internet. The Cuban government maintains tight control over citizen connectivity, so this case was considered a political priority. As such, there was great pressure on the judges to deliver an expedited judgment.

When the case landed on Yaremis's desk, she wasn't satisfied with the evidence presented to her. She thought the man deserved proper deliberation, especially given that someone of his age would not be well suited for the prison system. Yaremis said that she didn't feel comfortable making a decision so quickly. She was ultimately taken off the case, and it was given to someone else. She didn't know the final outcome, but she thought there was a possibility that the man got sentenced to three years in jail. Had she remained on the case, she said, she wouldn't have been able to sleep at night. But the problem was that even if you take a principled stance and say you won't do something unethical, "there's always someone who will."

Feeling alienated at work, in 2011 Yaremis started writing anonymously on a blog for an independent lawyers group called the Cuban Law Association, whose goals include increasing legal awareness among Cuban citizens. The group was not legally recognized in Cuba. Because she couldn't afford to use the Internet from hotels, she would sometimes connect at the U.S. Interests Section, which stands in place of an embassy. This was hardly an ideal scenario, as even the slightest interaction with the U.S. government gave Yaremis the appearance of a "*mercenario.*"

Strange things started happening at work. A woman showed up to meet Yaremis, saying she was a family member of a defendant. But the woman, who claimed to be pleading for justice for her relative, was dressed in a military uniform. Something didn't feel right. Yaremis saw the encounter as a visit from an official. She took it as a subtle warning.

And before long, the inevitable came to pass. "They fired me in a very diplomatic way," she said. Judges have to take semiregular exams, and now Yaremis was told that she had failed. She believed it was just a pretext. "I was very upset, very disappointed because I was doing good work," she said. "All my evaluations were excellent." But she was also a critic who associated with dissidents and who would not be pressured by her superiors. In other words, she wouldn't get another job for the state. The pretty young professional suddenly found herself cast outside the system.

But Yaremis didn't regret her defiance. "I was doing exactly what I learned in school," she said. "A judge administers justice in the name of the Cuban people, not in the name of the government."

Yaremis Flores was born in Havana in 1983. Her childhood was rather solitary, as her brother wasn't born until she was fifteen. Her parents tended to be overprotective and wouldn't let her go anywhere by herself. She was afraid of animals, afraid of the dark, afraid of everything. "I didn't have many friends when I was growing up. I was raised with many fears, and shyness was instilled in me," she said. She read and studied a lot, but found it painful to raise her hand in class. Her parents had to work hard just to support her. Her father was a professor of physics and astronomy, but his salary was a "*miseria*." Her mother worked for a trading company, but her pay was also very low.

Yaremis said that she started writing a blog "out of the necessity to express myself and the necessity to communicate, out of the necessity that people know what's really happening in the streets." When she first started blogging, her prose was rigid and cautious. Laritza taught her that a successful blog requires much more than recording the facts. There needs to be a story, including a hook that draws readers in. Yaremis began writing posts on Laritza's own blog, and soon after, her prose became more expressive.

In late 2011 Yaremis wrote a post about *Granma*, the official Cuban newspaper. She described seeing a recent article about a debate by the Parliamentary Commission regarding the effectiveness of the Cuban economic model. The commission unsurprisingly found that things were going rather well. In places where success appeared lacking, the commission responded with empty promises about working toward the "development" of the country and the "satisfaction" of the people.

In her blog post, Yaremis compared that recent issue of *Granma* with those of the past: "A few days ago, dusting off memories, my grandmother found an edition of *Granma* dated Wednesday, July 12, 1989. It was yellow with age. She had saved it as though it were a relic." That old issue of *Granma* discussed the topics to be debated during the Fifth National Assembly. They included the subjects of construction, public services, and worker protections. Yaremis wrote that from the standpoint of the present, the failures were obvious. "The housing situation is precarious; the shortage of building materials; public services in decline; and don't even talk about the protection of the workers." She observed that the two issues of the state newspaper, while nearly two decades apart, were disturbingly similar. She wrote, "So I ask myself, do I have to wait another 20 years to read another edition of Granma which will capture the same thing?"

In addition to occasionally writing for websites outside Cuba, Yaremis blogged on *Jurisconsulto*, which was administered by Laritza. The blog's goal was to highlight legal violations in Cuba, with the hope that citizens would become more vociferous about demanding their rights. According to the blog's mission statement, Cubans' "ignorance in these basic, human rights–related matters is what allows the regime to politically manipulate the population."

Laritza and Yaremis set out to remedy this problem. Both women went on to work at Cubalex, which offers free legal advice to any Cuban who needs it. The company's aim was to educate

Cubans about the rights that they have, at least on paper. Cubalex consisted of Laritza, Yaremis, and a couple other people, plus a secretary. The office was Laritza's house. Nobody got a salary. The services were free not only out of altruism, but because charging for them could have been considered an "economic crime." Laritza and Yaremis survived on the money they made by writing for such overseas websites as the Spain-based Diario de Cuba, or the Miami-based Cubanet. They emphatically claimed that they did not accept money from any foreign government.

They also relied on the kindness of strangers: sometimes one of the foreign readers of Laritza's blog would come to the island and buy office supplies for her. She proudly showed me a staple remover and ink cartridges she got in this manner. One Spanish reader bought her meat and oil from a Cuban website, and yet another fan, also from Spain, bought her a new pair of eyeglasses. It is also possible to add money to Cuban cell phones from abroad, and sometimes Laritza would find that her phone had been miraculously recharged.

Laritza has won some small victories. One man told Laritza that the authorities confiscated his camera. The police were apparently dubious that he could legally own such an expensive object, so they assumed it was stolen. The man said that the camera was a gift from a relative overseas, but the police wouldn't return it.

Many stories of this kind end here. But in this case Laritza accompanied the man to the police station. According to the law of civil procedure, she said, the police have to return the camera to its owner. After fifteen days, the police returned it.

Laritza believes that often the Cuban police are not familiar with the laws they are supposed to be enforcing. It usually doesn't matter, because citizens are so passive. But knowledge of the law does afford a certain degree of power. Officers don't want to get into trouble with their superiors because a citizen filed a complaint against them, nor do they want to be publicly shamed on some troublesome Cuban blog. Yaremis thought that the Cuban police were afraid of having their names appear on the Internet, as they may want to apply for a U.S. visa one day.

In 2011 Laritza first took me to see Cubalex headquarters, aka her house. She lived in Calvario, which while still in Havana is rather far from the heart of the city. We met in Vedado, not far from the Hotel Nacional, then jumped into one of the bright blue 1950s-era American cars for which Havana is well known. This one was acting as a kind of collective taxi or, more accurately, a public bus. People got in and out at various locations. At one point we were joined by a woman in a hot-pink shirt, at another, a man in ripped jeans eating a hot dog. The interior of the car was torn vinyl.

The car trundled through the streets, which became dirtier and livelier. Women sold fruit on the street. Police in blue-and-gray uniforms stood against a wall; an officer cleaned his car with a cloth. The architecture remained grand, with pink arches and sculptured window frames, but the paint seemed to peel faster as we bumped down the road. Cuban music blared on the radio. "The music was agreeable enough," Laritza commented after we arrived at her house, "but usually it is much louder, and reggaeton." She was referring to the ubiquitous Latin-Jamaican dancehall music that she despises. We got out of the blue car and hailed a different one, which took us directly to Laritza's home. The whole journey lasted nearly an hour.

Laritza's house was messy and run-down, but homey nonetheless. The backyard was lush with vegetation, and I thought I heard the sound of a rooster. There was a television in the kitchen. Laritza lived with her mother, her husband, and her son. Her mother was heavyset, and for most of my visit she sat on a folding chair in the kitchen, watching TV. Laritza's husband had a hulking frame and a gentle face. He seemed shy around me and answered my questions in as few words as possible. Her son was a typical eleven-year-old, restlessly moving through the house.

Laritza's office was right off the kitchen. There was a large wooden desk, a computer, and a diploma from the University of Havana hanging on the wall. Her shelves were filled with books about the law. I also noticed the Spanish-language version of Obama's *Dreams from My Father*, which Laritza had gotten from a friend.

It wasn't long before visitors arrived, seeking advice. Laritza welcomed an older woman who had a protruding belly and hair pulled back into a ponytail. She was accompanied by her teenage daughter, who was wearing studded jeans and was inexplicably sucking her thumb. The girl sat silently, slumped in a chair across from her mother. I was sitting by the windowsill when the pair entered the room. The woman shot me a quizzical look. "She's an independent journalist," Laritza explained. The woman seemed satisfied. I once met a friendly young woman who described herself as a journalist. When I asked her if she was independent, she blanched and lowered her voice. "Oh, no. 'Independent' is a very bad word," she told me. "It means you can't write for official publications."

The mother launched into a nearly hysterical stream of verbiage, and Laritza looked concerned but calm. I soon deduced the basic facts of the situation. This woman's son was convicted of murder. He was in jail, on a hunger strike. Now his mother was threatening to go on a hunger strike as well.

"I'm going to do it," she said, her voice strained with anguish.

"No," Laritza said. "You have to stay strong and fight for your son."

"I'm going to do it!" the woman persisted, her voice splitting into a sob.

"No!" Laritza said. She was wearing white pants and a white shirt. She stood by the wall, coolly smoking her cigarette.

"I'm going to!"

"No! No! No!"

The woman believed that her son had been wrongly convicted. She had no legal recourse other than Laritza, who gave free advice from her home. Laritza knew that if this woman went on a hunger strike, it wouldn't do any good. Nobody knew who she was. It would be far more effective for Laritza, an increasingly known quantity, to publicize the case on her blog and overseas websites.

"He found a good lawyer," the woman said of her son, "but he is asking for too much money."

"That's not a good lawyer," Laritza retorted.

This particular case involved a jeweler who was apparently murdered in his home as part of a robbery. Six men, including the son of the woman at Laritza's house, were arrested for the crime. Laritza thought that the legal proceedings were flawed, and she documented all the violations on her blog. In one of her posts on the topic she wrote, "There is also no physical evidence to put the suspects at the scene of the crime. Yet the authorities are keeping them detained, even where the preparatory acts to the commission of a crime and the withdrawal, according to the Cuban Penal Code, are not punishable."

Laritza also wrote about the case for the Spain-based Diario de Cuba website. Meanwhile, she helped the mother of the accused submit a written complaint before the prosecution, the Interior Ministry, and the court of justice in Havana. Laritza suspected that the young men had been presumed guilty from the beginning. They came from a poor neighborhood, not far from where she lived, and had questionable backgrounds. But for Laritza, these details shouldn't determine their fate. "I learned in school that you are innocent until proven guilty," she told me.

The mother of the accused clearly had an uphill battle. It was highly likely that her son would end up spending the better part of his life behind bars. Still, Laritza's words were having a calming effect. The first order of business was to get her son to stop this hunger strike. "Look, this is what I'm going to do," Laritza said. "On Tuesday I'm going to go to the jail and visit your son. I am going to say, Look at what you are doing to your mother." The woman nodded obediently.

"WHEN SOMEONE IS DETAINED, EVERYONE KNOWS ABOUT IT"

Cuba has two kinds of people. There are the independent bloggers and other liberated individuals, who glide confidently through the streets, willing to tell pretty much anyone what they think. Then there's everyone else. When I first met Yaremis, in 2011, I could see that she had already moved over to the other side. Once you cross that threshold of fear, she told me, "you can't go back." She said that she felt protected. "We have a strong weapon," she said of the Internet. She understood that she was not yet famous. She also knew, however, that "if anything happens to me, I can call Laritza and everyone will know that I was detained."

Less than a year later, this is exactly what happened.

In November 2012 I was sitting at my desk in New York City, casually scrolling through my Twitter feed. Yoani Sánchez was tweeting up a storm as usual. It was hardly extraordinary to see tweets about some dissident in Cuba who had been arrested or even beaten. But this time I saw a message that made me jolt upright in my chair. Yaremis Flores had been arrested. I soon learned that Laritza and others went to the state security building to find out what had happened to Yaremis. They were promptly arrested too. So another group of activists, including Yoani, set out to inquire not only about Yaremis, but about Laritza and the others. That group was arrested as well. In total, more than two dozen people were detained. I watched all this from New York, practically in real time, via Twitter and the Diario de Cuba website. Yoani used the hashtag #liberaciondeyaremis.

Earlier that day, Yaremis had left her house to bring soup to her father, who was in the hospital. She was crossing the street when she heard a car brake sharply. Inside the car was an agent from state security and two police officers. The state security agent identified himself as Tomas, although that wasn't necessarily his real name. Tomas was a young mestizo, and he seemed to have some respiratory issue that caused him to breathe through the mouth. He called Yaremis by her name and said, "You have to come with us and turn off your cell phone." Yaremis replied that she had a right to make a phone call.

She immediately called Laritza. Yaremis didn't cry or demonstrate any signs of nervousness. "I don't know where the calm came from," she said. She told Laritza that she was being detained, but she didn't know where they were taking her. She also made a point of telling Laritza the identifying numbers on the shirts of the two police officers, as well as the number of the police car. She knew that in cases of arbitrary detention, these were critical pieces of information. Laritza, on the receiving end of the call, was far less composed then her friend. *"Que!?"* she shouted into the receiver. *"Como?!"*

Then Yaremis was led into the backseat of the police car. When she asked Tomas about her destination, he replied, "You'll see where we take you. I felt like meeting you, but today you're going to find out who I am."

———

Yaremis was accused of "disseminating false information against international peace." This was apparently in reference to an article on the Miami-based Cubanet website that quoted Yaremis as saying that some prisoners died in a prison in Santiago de Cuba. Yaremis said that she had no way to confirm if this was true or not; she was only repeating what her sources had told her.

Yaremis believed that the Cubanet article was an excuse. She said that once she was detained, the authorities brought up her other Internet articles. She thought she was targeted because she was relatively new to dissidence. Arresting Yoani, or even Laritza, would get the attention of Cuban exiles and the international human rights community. "They didn't think that so many people would pay attention to me," Yaremis said. This turned out to be a serious miscalculation.

As soon as Laritza got Yaremis's call, she sprang into action. She had copied down the numbers of the police officers and also of the police car. She called a police information phone line and demanded to know where Yaremis had been taken. But it appeared as if Yaremis wasn't in any police station.

If Laritza couldn't get answers from the police, she would have to go straight to state security. So she and a group of other activists went to section 21, which houses state security. The group included the blogger Antonio Rodiles, who had founded a well-known online debate series called *Estado de SATS*. They all wanted to know where the officers had taken Yaremis.

Laritza said that they didn't shout or carry placards. The activists waited calmly across the street from the security building. Some of them talked on their cell phones. Meanwhile, more police gathered. They blocked traffic and closed off the street. Ultimately, around a dozen people were reportedly arrested, including Laritza. Laritza claimed that Rodiles was treated especially roughly and ended up getting a particularly long sentence, apparently for resisting arrest.

Laritza didn't offer any physical resistance, but she recorded the identifying numbers of the people she spoke to. When the agent "Camilo" said that she was being charged with disturbing public order, Laritza laughed out loud. "You're the ones disturbing public order," she said. She had just been standing there. It was the police who diverted traffic, closed off the street, and generally made a scene. "We'll talk about that tomorrow," Camilo said. She never saw him again. She told me that nobody seemed particularly eager to talk to her.

Laritza was taken directly to her cell. The next day, she demanded to see someone in charge. She said that she needed to know the cause of her arrest, as she had already been detained more than fifteen hours. She said that she would not accept selective application of the law, "because I am a citizen that is protected by the Constitution, which recognizes the right of equality." Finally Laritza was told that she was arrested for counterrevolutionary activity. She responded that she was a lawyer who knew the penal code inside and out, and they needed to identify a crime in the penal code.

The following day, another wave of activists came out to protest the detentions not only of Yaremis but also of Laritza, Rodiles, and others. More than a dozen additional people were detained, including Yoani Sánchez. Reports appeared on Twitter and other overseas websites. Videos of the activists arguing with police were posted on YouTube. On November 9, the U.S.-based Committee to Protect Journalists put out a press release titled "Cuban Reporter Flores Arrested on Anti-State Charges." When Yaremis later learned of this astonishing show of support, she said she had "no words."

Most notable was the reaction inside Cuba. People came out to demonstrate their solidarity with Yaremis and were detained as a result. The chain of events reminded me of something that Miriam Celaya had said a year earlier. She talked about the particular "blogger spirit" that differentiated her contemporaries from

Cuban dissidents of the past. Whereas previous waves of dissidents were often divided by political affiliations, Cuban bloggers had no particular ideology or hierarchy. As such, they enjoyed a special kind of solidarity.

A year before Yaremis's arrest, Miriam presciently remarked of the Cuban blogger community: "This horizontality allows us to support each other, to form networks. And in this way when someone is detained, everyone knows about it, it creates a circle of solidarity that protects the person, one by the other, as if we are in a community without laws, where everyone can think the way they want, express themselves as they wish, and everyone is responsible for what they say."

After she was arrested, Laritza was left alone in a little cell with three concrete beds, white walls, and a window with bars. When someone used the bathroom upstairs, there would be a terrible smell in her room. It was impossible to sleep. She was worried about Yaremis, not to mention her own family. While she was awake, she spotted a huge gray rat. "It was an incredible experience," she told me, her voice tinged with disbelief. She said she was held for twenty-seven hours.

Laritza had never been in a jail cell. At one point she looked out the window, and she could see the trees and vegetation outside. And at that moment it hit her: she was a prisoner. She couldn't get her mind around it. She thought, I didn't kill, I didn't steal, I didn't commit a single crime.

Yaremis had similar feelings of despair. She was in jail in Aldabó with women who had committed economic crimes. She chatted with them to pass the time and tried to give them legal advice. When the authorities talked to her, they kept repeating the same revolutionary rhetoric, as if "they had a chip in their heads." They also used subtle, devastating forms of pressure. "Your daughter is so small," they said of her young child.

But at that point Yaremis was not yet aware of the damage that had been inflicted on her family. Not long before her arrest she had noticed something strange in her house. She lived with her grandmother, her husband, her young daughter, and her uncle. "He raised me like a father," Yaremis said of her uncle.

In the days leading up to her detention she noticed that her uncle was taking an abnormal amount of interest in her comings and goings. He would ask her what time she planned to be in the house the next day, and what time she planned to leave. He would give bizarre explanations for his questions, saying that he needed her to be at home to pick up the phone at a certain time. Yaremis was confused. Why couldn't her grandmother pick up the phone? Her uncle didn't seem nervous, but his behavior wasn't natural.

She mentioned his behavior to Laritza. Yaremis had a bad feeling about leaving the house by herself, although she didn't know exactly what she thought would happen. Detention never crossed her mind, though she thought maybe her possessions weren't safe. When she mentioned her uncle, Laritza was unruffled. At that point Laritza had been in the world of dissidence for several years. Yaremis was a relative newcomer to this shadowy place. Laritza told her friend not to worry. It's perfectly normal to feel a heightened sense of paranoia, but you can't let yourself be crippled by it.

After Yaremis got out of jail, her uncle confessed that state security had contacted him and informed him that his niece was a counterrevolutionary. When Yaremis's husband asked her uncle why he didn't say anything, her uncle replied that he couldn't, because an agreement had been struck. Yaremis knew her grandmother to be loyal to the revolution, but she was less clear about her uncle's politics. It's hard to know what people really think, she told me. Maybe her uncle was just afraid. Maybe he was blackmailed; perhaps he was bribed. "I don't know what they promised him," Yaremis said sadly. "I don't want to know."

Her uncle's love for Yaremis bordered on possessiveness, and he had long been jealous of her husband, Veizant. After Yaremis returned from jail, the relationship between the two men became even more strained, so Yaremis and her husband decided to leave the house and move in with Laritza's family. "He was a father to me," Yaremis repeated. "I couldn't imagine that he would do this." She said that it's possible that one day she will forgive her uncle, but by successfully turning him against his niece, the authorities had created a rift in her family. Yaremis now says of her uncle, "He was a coward. I'm never going to forget it."

But she also says she is not going to stop writing on the Internet or educating Cubans about their rights. "I know what they are capable of," she said of the authorities. "To manipulate my family. I'm going to continue what I'm doing, maybe more carefully. But they didn't change at all the way I think."

I saw Laritza and Yaremis shortly after their stint in jail. Yaremis was released after several days but was still under investigation. It was December 2012, and I went to Laritza's house. Yaremis and her husband were now living there, while Yaremis's young daughter was staying with her paternal grandmother. Laritza, in a worn sundress, was more animated than ever. She made us all dinner: chicken, rice and beans, and a salad made of shredded lettuce. We chatted in her increasingly cluttered office, surrounded by papers. Laritza told me that her son already thought like a dissident. At one point he put on a T-shirt with a picture of Antonio Rodiles, who was arrested alongside Laritza. Laritza's son said, "Let's go to the station to protest!"

Yaremis had lost that crisp, professional look. She was wearing hot-pink pants and several layers of cotton shirts. She looked tired, but she had a quiet fierceness about her. For those who lived and breathed the law, there was no greater insult than being made a prisoner. "I am a person who is doing good things for other people. I am a professional, and to be treated like the lowest rung of society . . . ," she said. She wasn't physically mistreated, but psychological damage was done. "They made me wear a prison uniform. They took a photo of me from the front and from the profile."

Yet despite the trials of the past few months, Yaremis and Laritza said that for the first time, they were professionally satisfied. Every day they learned so many new things! They investigated previously unknown areas of law. Most important, they felt useful. They were giving legal counsel in a country where the wrong advice can have terrible consequences. They heard about some people who were fined for trying to escape Cuba on a makeshift boat. After following bad advice to ignore the fine, the men were sentenced to jail. Laritza and Yaremis were horrified. They would have advised them to pay and then reclaim the money later. Laritza told me that the son of the mother I had met earlier was indeed convicted and sentenced to a long prison term. But Laritza planned to continue fighting the decision. Laritza and Yaremis got constant phone calls and visitors. They showed me a letter that apparently came from someone in prison. By the time it got to them, likely as a result of tampering, the envelope was empty. Everyone wanted their advice.

Yaremis and Laritza also continued to attract international support, in large part thanks to their Internet presence. In 2013, after the Cuban government made it easier to travel, both women received invitations from abroad, even making it to the United Nations in Geneva. In August I caught up with Laritza in Miami, where we were both presenting at a conference organized by the Association for the Study of the Cuban Economy. I was awestruck to see Laritza outside Cuba, composed as always and wearing smart black heels. Laritza was totally unfazed by her first trip to the United States. She told me her most striking impression of life abroad was that there were so few police in the streets.

As for Yaremis, she will probably get into trouble again, but she is prepared. After so many years of scared silence, blogging helped her discover her voice. And now she was ready to raise it. Or, as she put it, "I know my rights, and that's going to be my principal defense."

PART THREE

RUSSIA (APATHY)

"PEOPLE WERE SILENT AND KEPT THE CONSTITUTION OVER THEIR HEADS"

"Eto nash gorod!" the people chanted. This is our city! That's when the police moved in. Blue-shirted cops charged the crowd and began pulling at arms and legs. *"Eto nash gorod!"* The car engines suddenly grew louder, sounding like a swarm of bees. The police grabbed a young man in a red-and-white-checkered shirt who was just standing there. They played a brief tug-of-war with a woman who tried to pull the man toward her. The police easily prevailed, holding the man by his limbs while his button-down shirt flew open and his glasses slid down his face. The cops grabbed another man in olive-green pants and sandals. He seemed almost amused as they clutched his arms and legs, his back arching toward the ground.

"Let's get out of here," Veronika said. "Now." We weaved our way through the knot of agitated protesters. A cop blocked our path, as if to check our papers, then inexplicably changed his mind and let us through. We arrived at the Mayakovskaya Metro station, where the platform was silent and grand. There were marble floors and art deco pillars, stainless steel and pink stone. The police were everywhere. We jumped on the first train that arrived, not looking to see which direction it was going. I slid down into my seat.

Driven mostly by curiosity, I had asked Veronika if she wanted to check out the scene at Triumfalnaya. Veronika, petite and blond, was a Russian American graduate student who was also in Moscow for the summer. She started out as my research assistant in

Moscow and quickly became a friend. Now she touched my arm. "Are you okay?" she asked. I nodded quickly, feeling silly. Russia is a police state, everyone knows that. The whole thing just felt so pointless. I now understood why so many Russians had given up on political demonstrations.

The protesters weren't even asking for much. It was July 31, 2010. Article 31 of the Russian Constitution guarantees freedom of assembly, at least in theory. So on the thirty-first of the month, people came to Moscow's Triumfalnaya Square. They demanded the right to stand there, together. They carried thin white sheets of paper with the number 31 and the text of the constitution.

The police looked bored. A cop with a potbelly and a thick mustache shouted halfheartedly into a megaphone. The younger officers seemed dazed, smiling in confusion. The crowd turned its chorus on them. *"Pozor! Pozor!"* They cried. Shame! Shame! A middle-aged woman tried to protect one of the younger female protesters who was huddled on the ground. Both were quickly overtaken by a mass of police, some in blue, others in camouflage. Someone exclaimed, "Where are you dragging them? What have they done? Who gave you the right?" Car engines roared. The police dragged more people away, hauling them onto buses that were stationed nearby.

Strategy 31 had been initiated in 2009 by Eduard Limonov, founder of the unofficial opposition movement known as the National Bolshevik Party. The protests have attracted the attention of human rights groups and international media. They were held in other Russian cities as well, and even in London and New York. But in Moscow, at least, one thing had remained constant since 2009: authorities denied permission for every one of the Strategy 31 protests, on the grounds that other activities were scheduled to take place on Triumfalnaya Square.

This time, Russian city officials had given a permit to a sports car federation to hold its event at the site where the opposition protest was supposed to take place. A temporary racetrack covered much of the square. Stock cars thundered along while people watched listlessly. Veronika and I went over to the track, and I glimpsed flashes of yellow and white metal zooming by, wheels screeching.

The track seemed to be openly mocking ordinary Russians, asking them: Are you really going to carry on about your rights when you can just look at these cars? The sound of the car engines dwarfed the cries of the protesters. The engines' volume noticeably increased as the police stormed the crowd, suggesting some cynical act of synchronization.

The racetrack easily served its purpose: it ate up the majority of the protest area. The demonstrators were wedged into a tight space, about a block long, near the Tchaikovsky Concert Hall. There were hundreds of them. Student types wearing T-shirts. A young woman with dirty-blond hair messily held by a barrette. The spaghetti straps of her white tank top slid down her shoulders as she was jostled by the crowd. A balding man with a gray-white mustache. Journalists snapped photos and shot video. The police looked oblivious of the cameras. Embarrassing footage of cops pushing around peaceful citizens would later appear on the Web, and nothing would come of it.

Earlier in the day, I had coffee with Max, an acquaintance in a high-level position at a Russian Internet company. We sat at one of the familiar wooden tables of Le Pain Quotidien and talked about Russian search engines. Max loved chatting about technology but seemed bored by Russian politics, so I was surprised when he mentioned that he might stop by Triumfalnaya. Most Russians I spoke to were unhappy with the country's political situation but didn't think there was anything they could do about it.

Russia in 2010 was plagued by apathy born of a deep disappointment. The democracy that so many had idealized during the Soviet era had played out like a mean-spirited joke. President Dmitry Medvedev was handpicked by his predecessor, Vladimir Putin, who still ruled behind the scenes. Elections were widely considered to be unfair, even fraudulent, and I hadn't met a single Russian who thought he would have the slightest say in choosing his next leader. An oft-cited survey found that 85 percent of Russians didn't feel they had any effect on their political process. So although many Russians I spoke to were unhappy with the Kremlin and the corruption that surrounded it, they weren't about to waste their time and energy agitating for change.

It turned out that the Strategy 31 protests were so grimly predictable, I could have known the outcome several months earlier by reading Oleg Kashin's article about the May 31 rally. Kashin, a popular journalist and blogger, had written in the national *Kommersant* newspaper, "History is not made—indeed politics isn't even practiced." Instead, people adhered to well-defined roles. "Someone gets to stand and yell 'Shame!,' someone else gets to be dragged to the bus, another is the photographer, and yet another person later uploads the pictures to the blogs."

The May 31 and July 31 protests were not completely indistinguishable. In May, race cars did not dominate the square. Rather, protesters were told to make way for a blood drive.

In his article, Kashin continued to predict what would happen after the protests. The people carted away on buses would be let off close to midnight with nothing more serious then jaywalking violations. The other protesters would drink cider at a bohemian pub on Nikitsky Boulevard. Maybe a few would go to the police station to hand out water to the detained.

Kashin wrote, "I know this all in advance not because I'm so smart, but because everyone knows this. Everyone—the excited babushka with the number '31' written in marker on the palms of her hands, the quiet intellectual with the thick glasses, and the young leftist in the Che Guevara T-shirt." Kashin said that the only unexpected event of the May 31 demonstration was that a protester's hand was broken by the police. Although it was unfortunate, "it will hardly launch a wave of change across the country."

This was certainly true. Forget the rest of the country; most Moscovites were supremely uninterested in the drama playing out in the heart of their city. That same afternoon, Veronika and I went to an outdoor picnic hosted by *Afisha*, a hipster magazine. Girls in cotton sundresses sprawled in the grass with their T-shirted boyfriends, listening to a rock concert. Veronika and I bought black-and-white-patterned jewelry from a St. Petersburg artisan. Life went on.

I later learned that another thirty-first demonstration was held in St. Petersburg and that around a hundred people were arrested in the two cities, including two well-known activists, Sergei Udaltsov and Boris Nemtsov. After the protests, I texted Max to see what he thought. I hadn't seen him in all the commotion.

"As usual," he replied coolly, "I spent 20-25 minutes there. Met a couple of friends and left before major arrests." He went on to say, to my amazement, that he thought the protest had gone relatively well. "Less fights," he explained. "People were silent and kept the constitution over their heads."

The ultimate futility of Strategy 31 helped explain why ordinary Russians were apathetic about political protests. Without a critical mass, street protesters were weak and vulnerable. If people turned up by the thousands, they would at least pose a challenge to the police. But when they came in the dozens, it was all too easy for cops to pluck them up and throw them onto a bus. It became a vicious cycle: nobody wanted to attend a protest if nobody would be there. Besides, it's not as if anything would change.

There was, however, at least one man in Russia who didn't

subscribe to this fatalistic view. Forget the sad protests of Triumfalnaya Square! He had discovered a space where ordinary Russians could actually have an impact. That space was the Internet, and the man was Alexey Navalny.

"YOU HAVE TO PROPOSE TO PEOPLE THE COMFORTABLE WAY OF STRUGGLE"

When I first met Alexey Navalny, in 2010, he was still fairly unknown outside Russia. Three years later, he was one of the most prominent opposition figures to go on trial since the fall of the Soviet Union. Navalny was charged with embezzlement in a case that was widely seen as politically motivated. In July 2013 he was sentenced to five years in jail, sparking protests in Russia and international condemnation. Navalny had long been barred from state-controlled television, and so his fame was essentially created by the Internet. Even as his trial was featured in headlines all over the world, he said, "My laptop—that's the only media resource I have."

I first met him over Skype. I was sitting in my office at the Carnegie Moscow Center, where I was a global policy fellow. The window sloped sharply down, as in an attic, and overlooked the low roofs of the city. I could see a red church with a gold dome.

It was the summer of 2010, and I had come to Moscow to research the Russian blogosphere. I supposedly had a private office for several months, although my Russian colleagues didn't see it that way. Once, I opened the door to find an unfamiliar woman chatting on the phone. Someone would randomly leave a potted plant on my desk. I didn't take it personally. As I was not a permanent fixture in the office, my Russian colleagues politely ignored my presence. One day I discovered a man's suit hanging from my office door. I took it down and presented it, quizzically, to a secretary sitting outside the office. "Oh, it must belong to Alexey," she said casually, taking the suit. I had no idea who Alexey was or why he was leaving his clothing in my office. After that interaction, the strange objects stopped appearing.

It was from this office that I called Navalny on his cell phone to set up a meeting, and he suggested a video call. I agreed, not understanding that he meant *right now*. Before I truly understood what was happening, the rising star of the Russian Internet was staring at me from my laptop. My office suddenly felt too small.

Navalny, then in his early thirties, was tall and fair, with a blue gaze. He is a good-looking man, a fact that has escaped no one's attention. This isn't what I was thinking when I first saw him, however. It felt as if his blond head were straining to crash through the computer screen. He spoke to me, a complete stranger, as if he had to convey a crucial message in a limited amount of time. I shifted in my chair, backing away from my laptop.

Not only a blogger, Navalny was also a commercial lawyer and shareholder activist. He figured out that by buying small stakes in companies, he could wield those shares to press senior management on their business practices. In 2008 he showed up at the annual shareholders meeting of the oil company Surgutneftegas, in which he owned about $2,000 in stock. In front of hundreds of bewildered shareholders, he interrogated senior management about the company's lack of dividends and transparency. When he was done, a small group of shareholders burst into applause.

Navalny used his blog to detail corruption cases or launch campaigns against specific corporations. He told me, proudly, that his own campaign against Gazprom, Russia's state-owned gas monopoly, spurred officials to reopen a criminal investigation. From

2005 to 2006 Mezhregiongaz (a 100 percent Gazprom-owned subsidiary) was purchasing gas from a small company, Novatek, through an intermediary, Transinvestgas. A police investigation discovered that by using this intermediary, Gazprom was buying gas for a 70 percent markup over purchasing the gas directly. The investigation concluded that the management of Mezhregiongaz and Transinvestgas had organized the scheme to make money off Gazprom. The intermediary later funneled at least $10 million of the excess payments to a consulting company that had been registered with fraudulent documents.

In March 2009, six suspects were indicted in the case, which then got transferred to a different investigative group. In August, Russia's *Vedomosti* newspaper reported that the new investigators dealt a blow to the case by concluding that suspicions against Igor Dmitriev, deputy general director of Mezhregiongaz, were unfounded. Thus ended his criminal investigation.

Navalny, a Gazprom shareholder, decided to fight back. In August he wrote a blog post asking other shareholders to send letters of complaint to the Ministry of Interior and to post comments to Medvedev's blog. Navalny's blog post deftly blended legal detail with sweeping prose. He anticipated that his readers would be loath to strike at Gazprom, so he addressed this problem with a dose of sunny Russian humor: "If you think that a small group of people cannot change anything and everything is useless—kill yourself!"

Hundreds of people filed complaints. And on September 1 the investigators' decision regarding Dmitriev was annulled. In an exuberant post in October, Navalny wrote, "The Interior Ministry has received 512 formal complaints. This has not happened in history." Five hundred and twelve may not seem like a lot, but in Russia at the time, considering the suspension of disbelief required for a group of ordinary people to wage a battle against Gazprom, it was nothing short of extraordinary.

Gazprom was not only Russia's biggest company, it was the largest natural gas producer in the world. A descendant of the Soviet Ministry of Gas, Gazprom was privatized by Boris Yeltsin in the 1990s, with the state keeping around 40 percent of the shares. By the time Putin came to power, in 2000, Gazprom had sunk into a corrupt mess. Putin decided to address this by putting two of his own men, Dmitry Medvedev and Alexey Miller, in charge of the company.

Under Putin's rule, Gazprom effectively became an arm of the Kremlin. In 2001 Gazprom took over NTV, turning a once-provocative independent television station into a mouthpiece of the state. Gazprom also became an instrument of foreign policy. After Ukraine's 2004–2005 Orange Revolution unseated the Kremlin-backed prime minister Viktor Yanukovych in favor of his Western-supported opponent, Viktor Yushchenko, Putin decided to "punish" the Ukrainians by determining that Gazprom would more than quadruple the price of its exports to Ukraine.

Given Gazprom's power, most Russians weren't eager to pick a fight with the company. And despite Navalny's modest but notable victory in reopening the criminal investigation, by 2012 there were still no convictions in the Gazprom case.

But Navalny knew his crusade wasn't going to be easy. The power of the Russian state wasn't just formidable, it was incredibly opaque. Graft had long been sky-high: Transparency International rated Russia as one of the most corrupt countries in the world. Bribes were commonplace. Every year, tens of billions of dollars for supposed government contracts were unaccounted for. Fortunes passed through such companies as Gazprom and Rosneft, the national oil company. The conspiracy theories were so tangled that one could get a headache trying to figure out who was paying whom just to conceal the fact that they were really being paid by someone else.

Navalny was one of the rare Russians who dove into this murk.

In 2009, in another of his more famous campaigns, he blogged about the alleged embezzlement of over $150 million by officials at a subsidiary of VTB, a state-owned bank. He organized other VTB shareholders to help him write an official complaint. He found specialists and insiders who could provide more information on the corruption, which was related to drilling rigs. This led Russian authorities to review a case that had once been dismissed. It also drew the attention of shareholders and became a thorn in the bank's side.

Navalny later said, "I am confident that this investigation made corruption in the bank more subtle and complicated. They probably steal 40 percent instead of 70 percent. They continue to steal but at least they are afraid to do it openly." Again, this may sound like dubious progress, but in Russia it represented a rare instance when ordinary citizens made a difference.

Navalny was a realist. He understood early that he was one man trying to get a cynical, weary population to rally for change. They weren't going to spring into action overnight. He had to start small. "You have to propose to people the comfortable way of struggle," he told me in 2010. In other words, now's not the time to call people into the streets. It would be far more effective to say, Please, just fill out this online form.

And that's exactly what Navalny did. Encouraging lazy, non-committal Internet activism, which some Western commentators derisively call "slacktivism," was all part of Navalny's master plan. In the 1990s, he said, people demonstrated constantly and failed to see improvements. They were still exhausted from this "mass political activity." He wanted to show Russians that they could fight corruption from the convenience of their living rooms, and that they could win.

Navalny had proposed this "comfortable way of struggle" earlier in 2010, after U.S. prosecutors said that the German carmaker Daimler had bribed officials in Russia. Navalny wanted to know who was on the receiving end of these bribes. In Russia, the case was initially met with silence. So Navalny called on readers of his blog to write letters to the Russian Interior Ministry to demand that they investigate the corruption surrounding the Daimler case.

With Daimler, the U.S. Department of Justice suddenly breathed new life into Navalny's anticorruption fight. In March the DOJ charged Daimler with violation of the Foreign Corrupt Practices Act. (The law applied to Daimler, a German company, because it was listed on a U.S. stock exchange.) The DOJ found that Daimler made "improper payments" to officials in more than twenty countries, including Russia, China, Egypt, Greece, Hungary, and Thailand. According to the DOJ, Russian parties received nearly $7 million in payoffs from Daimler between 2000 and 2005. The payments were sometimes made by overcharging customers and giving the excess sums to government officials or their proxies.

In early April, Navalny complained on his blog that Russian officials had been silent on the corruption scandal for a week. He set out to ensure that the case saw daylight. He wanted a criminal investigation, and he asked his followers to help him get one.

Navalny knew that he needed to make it easy for readers. He would have to propose the comfortable way of struggle. He provided a template and detailed instructions for sending individual petitions to the Interior Ministry, which investigates economic crimes, and the Prosecutor General's Office. He directed his readers to the appropriate websites, instructing them to write their names and addresses clearly and carefully so that they would receive a reply in the mail. He even provided suggested language for the complaint, so that all people had to do was copy and paste. He also asked people to send messages to Medvedev via the president's website. He referred to the overall effort as a "civic flash mob."

Once again, Navalny's blog post combined meticulous detail with soaring calls to patriotism. "I urge all to show citizenship," he pleaded. By doing nothing, he warned his readers, "you play into the hands of corrupt officials. All they want to achieve—is your personal passivity." He explained that if there was no announcement of a criminal case within two weeks, then the top officials had decided to protect their bribe-taking subordinates. If the case got transferred to regional authorities, it would likely die there. He concluded his blog with a direct appeal to his readership, whom he described as "the hope of our country."

A day later, Navalny presented his readers with what appeared to be evidence of the first results of his campaign. He posted a screenshot of the Prosecutor General's Office website. The online form through which corruption reports could be submitted was temporarily down, apparently for "technical reasons." One commenter quipped, "For technical reasons, we are not fighting corruption." That same day, President Medvedev, who had made fighting corruption one of his signature issues, posted a video on his own blog of him speaking at a meeting of the anticorruption committee. He did not mention Daimler directly, but he underscored the need for high-ranking officials to personally follow and respond to claims of corruption. Medvedev asked the officials at the meeting to not wait for his orders, but to initiate action themselves.

Less than a week later, Navalny claimed that a thousand letters had been submitted to the Interior Ministry, the Prosecutor General's Office, and President Medvedev. This was based on the number of people who notified him that they had written to the authorities.

In a January 12 blog post Navalny wrote that two criminal cases related to Daimler were initiated in 2010. As of early 2012, suspects had been identified, but no formal accusations made. Around that same time, the Russian newspaper *Vedomosti* reported that there were unnamed suspects within the Ministry of Interior and the Federal Guard Service, but there were still no formal accusations or cases initiated in the other implicated government bodies.

As with the Gazprom case, several years later Navalny's Daimler campaign had still not produced any actual convictions. But by another measure, the campaign was a success. Navalny had taken a powerful swipe at the widespread apathy that anesthetized the public and helped keep corrupt officials in business. With Daimler, he had spurred a ragtag civic army to provoke a notoriously corrupt regime. And he was just getting started. "Now people are ready for the next step," he told me. "We just need energy."

"WE HAVE OUR OWN WORDS"

Navalny was born in 1976 in Butyn', a military town near Moscow. His father was from Chernobyl, Ukraine, and was in the army. Navalny behaved badly in school and often had conflicts with his teachers. But when I asked him if he had a sense, growing up, that he was different from other kids, he responded, "No. Everyone thinks that he's different."

Navalny sees himself as part of a distinct generation of Russians who were born in time to experience the Soviet Union but too late to subscribe to its myths. He grew up under the leadership of Leonid Brezhnev and the era of stagnation that began in the early

1970s, when the cracks in the planned economy became impossible to conceal. He described his generation as one that was raised in Soviet times but was "not so poisoned by this style of life, this mentality."

Navalny grew up at a time when it was getting harder to hail the superiority of the Soviet model. Such basic goods as food and clothing were increasingly scarce. At the same time, more people owned televisions, and occasional Western programs offered a glimpse of relatively comfortable lives abroad. Navalny remembers the first time he met someone who had traveled overseas. He was sixteen. The first things he thought to ask were, "Is it true that they have twenty types of sausages in the stores?" and "Is it true that you can just go to the store and buy chewing gum?"

When Navalny talks about his "generation," he is referring to a specific group of people born roughly between 1976 and 1982. This is a generation that had Soviet childhoods and educations before entering the chaos of the 1990s. They were still adolescents when the Soviet Union fell apart. They don't romanticize the Brezhnev era, which even now some Russians view as an oasis of relative stability. "There is a generation who remembers how everything was awful after [World War II] and then became much better when it was Brezhnev," Navalny said. "But we just saw when everything just went bad and bad and bad and bad, and then the Soviet Union collapsed."

He recalls being one of the Young Pioneers, a Communist Party children's organization. He grew up singing patriotic songs, which he described as a kind of "agony." He added, "But we have our own words, we kind of pervert it . . . No one really believed in it."

Unlike some of the younger Russians who were born after him, he also knew better than to glorify the past. "Now we have a lot of young people in their twenties who are just ready to fight for the Soviet Union, and they are trying to prove that the Soviet Union was a very good country, and it was very big, and America was afraid of us, and we were so cool and powerful," Navalny said. "For me, the Soviet Union was just standing in the line all the time."

Navalny feels a special connection to those who were born around the same time. He remembers being part of a blogging community for those born between 1976 and 1982. The online community, started in 2002, became one of the more popular communities on LiveJournal, Russia's leading blogging platform. Many posts describe films, books, or songs from the 1980s to the early 1990s and ask other members of the community if they know these titles or where the items can be found. Navalny recalled, "People were posting jokes, funny stories, slang, which no one understands except us."

The LiveJournal blogging community is not only a gathering place for members of a distinct generation, it is a virtual shrine to the twilight of the Soviet era. One blogger recalled the opening of the Soviet Union's first McDonald's, in 1990. Thirty thousand visited that first day, including his father, who went to McDonald's instead of his office. When he arrived, he received a commemorative red pin of the Golden Arches. He bought a Big Mac and took this foreign food, packed in a little box made of special insulation material, back to his office, where he shared it with the entire department.

Another blogger remembered the country's first telethon, which also happened in 1990. There were short videos of children in need, which were shocking because such material had never been shown before. Everyone thought that the state was doing a fine job of taking care of the sick, the elderly, and the orphaned. The telethon aired for a full twenty-four hours. People watched and discussed it for a long time.

The precise window of 1976 to 1982 is somewhat arbitrary.

Another website, Encyclopedia of Our Childhood, also dedicated to those years, explains, "Childhoods of those born in 1970 are hardly different from those born in 1976. Which means this project is created for all those who were born in the gigantic country called the USSR."

Encyclopedia of Our Childhood includes articles on movies, mass media, games, school, science and technology, and miscellaneous topics such as music, food, and sports. Within the "school" category, there are several entries dedicated to the Young Pioneers organization, including an article about how the Young Pioneers tie was a source of pride for new pioneers, and how sad and ashamed children felt if they lost their ties. The article recalled that once, the ties were made out of bright red, stiff cotton, and later they were a red-orange synthetic material. By the time the Young Pioneers reached the age of fourteen, the ties had lost their mystique. They became crumpled and dirty. People drew on them with pens.

Navalny's skeptical worldview wasn't simply a product of being born into a certain generation. His family weren't true believers in the Soviet system either. Navalny told me that when he was young, his Orthodox grandmother secretly took him to church and baptized him, a practice that wasn't widespread in those days. He heard stories about how his family had suffered under collectivization.

Navalny's description of his childhood is revealing. He clearly grew up with a distrust of authorities, but he would hardly describe his family as "dissident." His opposition was not grounded in lofty ideology, but rather in annoyance that things didn't work. In that sense, he hasn't changed much at all. He described the attitudes around him when he was growing up: "It was criticizing on the level of, 'These stupid authorities. We don't have milk in our store. Where is the butter? Like this.' It was on the level of jokes and anecdotes." He remembered everyone listening to the Voice of America, "not because of politics, but because of music." When I asked him if there were any books that were influential in his thinking, he said there was nothing in particular.

He was, however, fascinated by politics. He remembers reading newspapers. In the 1980s and '90s he and his mother, who was an economist, watched TV programs such as *Vzglyad*, *Itogi*, and *Vremya*, and Navalny learned the names of various ministers.

In 1999 Navalny joined the liberal opposition "Yabloko" Party. A few years later, he joined forces with Maria Gaidar, another opposition activist, to start a series of political debates. The idea was to get more young Russians engaged in politics. These debates, funded by an overseas grant and hosted in bars, were enormously popular. Trouble began when thugs started coming to the bars and roughing up the participants. Navalny himself was arrested after a scuffle. He believes that these thugs were there at the Kremlin's bidding. "We stopped this project because we couldn't guarantee the safety anymore," he told me.

Not too much later, after fights with the party's leadership and accusations of nationalism forced him out, Navalny left Yabloko. The liberal party was not pleased that he had been photographed at planning meetings for the nationalist "Russian March," which is widely known for intolerance.

In any event, Navalny was ready to move on. He wasn't sure that party politics were the best platform from which to effect change, and in 2006 he started his blog. He was never the type to wax poetic about the transformative power of technology. Rather, he embraced the Web because it was cheap and effective. "If I have a nonprofit organization in Russia, it's really expensive to have a meeting," he explained. You have to rent a room, draft an agenda, and wrestle with various other administrative headaches.

This was not to mention the physical dangers of holding an opposition gathering, which Navalny experienced during his ill-fated debate series. It was far more efficient to host gatherings online.

"THE PROBLEM IS THAT PEOPLE DON'T SEARCH FOR IT"

The Internet has long been the best place for a fierce critic of the Kremlin to establish something resembling a public presence. Television, from which the vast majority of Russians get their information, is a non-option. Before Putin came to power in 2000, Russia's privatized television stations were home to diverse opinions, hard-hitting news, and political satire. Yet over the course of Putin's tenure, all of Russia's federal television stations fell under the control of either the Kremlin or state-owned enterprises. The Web thus became the primary space for Russia's opposition to congregate, as well as to spread and receive information.

Although radio stations and newspapers were far more open than TV, the Internet remained the freest space in Russia. And its popularity had soared. In the fall of 2010, 40 percent of Russians reported having used the Internet in the last month, compared with 6 percent in 2002. Of course, Internet use varied greatly across the country. In 2010 the proportion of Internet users in Moscow and St. Petersburg was three times higher than in the villages. However, more than 90 percent of new Internet users lived outside those two cities.

In 2010 about one-quarter of Russia's population had broadband Internet access, roughly 17 percent of the population had mobile Internet access, and 9 percent had wireless. In Moscow at least, so many cafés had free Wi-Fi that if you switched on your laptop near a busy avenue, you could pick up a signal outside.

Russian Internet users flocked to social networking sites so much that Russians became the most active social media users in the world. In August 2010 some 35 million Russian Internet users (roughly 75 percent of the online population) visited at least one social networking site. With an average of ten hours per visitor each month, Russians spent more than double the worldwide average (4.5 hours per visitor) on social networks.

The most popular of these sites (27.8 million visitors a month) was VKontakte.ru, basically a Russian version of Facebook, followed by Odnoklassniki.ru, a site for reconnecting with former classmates (16.7 million visitors). At the time, Facebook couldn't compete with these domestic sites. It ranked fifth, with just 4.5 million visitors. But Facebook was growing quickly in Russia, as was Twitter. As of March 2010, Twitter had 183,000 Russian-language accounts.

The shining star of the Russian blogosphere has long been LiveJournal, a blog-hosting platform with such social networking functions as communities and friends lists. LiveJournal has become such a central feature of the Russian Internet that one could forget that the company originated in the United States. LiveJournal was created by a U.S. developer named Brad Fitzpatrick in the late nineties. Its Russian assimilation began one fateful day in 2001, when a Slavic literature lecturer in Estonia came to the site via a link on another forum. "First attempt at writing. Let's try in Russian . . . how funny!" he wrote.

Before long, the Russian word for LiveJournal, "ZheZhe," also became the Russian word for blogging. By the fall of 2010, there were 4 million accounts registered in LiveJournal's Russian-language section. On average, some five thousand accounts were registered each day. In America, LiveJournal still had more users but far less cultural importance; the site was sometimes viewed as a place where teenagers write online diaries. In Russia, however, it has grown into a vibrant social networking site and a key forum for free expression.

In 2006 some Russian bloggers worried that this freedom might come to an end. LiveJournal's Russian-language pages were licensed to the Russian company SUP Media, founded by the U.S. entrepreneur Andrew Paulson and the Russian banker Alexander Mamut, who appeared to have close ties to the Kremlin. A year later, SUP bought LiveJournal for around $30 million, in what was the biggest-ever Russian takeover of a U.S. Internet company. But despite fears of a Kremlin takeover, LiveJournal continued to gain influence and seemed generally free of serious government intervention. Anti-Kremlin bloggers like Navalny eventually used it to reach millions of readers.

You could find some amazing pieces of information on the Russian Internet. According to a 2005 law intending to clean up official corruption, the Russian government has to post its purchases on a website called zakupki.gov.ru. In 2010 bloggers and journalists pounced on some suspicious purchases that were buried deep within the site. A year earlier, the Russian Interior Ministry declared its plans to buy around $800,000 worth of furniture, including a bed "covered with a thin layer of 24-carat gold," according to the official tender documents.

The officials, once exposed to public mockery, tried to explain that the bed was needed to host foreign officials in a special VIP guesthouse in Moscow. If this wasn't ridiculous enough, a regional procurement website revealed that a governor of Russia's far eastern Sakhalin Province planned to bring African drummers from Burundi to perform at his New Year's party. The outcry over these purchases did not prevent the Interior Ministry from buying more gilded furniture the following year, nor did it deter members of President Medvedev's security detail from spending thousands of dollars on a "luxury bathtub."

This underscored a broader problem. Despite its relative freedom and openness, the Internet was not yet changing the overall situation. This was largely because, aside from a handful of outspoken bloggers, there wasn't a critical mass to demand justice and accountability. In any country, the culture of the Web simply reflects the realities on the ground. In Russia, the Internet was not immune to the apathy that plagued real life. "You can pretty much find any information you want on the Russian Internet," a Russian journalist told me in 2010. "The problem is that people don't search for it."

Polls bore this out. Despite decent and growing Internet access, a 2010 report found that a staggering 94 percent of Russians learned about the latest news from state-controlled TV; 41 percent got news from the radio, 37 percent from newspapers, and only 9 percent from the Internet (respondents were able to pick more than one media source). One poll asked Russians to which media they would first turn to learn the details of an extraordinary piece of news. Overall, 74 percent said television, while only 6 percent said Internet publications. As a result, most Russians were unaware of or uninterested in stories about corruption, abuses of official power, government repression, or opposition movements, which were readily available online.

Nor was the Web widely seen as an effective political force. One of the most definitive early academic studies of the Russian Internet is tellingly titled "The Web That Failed." The paper, published in 2008 by Floriana Fossato, John Lloyd, and Alexander Verkhovsky, paints a dismal picture of opposition politics on the Russian Internet. It concludes that "new communications developments are not yet breaking down well-established patterns of power. The state remains the main mobilizing agent in Russia." The Russian Internet does help spread information, "but largely among closed clusters of like-minded users who are seldom able or willing to cooperate."

The article also detailed manipulation by the Russian government—for example, in the form of brigades of bloggers who spread the Kremlin's message. These bloggers use abusive language to obstruct discussions, or they organize to prevent certain topics from making the headlines on the top-twenty issues of the day by Yandex, Russia's leading search engine.

There are indeed stories of Kremlin interference on the Web, either via surveillance, cyberattacks, or government-sponsored commentary. But at least early on, censorship was not a key element of the Russian Internet story. Unlike in China, Russia has never had a comprehensive system of filtering or blocking. Most likely this is because in the early years, the Kremlin didn't see the Internet as a serious threat.

Once, over coffee in a Moscow Starbucks, a Russian graduate student asked me about the difference between the Internet in Russia and China. "Well, in China we wouldn't be doing this," I said. He had his laptop open on the table, and we had been browsing opposition Twitter feeds and discussing the various rants against the Kremlin. In China, Twitter is blocked entirely, and on other sites such blatant antigovernment material would be blocked or deleted.

Russia was a completely different story. When I lived in Moscow in 2010, on a day-to-day level it didn't feel like an authoritarian country. Sure, police officers were a constant menacing presence on the Metro platforms. They often seemed to be looking for ways to harass people and extract bribes from them. But I also spent hours in crowded cafés listening to bloggers and journalists loudly complain about Putin while drinking $8 cappuccinos. Nobody lowered their voices, nobody cared who was sitting at the next table. People could speak freely because their speech ultimately didn't matter.

The Internet reflected the country's political realities. Yes, Russians were free to agitate for change online. But to what end? Like Putin or not, there didn't appear to be any viable alternatives. The Kremlin and its network of business and media ties made it impossible for a serious opposition figure to make a name for himself. He certainly wouldn't be campaigning on television.

In the absence of political alternatives, many Russians sincerely believed that Putin's leadership was key to the country's stability. People were still reeling from the crime and economic uncertainty that followed the collapse of the Soviet Union. This helped prevent a critical mass from rallying against Putin, and a handful of would-be reformers weren't going to overturn the system by themselves.

"IN RUSSIA, CHANGE NEVER COMES FROM THE BOTTOM"

In 2010 the most popular blogger in Russia was not Alexey Navalny, but Rustem Adagamov, otherwise known by his blog handle, "Drugoi." The first time we met, Adagamov smiled shyly and then handed me a business card that said he was the most popular blogger in Russia. He was tall and stem thin, with a straight, sharp nose and deep creases around his smile. He wore glasses, a striped shirt, jeans, and loafers with no socks. He was forty-eight.

Drugoi was better known for his photography than his writing. Adagamov, born in Kazan, had lived in Norway from 1996 to 2003. Employed as a graphic designer, in 2002 he started blogging to connect with Russian friends back in Moscow. He wrote about his life abroad, depicting Norway through photographs. In 2005 he had a few thousand readers. By 2010 his blog had about half a million hits every twenty-four hours, with some forty thousand unique hits. His blog also had fifty-five thousand regular subscribers, making him the most popular blogger on Live-Journal, which was the only blogging platform that mattered in Russia.

Drugoi literally means "other." Adagamov explained that this reflects the sense of "otherness" he feels everywhere in the world. "It's my style of life," he said matter-of-factly. "I'm not a foreigner . . . I'm alone." I later understood that by "otherness," he was referring to an invisible window that separated him from the world, as if he were an observer of his own life. Despite the fact that he had a unique platform for influencing society, he embodied Russia's political apathy. In person he came off as curiously dispassionate, so much so that nothing seemed to rouse him.

I saw this firsthand the second time we met. We were in a generic chain café in Moscow that had yellowish walls, big windows, wooden tables, and comfortable armchairs. The walls were decorated with framed, instantly forgettable artwork. It was the kind of café where you could sit for hours, using the free Wi-Fi and being ignored by staff who didn't care if you ordered coffee or not.

Adagamov greeted me with his slow, modest smile. We found a table on the second floor. I looked down for a moment, and when I glanced up again, I saw him in front of me, looking stunned, his hand clasped to his forehead. I first noticed the small red drops on the floor. Then I looked up to see blood streaming down his face.

We stared at each other. The ceiling had a low, rectangular protrusion, and he had hit himself on its sharp corner. "I'll get help," I said. Adagamov just stood there, swaying gently from side to side. I ran downstairs to alert the café staff. Some employees took Adagamov into a little room near the counter and discreetly shut the door. "Watch my bag," he ordered me before following them down the stairs. Around ten minutes later he emerged, his wet hair plastered to his forehead. He looked at me solemnly. "I am sorry. Let's forget about it. Shit happens."

Adagamov, with characteristic nonchalance, had stumbled into a unique position in the Russian blogosphere. Although he claimed to be his own man, he had some powerful backers. He was employed by SUP Media, the parent company of LiveJournal. "My blog was a leader, and people who were owners of this company needed to have this leader blog, it was good PR for the service," he explained to me in 2010. He received income from other sources as well. Adagamov had a contract with MegaFon, a major Russian mobile phone company. In return for the sponsorship, he photographed the company's social events, such as a soccer championship for orphans.

Adagamov showed me a photo of a brightly colored MegaFon blimp that the company asked him to photograph. He flew all over the country in that blimp, taking photos. He also had a contract with VTB Bank, which would use his photographs for its own publicity purposes. None of this was a secret: both MegaFon and VTB put their logos on Adagamov's blog.

If this wasn't enough to call his editorial independence into question, then his relationship with President Medvedev would do the trick. Medvedev talked a big game about blogging and social media. He had a blog and a Twitter account and was a high-level supporter of Skolkovo, Russia's attempted version of Silicon Valley. So it was hardly surprising that he would take a prominent blogger under his wing.

In 2009 the Kremlin invited Adagamov to cover a meeting between Medvedev and his visiting Indian counterpart, Pratibha

Patil. Adagamov was initially stunned by the Kremlin's interior. "The abundance of gold stucco and bright yellow light drove both of my cameras mad," he commented. He was also invited to travel around the country with Medvedev. This all inevitably led to suspicions that Adagamov had been co-opted by the Kremlin.

He seemed to be enjoying the perks of his position. Demonstrating something close to excitement, he showed me a photo of Steve Jobs and Dmitry Medvedev in California. "I've been working with Macintosh products for many years, and Jobs for me, he's like a God," he said. He seemed considerably less moved by having been in the same room as the president of the Russian Federation. He posted a picture of Medvedev and Jobs on his blog, with the title "I Saw Jobs."

Adagamov liked that Medvedev could hang out in Silicon Valley, that he talked about technology and innovation. He told me that Medvedev was Russia's "best hope for change." He added, "I like that he is also a photographer."

"Is he a good photographer?" I asked. Adagamov cocked his head and smiled. "So-so. He likes it, which is good."

Adagamov told me that he was proudest of a post he wrote in 2007 about his friend Ilya, which years later still attracted attention. For more than two decades Ilya picked up street dogs and brought them to his home in the suburbs of Moscow. Adagamov went to visit his friend and then posted a photo montage of bedraggled canines lounging around a home that had clean wooden floors and a comfortable-looking sofa. One picture showed a dog that was missing two paws, standing in the snow. "Beaten, mutilated, half-dead they come here and receive treatment, shelter, food and human warmth," Adagamov wrote.

The post was particularly striking in Russia, a country not known for such charitable acts. According to one poll, in one month 5 percent of Russians gave money to charity and 36 percent helped a stranger. During one particularly cold winter some people asked Adagamov to post an appeal for warm clothes for the homeless. Many people helped, he said, but he also got pushback from those who felt that the homeless "are not people, but trash, and they have to die." One commenter wrote that helping the homeless is just "prolonging their agony." So it's hardly surprising that not all his readers were supportive of Ilya's decision to harbor stray dogs. Adagamov told me that some of his readers "don't understand how people can help homeless dogs. They think it is some kind of big mistake."

He said that his readers particularly liked "hero" stories, such as the tale from the north of Russia, in which a pilot had to make an emergency landing in the forest: thankfully, an aviation worker who was in charge of this unused airport had dutifully kept the field clean for twenty years, allowing for a smooth landing. Adagamov used his blog to direct readers to a site that collected money to buy a ski scooter for the aviation worker and his wife.

Occasionally he broached social and political issues. Adagamov said he liked to describe life in Norway "just to show Russians how people live in a democratic country." He also made a point of telling his Russian readers about Norway's tolerance for homosexuality, triggering such comments as "What is it with you and pederasty?"

He also posted videos of police excesses in the Strategy 31 demonstrations, although he thought the protests were an exercise in futility. "It's not the right way to change something here. In Russia, change never comes from the bottom. All changes must come from people in power." He said he had readers who were more supportive of the police than of the protesters. "No one likes a struggle for human rights," he told me. "We need stability. It's this feeling when you are sitting in a boat." Adagamov swayed back and forth in his chair. "Don't rock the boat."

Some may have believed that Adagamov was cowed by his corporate connections or his relationship with the Kremlin, and he wasn't blind to the risks of his profession. "This popularity, it's nothing if some people want to punish me," he told me between calm draws of his cigarette. "It's absolutely nothing."

Yet I didn't have the impression that he was deterred by fear. He just didn't think opposition activism was a good use of his time and energy. "We have no political life in Russia," he said in 2010. "People live their lives, and the government lives its own. They are two different groups. We have no real political parties. We have no elections, because elections are artificial, for show." He was skeptical of Navalny's effectiveness, arguing that his online anticorruption campaigns sparked a few days of collective horror and then nothing changed. He was also wary of Navalny's larger ambitions: "He's trying to be a politician in a country that doesn't need politicians."

Adagamov liked the Internet because it allowed him to communicate to the public without an intermediary and because it sent his photographs out into the world. But the Web was hardly going to change the fate of his country. He told me that his son, then in his twenties, was frustrated with his father's pessimism. Adagamov ascribed this worldview to his personality, not his generation. "I'm a clever man," he said. "I think only idiots are optimistic." I asked him if he thought bloggers mattered in Russia. The most popular blogger in Russia didn't even pause. "No," he said. "Absolutely not."

Adagamov's views were in sync with the mood at the time. Anton Nossik, an influential blogger and Russian Internet expert, put it succinctly in 2010: "If you have what Lenin used to call a revolutionary situation, of course the revolutionaries will make use of the Internet for organizing all sorts of political activity, spreading the word." He added, "On the other hand, if there is no revolutionary situation, no critical mass of people who need to overthrow or confront the regime, this will not be created by virtue of the

Internet being there. This is a big disappointment for people who believed otherwise, such as Putin's opponents."

As Nossik said, the mere existence of the Internet would not topple the Kremlin. There would have to be a spark. Perhaps it would be an economic or political crisis, or a popular loss of faith in the current regime. People like Navalny believed that it was only a matter of time before that spark was lit. And when the moment came, Russians had to be prepared. To do that, they must first overcome the apathy that had become the Kremlin's best protection.

"YOU CAN KEEP SILENT, YOU CAN EMIGRATE, OR YOU CAN STAY HERE AND FIGHT"

What Alexey Navalny was doing in Russia, essentially a combination of investigative journalism and whistle-blowing, was not only unusual, it was incredibly dangerous. Challenging official corruption could have deadly consequences. One of the most notorious cases was that of the attorney Sergei Magnitsky, who accused Russian officials of stealing from the government. He was held without trial for eleven months, during which time he fell ill and was denied medical treatment. In 2009 he died in a Russian Jail.

After his death Magnitsky became an international cause célèbre. In June 2012 the U.S. House Foreign Affairs Committee passed a bipartisan bill called the Sergei Magnitsky Rule of Law Accountability Act. Shortly thereafter, the Senate Foreign

Relations Committee also passed the bill. It imposes banking and visa restrictions on Russian officials who are implicated in human rights abuses. Former House Committee on Foreign Affairs Chairman Ileana Ros-Lehtinen said that corruption in Russia is "widely accepted as normal and a way of life . . . Tragically, those who challenge the authorities and take on this forbidden subject are dealt with harshly, and several of those who have investigated it have been assaulted, jailed, and even killed." In November 2012 the bill passed through the U.S. House of Representatives. In December President Obama signed the bill into law. Russia responded swiftly and angrily by passing a ban on U.S. adoptions of Russian children.

Although Russian apathy did have some fear at its root, most Russians had long ago given up on challenging the rich and powerful. As a result, the individuals who did push the envelope became vulnerable targets of abuse. Those individuals were ruthlessly punished, and the punishers often got off scot-free. Often it was unclear who commissioned the violence. There was a strong but silent undercurrent of violence and lawlessness that streamed through daily life. It was everywhere and nowhere, easy to ignore and impossible to forget.

One summer evening I was accompanying Veronika back to her apartment in Moscow. Veronika lived near Belorusskaya Square, which has a little fountain and cafés where we would enjoy wine or coffee outdoors. We weren't far from the square when we came upon an ordinary if somewhat run-down apartment building that had a dark red door. Veronika called my attention to a small Russian plaque next to the door. This was nothing unusual: Moscow is dotted with plaques commemorating poets, writers, and various wartime heroes, and Veronika loved to point them out.

Underneath this particular plaque were two wilted white roses. We stopped walking, and I casually peered at its message. It said,

"This is the building in which Anna Politkovskaya lived and was viciously murdered."

Politkovskaya was a journalist and human rights activist who was fiercely critical of Vladimir Putin and the Chechen conflict. She wrote for *Novaya Gazeta*, a prominent opposition newspaper, and made powerful enemies in both the Kremlin and Chechnya. Politkovskaya's editor, Yuri Shchekochikhin, had died of poisoning, and Politkovskaya herself was the target of constant death threats. In 2004 she flew to North Ossetia to cover the tragedy in Beslan, where children in a school were being held hostage by terrorists.

The cautious Politkovskaya took her own food on the plane and accepted only a cup of tea. Apparently, that was all it took. She fell into a coma and was taken to Moscow, where doctors determined that she had been poisoned by a toxin that damaged her kidneys, liver, and endocrine system. Thus, as the journalist and author Masha Gessen observed, Politkovskaya "was effectively prevented from covering and investigating the tragedy in Beslan." Politkovskaya never fully recovered from the poisoning and continued to have health problems.

On October 7, 2006, she was shot to death in the elevator of the very building Veronika and I were facing. Her death, which drew gasps of horror from around the world, happened to take place on Putin's fifty-fourth birthday. According to Gessen, the day after Politkovskaya's death, Putin sent his own birthday wishes to a figure skater and a popular actor, but didn't make any public comment about the murder. Three days later, he met with German chancellor Angela Merkel in Dresden. When he got out of his car, he found a picket line of some thirty people holding signs with the word KILLER.

At the press conference that followed his meeting with Merkel, Putin apparently had no choice but to comment on Politkovskaya's death. He did say that the murder was "an unacceptable crime that cannot go unpunished."

He acknowledged that Politkovskaya was a harsh critic of the Russian government, then added, "Her ability to influence political life in Russia was extremely insignificant." Eventually an accomplice to the murder was sentenced to prison. In 2013 five suspects in the case went on a trial that Politkovskaya's children called "illegitimate."

On the same street as Politkovskaya's building was a pharmacy and store that appeared to sell men's underwear. The only reminder of what happened there is a little black sign, put up by the opposition activist and former chess champion Garry Kasparov, that many Russians don't stop to read.

Russia is a notoriously dangerous place for journalists, largely because so many crimes against them go unpunished. "The impunity the masterminds enjoy—this is the main part of the mechanism, which breeds new murders," said Sergey Sokolov, deputy editor of *Novaya Gazeta*. In 2012 the Committee to Protect Journalists ranked Russia ninth on its "impunity index"—the list of countries where journalists' murderers roam free. At the time, Russia had sixteen unsolved journalist murders.

Oleg Kashin, the popular blogger and *Kommersant* writer, returned home late one night to find two men waiting for him outside his house. One was holding a bouquet of flowers. They proceeded to beat him with their fists and metal objects. Kashin's jaw and leg were broken, his skull was fractured, and his fingers were partially torn off. His editor at *Kommersant* interpreted the damage to his hands as a clear attempt to get him to stop writing.

Like Politkovskaya, Kashin had an assortment of enemies. He covered the environmentalist and resident group protests against the cutting down of Khimki Forest in order to make room for a highway between Moscow and St. Petersburg. Backed by powerful figures, it appeared as if the federal project would yield dividends for the Khimki administration and its mayor, Vladimir Strelchenko.

One of the highway's strongest critics, the journalist Mikhail Beketov, was beaten nearly to death in 2008. Beketov had defended the forest, which was home to old trees and wild animals, and he also suggested that local officials were profiting from the project. Local officials were not happy. Beketov received phone threats. His dog was killed. His car was blown up. And then he was severely beaten and left lying in the snow. Like Kashin's, his hands had also been bashed.

If that wasn't bad enough, in 2010 a judge found Beketov guilty of slandering Strelchenko by accusing him of involvement in blowing up Beketov's car. Beketov was fined a small amount, which was then suspended. His own brutal attack went unpunished, and he died in 2013.

In Kashin's case, there were various possible motives for the beating. One theory was that his attack was linked to his blog post about Andrei Turchak, the governor of the Pskov region, which argued that he had gotten his position through his Kremlin ties. Turchak had threatened Kashin months before the attack.

Another theory, and the one Kashin himself believed, was that he was attacked for crossing Nashi, an ultranationalist youth group founded by the Kremlin. He was highly critical of their violent tactics, claiming that they were launching attacks and beating up the opposition. He questioned their impunity and the fact that they were not being tried for their violence.

I first met Kashin in a small, dimly lit Starbucks on Moscow's bustling Tverskaya Street. It was a few months after his attack. He was determinedly cheerful, although he looked vaguely lost. He was missing some of his teeth, and one of his fingers had been amputated. He told me that President Medvedev had promised to catch the killers. In fact, President Medvedev had tweeted, "I have ordered the office of the Prosecutor General and the Interior Ministry to take the case of the attempted murder of the journalist Kashin under special control. The criminals must be found and punished."

"I feel optimism about journalism in Russia," Kashin told me, while I tried not to look at his mutilated hand. "I think the Kremlin understands that a kind of new perestroika is needed." Then he ended our meeting rather abruptly, and I walked him outside. A young guy on the street inexplicably took a cell phone photo of him. I realized that Kashin's bodyguards were sitting in a weathered-looking car, waiting in the dark. He told me they were being paid for by the Russian government. Neither Kashin's attackers nor those who commissioned the beating have yet been brought to justice.

If this is what can happen to journalists in Russia, imagine the possible fate of someone like Navalny. Not only was he trying to reveal corruption, but he wanted someone to pay for it. As a result of Navalny's anticorruption campaigns, corporations and individuals stood to lose real money. Many speculated that his days were numbered. He has a wife and small children, and he was known to keep guns in the house.

The one silver lining was that at least his disappearance wouldn't go unnoticed. In 2010 Navalny's blog had about fifty thousand daily readers. He had begun to attract the attention of the Western media. Navalny knew he was striking a nerve. People were sick of corruption, and now someone was offering the possibility of making things at least a little better. He still wasn't the most popular blogger in Russia, but he was well on the way to becoming the most powerful.

Fame alone, however, won't protect you in Russia. The disgraced businessman Mikhail Khodorkovsky, whose arrest generated great controversy throughout Russia and the world, was still behind bars. The first time I spoke with Navalny, I asked him if he was afraid. He didn't pause. "I know how easily people are killed in Russia," he said. "But in the end, it's a question of choice. You can keep silent, you can emigrate, or you can stay here and fight."

And a fight it would be. Not only was he putting himself in danger, but his activities started to cause trouble for his family. In 2011 he told me that his family had two very small shops, of which Navalny was cofounder and part owner. He believes that his activities led the authorities to constantly check the stores' licenses and certificates. "It's not a problem for me, but it's a problem for our parents," he said. "Not a big problem but it's, you know, annoying."

His wife, Julia, supported his activities, but his parents worried. Navalny finally had to have a frank conversation with his family. He told them squarely, "There will be a date when I will be arrested. So just consider it as a fact. Stop discussing. Just be prepared." He said that this conversation brought a sense of relief, and it became "taboo" for the family to pester him about his safety.

This is not to say that his mother slept more easily. "Unfortunately, I was stupid enough, and I showed her how to Google me on the Internet," he told me. He said she knows how to find all mentions of him on blogs and Twitter. "She reads everything which was written about me. And half of it is a kind of, 'he will be killed.'"

Still, Navalny was emboldened by the knowledge that he wasn't alone. The first time we spoke, he said proudly, "I feel the support of the people, and the support of the bloggers who are ready to join me in my action."

"WE DIDN'T APPLY TO THE AUTHORITIES, WE APPEALED TO THE PEOPLE"

There were increasing signs that Navalny would not have to battle on his own. Slowly but steadily, a dynamic opposition movement was growing online. This energy sometimes spilled over into the real world.

In 2010 I met Katya Parkhomenko, then an editor at *Snob*, a trendy website and magazine that catered to Russia's well-to-do. When we met for coffee, Katya showed up in a blue blouse that had pictures of animals, parrots, and flowers on it. She had an African-looking beaded bracelet around her wrist, and she smoked cigarettes throughout our conversation. She had a short, boyish haircut and a warm expression.

Snob, whose name is slightly tongue in cheek, was funded by Mikhail Prokhorov, oligarch, opposition politician, and eventual owner of the Brooklyn Nets basketball team. The site was supposed to appeal to the "global" Russian. *Snob* began as a kind of gated community. At first a collection of celebrities were invited to become members for free, and they enjoyed a different status from other users. The system was then simplified: everyone who paid had the same rights as invited celebrities. So membership grew from the hundreds to the thousands.

Still, *Snob*'s editors didn't want a free-for-all. They weren't interested in hosting a massive social networking site such as VKontakte. "Our idea was to have this place where we keep the order, we don't let people use nicknames. We promise them a place to speak," Katya said.

Katya, a Moscovite who was born in 1957, experienced firsthand how much the Internet had changed Russia. "I'm old enough to remember when just a copy of a book was a real threat," she told me. "When I was a child, I used to listen to VOA or BBC to learn what was going on in my own country." She added, "Now I don't need to. I have the Internet."

When Katya first went online some twelve years earlier, she was wary of interacting with strangers. She initially thought that she had to look into the eyes of someone in order to trust that person, but eventually she got over her uneasiness. She also convinced her bosses of the need to pay more attention to what was happening on the Web. From 2004 to 2008 she worked for Radio Liberty and Radio Free Europe's Russian-language service, where she had a weekly radio program devoted to discussing the content of Russian blogs.

Katya wasn't terribly concerned about authorities' interference on the Web. By the time President Medvedev started his own LiveJournal blog in 2009, she said, "we were already there; it was our place." The Web "was a place where everyone did what they wanted. Sometimes it was silly, sometimes it was rude. People realized they could post what they wanted without journalistic edits. By the time the Russian authorities realized the weight of this, the space was already occupied."

Katya was deeply skeptical of street protests such as the one I had witnessed on July 31. First of all, they didn't accomplish anything. And second, they were boring. Cosmopolitan Russians like Katya were tired of Russia's grim-faced street theater. "From time to time I try to take part in some street protests. Usually it is too serious, too dull," she told me. "I think it is useless to just go out in the streets with slogans, because nobody pays attention."

Earlier that year, however, *Snob* was at the heart of a very different kind of political demonstration. It became known as the blue bucket movement, and it proved that a successful protest doesn't have to follow the dreary conventional model. Protests could be creative, even fun. Moreover, the blue bucket movement showed that protests could be organized online.

The blue bucket protests were inspired by the traffic for which Moscow is notorious. People would be hours late to meetings that were short distances away. Making matters worse were the "VIP" cars of the rich and powerful. These cars were instantly recognizable by the blue lights, or *migalki*, that flashed on their roofs. Those lights signaled that these drivers could navigate the streets with impunity and, much like ambulances, were exempt from normal traffic rules. By official tallies, there were nearly a thousand of these blue-lighted vehicles, although unofficial accounts placed the number higher. These VIP cars flouted traffic laws and caused shocking accidents that were posted on YouTube.

In February 2010 the Lukoil executive Anatoly Barkov's Mercedes-Benz crashed into a Citroën hatchback, taking the lives of the two women inside. The Russian police blamed the female driver for the crime, saying she swerved into traffic, but the police were unable to produce any evidence to support this claim, despite the fact that there were security cameras in the street. Many people suspected a cover-up. Bloggers, along with the Federation of Russian Car Owners, identified witnesses and pressed for justice. The Russian rapper Noize MC wrote a catchy song about the accident, "Mercedes S666," and posted it on YouTube. The song featured such lyrics as "Get out of my way, plebeians, don't get under my wheels . . . We're late for hell, make way for the chariot." Within a few days the song had half a million hits on YouTube.

An older video also started making waves. A few years earlier, a Russian driver had put a blue bucket on the roof of his car, just to taunt the police. He filmed the event and posted it on YouTube. The vaguely absurdist video shows a guy in his car, earnestly explaining to a nonplussed officer that it is not illegal to transport cargo via car, which is what he was doing with the bucket.

One day Katya was talking to her sons, Leva and Petya, and their friends. Most of them were young drivers, in their twenties, and were wound up about how blue-light cars brazenly broke traffic rules. Katya recalled, "We were chatting in the kitchen, drinking vodka, just discussing this guy who made the video. And we were wondering what it would be like if there were more." Katya said that the next day, Leva made a regular visit to his father, her ex-husband, Sergei Parkhomenko. Leva floated the idea of using a simple blue bucket to mock government officials. Sergei, who happened to be a blogger, a *Snob* writer, and a host at the radio station Ekho Moskvy, thought it was a brilliant idea. He posted the video on his blog.

"I think this could be the beginning of a new mass movement," Sergei wrote on his blog. "I can imagine thousands and thousands of members of the Society of Blue Buckets leaving in the morning for work." The post got many replies, some encouraging and others questioning the legality of such an action. Sergei replied by posting about Article 23 of Russia's road regulations, which regulates the transport of goods by car. The blue buckets, which you could buy in a toy store and then tape to your vehicle, were simply goods to be transported.

Sergei and I met in Moscow a few months after the blue bucket movement began. Sergei was middle-aged, with a thick gray beard. He exuded charisma and self-assurance. Unlike most of the other Russian journalists I met, he seemed to have a hectic, tightly packed schedule. One of his old friends warned me that he would be difficult to nail down for a meeting. She then gave me a useful tip. Like many members of Moscow's chattering classes, Sergei was an ardent Francophile. He would be much more enthusiastic about meeting me if it offered him the opportunity to speak French, which, fortunately, I knew. So our interaction took place in French, which he spoke with a booming joie de vivre.

To Sergei, the blue bucket movement was not just about traffic. Rather, the *migalki* represented the elite's disdain for ordinary Russians. He told me that those lights signaled to ordinary people,

"I am more important than you." Moreover, Russia's common folk had no channel through which they could communicate their grievances. "There's no place where ordinary people come into contact with the powerful. There are no real elections in this country. Elections are theater," Sergei told me. A government official has "no possibility of seeing the reaction to what he does. And the common person has no possibility of showing his reaction."

"For me," he said, "the problem with the blue lights is the stratification of Russian society and the absence of contact between different elements." I asked him if the Internet could facilitate this contact, but he felt that Internet use was not yet widespread enough. For the time being, Russia's different classes shared one common space: traffic. "They drive together through the same streets. And that's where there is the possibility of an encounter between layers of society that would never otherwise meet—unless one is paying the other." Moscow's roads were thus the perfect place for ordinary people to send Russia's VIPs a message.

Sergei used his blog to call for action. He told people to bring their blue buckets out for a drive at Mayakovsky Square on Sunday, April 18, at 2:00 p.m. He also posted this appeal on *Snob*, and other online media picked it up. Like many movements that originate online, the blue bucket movement had no central organization. But it struck a chord. "In a week, it was impossible to buy a small blue bucket in a store for children," Katya said, still delighted by the memory.

Many viewed the event as a success. Katya recalled, "One day we went for a drive around Moscow, and there were fifty cars. It's not very much. But people saw it. We didn't apply to the authorities, we appealed to the people." Katya loved the joking and lighthearted mood of the protests, which were so different from the usual demonstrations. For once, protesters were actually having a good time. She told me the conversation between drivers and the police would go something like this:

"What is on your car?"

"Just a blue bucket."

"Why did you put it there?"

"I have to. It's my cargo."

The police stopped Katya in her car but just checked her papers and let her pass. Other cars on the road honked their horns in solidarity. Radio Kommersant reported live on the event. They happened to call Sergei for a comment just as he was being stopped by the police. The station's audience thus tuned in to Sergei's conversation with a police officer. He explained to the officer that he was carrying cargo in the form of a plastic bucket, fastened securely in accordance with regulations. He showed the officer his fire extinguisher and first-aid kit. "Everything is in order," he said. "You'll have to let me go." He made a point of reading the officer's badge number aloud for his audience to hear.

Videos of blue bucket drivers popped up online, and a Live-Journal community grew around it. "The media reaction was so hot," Katya said. "Newspapers, TV, blogs, news sites, whatever." For the first few weeks, she tried to monitor the number of links to Sergei's post on *Snob*. "I stopped when it was about two thousand. I thought it was useless to monitor it further."

The movement marked a turning point for Internet-led activism in Russia. It was also deeply inspiring to people like Navalny, who saw that a decentralized online campaign could spur off-line action. "Sergei proposed this funny action, but nobody thought it would be so popular," Navalny enthused to me a few months after the April drive. "Now on the Russian streets nobody lets cars with the blinking signals go. Nobody."

Although this was likely an exaggeration, the blue bucket drivers definitely got their point across. The number of *migalki* did decrease. But more important, at least some VIPs would think twice before flashing their lights. A group called the Society of Blue Buckets hosted a website where people could post videos of outrageous *migalki* antics. Katya said that the popularity of inexpensive, simple video cameras helped support the movement. Although you might not have been able to prove injustice in a Russian court, she said, at least you could "prove it for other people."

"RIGHTS ARE NOT GIVEN, THEY ARE TAKEN"

One of my first impressions of Moscow was that I had never been in a city with so many doors. When I arrived at my apartment, I would open a locked door, perhaps by typing in a password, and enter a small corridor that led to another locked door. After opening the second door, I would find myself in the downstairs lobby. I would then take a creaky old elevator, or maybe the stairs, to get to my landing. Once upstairs, I would inevitably encounter another locked door, but it would not open into my apartment. Instead, I would enter a vestibule with several other doors, each with multiple locks. One of these doors would be mine.

The other thing I noticed about Russian apartment buildings was the stark contrast between public and private spaces. The staircase would be dirty, with paint peeling off the walls or tiles missing from the floor. Once, I found a man passed out on the stairs. But then I would open my door to a modern apartment that was airy and immaculately clean.

Sometimes Russian society felt like one of these compartmentalized apartment buildings writ large. People tended to their own gardens and were more inclined to solve problems individually, not collectively. But the Internet was slowly changing that mind-set.

One early example of decentralized, collective action occurred in the summer of 2010, when Russia suffered from historically high temperatures and wildfires broke out across the country. Much of the western part of the country was suffocated by toxic smoke. In Moscow, the Kremlin literally faded from view, as did the brightly colored buildings in what Veronika and I called White Square. The air's carbon monoxide levels rose to six times higher than acceptable; spending an afternoon outdoors was like smoking several packs of cigarettes. Tens of thousands of people died.

A handful of Internet activists created an online wildfires map, which used crowdsourcing technology to link victims of the fires to those who could help. People could offer information about their need for food, clothes, or evacuation, and perfect strangers from all over the country would go to the "I wish to help" section to offer whatever they could. The site got hundreds of thousands of hits and even won a Russian Internet award.

The success of the wildfires map was a powerful rebuttal to the assumption that Russians looked out only for themselves and those around them. The Internet was also emboldening individual activists by showing them that they were not alone. Without the Internet, it's unlikely that a Siberian artist would have found himself at the center of an international protest movement.

In 2010 I traveled to Novosibirsk, Siberia, for an innovation conference. The conference consisted of Siberian government officials, U.S. embassy representatives, my colleagues from the Carnegie Moscow Center, and various others. I gave a presentation about the Internet in China, a topic of interest to approximately no one at the conference, but I was thrilled to be in Siberia. I had been studying how the Internet could bring even the most isolated individuals into larger communities. Would this phenomenon extend to Siberia, which to me at least was one of the most remote places imaginable? I did realize, of course, that Novosibirsk is the third-largest city in Russia, not a wide expanse of ice. There was a pleasant, wide promenade along the Ob River, but for the most part it felt like a big Russian city, colored in tones of white and gray.

Still, I was curious about the Siberian blogger scene. On my first night in Novosibirsk, I arranged to meet Elia Kabanov, who earlier that year had won the Deutsche Welle award for the best Russian blog. Elia wrote about his interests, which ranged from beekeeping to freedom of speech. He had blogged about everything from the economics of prostitution to climate change. He also posted old photos of Russian cities and scans from mid-twentieth-century magazines on science and technology.

Elia and I planned to meet in the lobby of my hotel after a dinner for the U.S. and Siberian delegations that were participating in the conference. The dinner consisted of salad that looked like cabbage and mayonnaise, followed by rough brown meat with a side of potatoes. I mentioned softly that I wasn't a big meat eater, and before I realized my mistake, a member of the Siberian delegation was having an animated dialogue with an annoyed-looking waitress whose hair was dyed in stripes.

"They will give you more potatoes," the Siberian told me. "You will survive?" he asked, though it wasn't really a question.

"Yes," I said.

"Good."

A new plate arrived. Instead of meat with potatoes, there was now potatoes with potatoes. The potatoes, grilled and garnished with herbs, were actually quite tasty. Once I finished this memorable meal, I stood up to go meet Elia. Dima, a friendly young Siberian who wore a cowboy hat, joked that I already had a date in Novosibirsk. A Russian man at our table nodded knowingly. "American women are fast," he said.

I can only imagine what this man would have thought had he

seen that there was not one but three young men waiting for me in the lobby of the River Park Hotel. Elia had brought two other bloggers with him, and I was struck by how trendy they were. Elia wore well-fitting dark jeans and stylish white sneakers with stripes. His friend Alex, whom he had met online, was tall, with soft suede shoes and an angelic face. Both Elia and Alex worked in public relations. Eugene, a news anchor, wore black pants and had sunglasses clipped to his button-down shirt. They had already ordered beer by the time I arrived.

They all loved the Internet, largely because it expanded their world. Alex described the Web as a place "to meet people with whom you share interests and life expectations." In Siberia, this was not always such an easy thing to do. "In our country, in our city, we don't have many platforms to meet people with the same interests," Eugene explained. They said they didn't have debate clubs or a vibrant civil society. At university, clubs tended to be for music and theater, or for people "who liked domestic animals." They joked that Russia's biggest secret society was the KGB, now known as the FSB.

"We don't have many opportunities to express our opinions, and blogs become the way that people can express themselves. An ordinary man can change things," Elia said. "One blogger in the middle of nowhere who writes a post about an issue that touches his life—say, local government—his post can reach a lot of people all over Russia." This blogger essentially becomes a media outlet, Elia said, doing "what newspapers or TV should do."

He gave the example of the Siberian artist and blogger Artem Loskutov. Before the authorities targeted him, Elia said, "he was just one of the strange modern artists who did strange events that no one understands. As soon as the authorities came after him, he became an icon. Every open-minded blogger felt that he should support Loskutov."

———

I met Artem Loskutov two days later. I was delayed getting back to my hotel and found him patiently waiting in the lobby. Artem, twenty-three at the time, brought his girlfriend, Masha. She wore black shorts and a royal blue T-shirt. Masha was a striking blonde, with pink lips and eyes like blue glass. She didn't say much but listened intensely to our conversation. Artem had a goatee, and he wore shorts and a yellow plaid short-sleeved shirt. He had a soft voice and a mellow expression, and he struck me as a serious, thoughtful person. We found a bench near the hotel and sat there for hours, all the while being bitten by aggressive Siberian mosquitoes. Artem slumped over, his elbows on his lap. He often seemed to be speaking to some point in front of him or to the ground. Occasionally he would catch a mosquito in his hands.

Artem worked as a videographer at Novosibirsk State Technical University. He told me that he became interested in politics several years earlier, when he went to university and learned about the war in Iraq. He didn't approve of what the United States was doing, nor did he approve of what Russia was doing in Chechnya. He thought Russian elections were a joke. Around that same time he started becoming more active on the Internet. In 2006 he began posting on LiveJournal. He started his colorfully titled *Kissmybabushka* blog in 2008, in which he blogged about various exhibitions and art events, most notably about *monstratsiya*, or monstrations.

Monstrations, of which Artem was a key organizer, are best defined as a blend of civic protest and performance art. The first monstration was held in Novosibirsk in May 2004, drawing some eighty participants. It was held on May Day, which in Soviet times included parades to celebrate workers. Monstrations, which over the years spread to other cities in Russia, were marked by absurdist banners with such slogans as "The guinea pig lied to me," "Earth for earthlings," and "Think globally, act idiotically!"

Artem said that the monstrations movement began in 2004 in reaction to a predictably boring presidential election that same year. Artem felt an urge to react. The last straw was the May Day celebrations. The participants didn't demand anything from the people in power or even make their views known. Artem believed that the only way to demonstrate the absurdity of the situation would be to come up with a completely nonsensical response. He later described monstration participants as the people who, if allowed, would vote against everyone in an election.

Young artists such as Artem felt alienated by both the government and its traditional opponents. Monstrations were a deliberate avoidance of dialogue with those in power as well as with those in the opposition. They reflected the widespread view that elections were theater and street demonstrations were farce. In 2006 Max Neroda, one of the original monstration organizers, wrote an article explaining that monstrations were intentional hyperbole, both a satire and a critique of traditional demonstrations. The organizers didn't even want to use the word "demonstrations." Artem explained that the prefix "de" had a negative, destructive connotation.

This absurd form of protest was hardly unprecedented in Russia. In the late 1920s, during the dark years of Stalin's rule, OBERIU (meaning the Union of Real Art) was founded by Daniil Kharms and Alexander Vvedensky. They incorporated parody, absurdity, and even circus tricks into their events. One 1928 event, *Three Leftist Hours*, featured a poetry reading on top of furniture left over from the staging of a play, while the emcee rode around on a tricycle. In 1931 Kharms and Vvedensky were jailed for counterrevolutionary activity.

Monstrations were part of a larger creative movement. Artem knew some of the members of the art group Voina, which means "war," and he occasionally promoted their performances on his blog. Voina's membership included Nadezhda Tolokonnikova and Yekaterina Samutsevich, two of the women who would later form the band Pussy Riot (Tolokonnikova is a cofounder of Voina). Voina became known for such stunts as painting an enormous phallus on a St. Petersburg drawbridge. When the bridge split in two and lifted up to let boats pass, Voina's artistic creation rose with it, pointing directly at the headquarters of the FSB.

In 2008 Tolokonnikova, nine months pregnant at the time, took part in a Voina orgy at the Biology Museum in Moscow. The event was meant to be a protest against the election of President Medvedev. Voina founder Oleg Vorotnikov explained the action: "Many said it was pornography that we got undressed and had an orgy—but we say the pornography is the fact that we had no elections and that people are scared of telling the truth."

In 2010 I met with Voina in the hope of interviewing them for this book. I had been corresponding by email with a woman named Sandra. Sandra agreed to meet me in St. Petersburg but initially refused to provide a phone number or any details of our meeting. My younger brother, who was visiting me in Russia at the time, gamely accompanied me to a random street corner in St. Petersburg. We waited there for "Sandra," who turned out to be a shirtless, potbellied man swinging a beer bottle.

He led us down a deserted block where other members of Voina were sitting on a stairway. Some were painting large signs that each had one Cyrillic letter. One woman had her baby with her. "Sandra" told us he had a plan, but he wouldn't tell us what it was, only that it involved a supermarket. He asked us to participate, we declined, and we thus parted ways. I later learned that their "plan" involved a blond woman named Natalia going to a public supermarket, spreading her legs, and inserting a raw chicken into herself.

Monstrations tended to be slightly more family friendly than Voina stunts, but they shared the same creative approach to activism. Following their inception in 2004, monstrations slowly picked up steam. In 2005 some two hundred people participated. Invitations to the event were circulated online, and organizers asked that people come with meaningless slogans and images, as well as musical instruments. They were encouraged to wear strange outfits. There were no clear political demands. One slogan was "No to the colonization of Mars," and participants carried banners with images of Pushkin, Marilyn Monroe, and others. When participants tried to join hands and dance in a circle, the authorities intervened, saying that such dancing was not appropriate at a political event. The authorities then made participants leave, telling them that they did not have permission to be there.

But the movement kept growing. In 2006 slogans included "Buy an elephant!" and "Land for the peasants! Sky for the aliens!" Hundreds showed up in 2007, and this time authorities largely left the participants alone. The 2008 monstration had at least five hundred participants. The authorities just didn't get it, Artem told me. Participants in monstrations weren't trying to make money, they figured, so it must be some kind of opposition thing.

In 2009 Artem was getting close to earning his bachelor's degree from Novosibirsk State Technical University, where he was studying film. Monstrations were planned for May Day, as usual. But this time the Novosibirsk authorities weren't having it. Artem learned that the monstrations' usual path would be occupied by a track-and-field relay in memory of the Soviet hero Valentin Podnevich, honored for his service during World War II. The authorities couldn't even keep their own story straight, Artem said. Other media reported that the event at City Hall was to be a United Russia rally.

Artem needed a plan. One idea, he told me, was for people to gather around City Hall and lift it into the air with the power of thought, returning it to the ground an hour later. "The authorities had taken our space," he explained, "so we should take theirs." On April 27, a few days before the monstrations were scheduled to take place, Artem and his comrades held an exhibition in a makeshift art gallery called White Cube.

Artem's blog said that the exhibition's purpose was to explore possible directions for the absurd procession known as monstrations, using "black magic, the Constitution of the Russian Federation, acrylic painting, little hats made out of foil, and the news that the Novosibirsk City Hall, on May 1, is holding a track-and-field relay on the path of the traditional monstration procession."

When exhibition day arrived, the festivities had hardly begun when authorities made an appearance. The gallery owner was taken into the police station for a little chat. He was not given any direct orders, but he took away a clear message that similar initiatives would not be appreciated.

Meanwhile, May 1 was quickly approaching. Artem informed his readers that the city had not granted permission to hold the May Day event. On his blog, he outlined the arguments both for and against attending monstrations. The reason not to go was simple: monstrations weren't allowed. The goal of monstrations was to have a good time, after all, and nothing throws cold water on a party like a band of police. Artem wrote on his blog that authorities had sent out notices to the administrations of local universities in an effort to keep students from attending monstrations.

But staying home would also come at a price. Artem's blog raised a series of questions: Is it worth living in a world where you are scared to go outside on a holiday? How does it feel to know that your activities bother the cops? How does it feel to realize that they are afraid of you, that you are a force not controlled by anyone? Is it worth living in a country where you are afraid to exercise your rights? He concluded, "Rights are not given; they are taken. And I know my rights."

Meanwhile, Artem said, he was getting phone calls at home from the counter-extremism center, a branch of the police. They also called his relatives, who told him to go talk to the authorities so they would be left alone. So he went to the counter-extremism center and explained that he just wanted to hold a peaceful protest, that the issue was that they weren't able to hold it in front of City Hall. He promised not to cause a problem.

In the end, May 1 came and went relatively peacefully. About two hundred people showed up for monstrations. Artem, busy making his case at the counter-extremism center, wasn't able to attend. Monstration participants broke up into two columns, one with cameras and one with posters. Some people stood on the steps of City Hall chanting "All are free" and "Who is the leader here?" Despite these efforts, Artem's blog noted, City Hall failed to rise up off the ground.

"BLOGGERS HAVE NOTHING TO FEAR FROM PUBLICITY"

The authorities' warning was loud and clear, but Artem kept forging ahead. Less than two weeks later, he announced on his blog that on May 17 there would be an event to commemorate the World Health Organization's decision that homosexuality is not a mental illness. Participants were told to go to a park with a helium balloon in one of the colors of the rainbow. They should affix to the balloon a rainbow flag or a note with their name, their occupation, and a message to the world. Then everyone would let the balloons float upward, forming a rainbow in the sky. Cities around the world would be holding similar events, Artem's blog said. The post was vague about the backers of the event, referring to "mysterious organizers."

On May 15 Artem said he got another call from the counter-extremism center, but the caller wouldn't say what he wanted. Artem told the caller that he didn't wish to meet if he didn't know what the meeting was about. According to Artem, the caller said, "Well, if you don't want to come in, we'll just come to you," and Artem was detained that evening on his way home from work.

He told me that he sat in the center for an hour and a half. Authorities asked him about monstrations. They took his bag and emptied it out. Artem saw a bag of marijuana, eleven grams, to be precise. He claimed that the police planted the drugs. He was actually a bit disappointed. If the authorities were going to go through all the trouble of planting something, couldn't it have been articles suggesting his extremist or antigovernment activities? But no, they resorted to a primitive planting of drugs.

While they were investigating whether these were Artem's drugs, the court decided that he might flee or continue conducting illegal drug sales. He was also accused of being a leader of a group of young people who intended to organize acts of public disorder, vandalism, and arson. Thus he should be kept in custody for two months. He was charged with the acquisition of and intent to sell drugs, which carried up to three years of prison time. There was also a discussion of his being charged for "extremism." This latter accusation was not surprising. A 2002 anti-extremism law that initially intended to target far-right nationalists had become widely criticized for becoming a tool to crack down on political dissent.

Up to this point, nothing that happened to Artem was particularly exceptional in Putin's Russia. What followed was. Once, an edgy Siberian artist would have been taken into custody, and that might have been the end of the story. But that was before the

Internet. Now the Siberian artist in question was an active blog-ger. "Before having a stand-alone blog, I had a pretty popular ac-count on LiveJournal, so people from the Novosibirsk blogosphere knew me in one way or another, and many of them are journal-ists," Artem explained.

Several people had access to edit *Kissmybabushka*, and they launched an information campaign that began on the evening of his detention. Several days after that, the courtroom was filled with press. Artem's side of the story—namely, his argument that drugs had been planted and that there was insufficient evidence against him—was widely reported. Many believed that he was being targeted for his role in monstrations.

Meanwhile, he waited in custody. He said that on May 15 he was placed in a detention center in a roughly fifteen-square-meter room with two bunk beds, a desk, a toilet, a sink, and two to four people who, like him, were waiting for their court date. After he was arrested, on May 20, he was put in jail. The room was roughly the same, but now there was a three-tiered bed, and sometimes people had to sleep in shifts. Showers were once a week. He shared a room with about ten other people whose charges ranged from theft to murder.

The story of Artem's case lit up the blogosphere. People talked about his arrest and the fact that he had been put in jail for alleg-edly using drugs. The blog Artem had been running for a year and a half became a communications center. His friends posted details of his arrest, as well as his side of the story. They also live-blogged the trial. One blogger encouraged people to come out on June 9, otherwise known as the day of "united action in support of Artem Loskutov": "Participate in events, come out to rallies, sign petitions, stir up the Internet and the media space—most impor-tantly, don't stay apathetic, don't stand on the side. This concerns each one of us, even if Artem to you isn't a colleague and a friend, but 'someone in Novosibirsk.' We get the state that we deserve. Today an artist is accused of extremism, tomorrow any one of us could be in his place."

Support spread off-line as well. Rallies were held in Novosibirsk, Moscow, and St. Petersburg. While Artem was in prison, the police told him that hundreds of people came out in protest for him. They even sent out riot police in Novosibirsk. There was also at least one "radiomob" in Novosibirsk, in which people called in to radio stations, flash mob style, to express their support for Artem. He said that people made stickers and leaflets to put in Metro stations and other public places.

In St. Petersburg, demonstrators protested by drawing pictures. They depicted City Hall as hell, and painted pictures of the lawlessness and impunity of police officers. Demonstrators left their paintings up on easels in a square near Smolny for passersby to see. Some protesters even went on a hunger strike until Artem was freed.

A libertarian movement known as Free Radicals started a petition asking that Artem be released and that trials be more fair and transparent. More than seven hundred people signed. The petition was sent to the Novosibirsk regional court, the Russian Presidential Press and Information Office, and various other offices.

Outrage over Artem's case extended beyond Russia's borders. One petition circulated in Germany and was signed by Herta Müller, winner of the 2009 Nobel Prize in Literature. There was also an art event in Berlin in support of Artem. The poet, musician, and journalist Alexander Delfinov read critical poems about Putin and walked across a stage wearing a clown hat with bells. The event included a funny cartoon clip, *Sekstremizm*, prepared jointly by Artem's defenders from Germany, Russia, Israel, and Lithuania. The cartoon depicted creatures and fairy-tale characters rapping and generally mocking the Russian police.

In Russia, Artem's arrest coincided with a wave of dissatisfaction over the brute force of the police. In one extreme incident that April, mere weeks before Artem's arrest, a drunk police officer walked into a Moscow supermarket and randomly opened fire. He killed three people and wounded several others. So when Artem was detained in a highly publicized trial, ordinary Russians saw an opportunity to vent their anger about the police.

Artem was supposed to be in custody for two months, but he appealed the court's decision and ended up being released after twenty-seven days, on June 10. The appeal panel discovered procedural issues with the trial. Now Artem had to wait for a new trial. He didn't want people to forget about his case. One unlikely piece of support came in January, when the state television channel NTV aired a documentary called *We Are Not Vegetables*, about Russians who were not apathetic. The documentary featured several cases, among which was Artem's.

The actual trial didn't occur until March of the following year. Artem was found guilty for unlawful possession of marijuana despite his claim that his fingerprints weren't on the drugs, and that a medical investigation reportedly found he hadn't used drugs. He got a 20,000 ruble (roughly $627) fine.

Both Artem and the Novosibirsk authorities tried to use the Internet to their advantage. But Artem and his friends were far more comfortable with the Web. Artem said that authorities sometimes tried to influence online conversations by pretending to be ordinary commenters. It got comical. In March 2010, as he was awaiting his trial, he found a comment on his blog that had a peculiar tone. The comment said, "This is nonsense, a smug guy from some Monstration :) How can you draw conclusions, listening to only one side? I hope they lock you up, because the Russian court is the most humane court in the world :))))." Artem told me that as an administrator of the blog, he had the ability to see the IP addresses of all commenters, and he believed the address of the commenter in question led to a Siberian police station.

Artem understood that the police were vulnerable to publicity. In June 2010 he planned to make a trip to Moscow, and a couple of days before he was supposed to go, he got a call from a woman in the Novosibirsk prosecutor's office. He turned on his audio recorder. The woman told him she understood that he planned to take part in extremist activities in Moscow and she needed him to come in and either confirm or deny it. He told her that it was not legal to call him in. She proceeded to tell him she needed a statement from him documenting that he would not be participating in extremist activities in Moscow.

He asked if he could fax or email a letter from the organization that invited him, but she said that he must deliver it in person. She threatened to talk to his boss at Novosibirsk State Technical University, where he was working as a videographer. She said she would send a notice to the university rector listing the reasons the authorities wanted to see him, noting that this act could in itself end his employment at the university. The conversation concluded with Artem declining her invitation to come in.

The battle was on. He posted the recording on his blog, and the prosecutor's office sent a fax to the rector of the university. The fax referred to "extremist" activity that Artem planned to participate in when he went to Moscow. Artem promptly posted the fax on his blog. He then went to the prosecutor's office and asked them to provide documentation of his extremist activity. They couldn't, so he went to Moscow.

While the Internet helped draw public attention to Artem's arrest, it also made it easier for authorities to monitor him. He admitted that he may have been called in before his trip to Moscow in response to a joking tweet about giving a master class on organizing monstrations. He told me that he has learned to be more careful about what information he puts online. If he were to do some artwork on a wall or a fence, for example, he would not be so quick to advertise this feat on the Internet.

He was comforted, however, by the fact that the level of tech savviness among police wasn't very high. He believes the authorities tapped his phone calls, but he doesn't think they had his text messages. Although it was clear that the authorities would eventually increase their technical capacities, none of the Russian bloggers I met were terribly concerned about Internet censorship. As Elia and his blogger friends told me, Russians have a history of samizdat. Elia said, "If Chinese bloggers found a way to fight censorship, we will fight it too."

Artem told me that his motivation is the same as any artist's: go out and create. If an artist isn't creating, he feels unhealthy. He and his friends just want to create art without being accused of a crime.

He described the events surrounding his case as a "victory over public apathy." Protests were not just in Novosibirsk, but in other places as well. People wanted to go out and be seen. Furthermore, ordinary people made a difference. He believes that the publicity surrounding the case helped secure his freedom.

In Soviet times, Artem said, standing up for your rights was usually not worth the risk. At best, nothing would change; at worst, you would end up in jail. After the Soviet Union collapsed, people still felt that they couldn't have an impact. "The government stayed in its world and the people were in theirs," he said. In the 1990s, he added, people's values shifted. It became more important to have a big television than to have objective coverage on that television.

When I met Artem in 2010, he said that he had the feeling

that things were changing bit by bit. He could tell by the kinds of people who were starting to stand up for their rights. In Novosibirsk, parents picketed to protest a shortage of kindergartens. In Moscow, office workers refused to yield the road to flashing blue lights.

On May 1, 2010, Novosibirsk monstrations were held legally for the first time. Artem said that he followed the letter of the law, and organizers obtained permission from the city to hold the event. Monstrations were held in fourteen cities, including a couple of cities abroad. All in all, thousands participated. In an ironic twist, Artem received an innovation award from the Russian Ministry of Culture for Monstration 2010.

In some places monstrations were still not allowed, but participants weren't deterred. In St. Petersburg, where permission for the event was not granted, organizers held a "burial" for the monstration. The dress code was "carnival mourning," and participants were asked to moo in a dejected, organized manner.

Artem saw his story as a win for "any Russian who wants to be active." His high-profile battle with the counter-extremism center clearly worked in his favor. "Bloggers have nothing to fear from publicity," he said. Artem told me that he was no longer afraid. He went and met with officials, and they put him in jail anyway. Once you go to jail, you don't fear it as much. He also felt that the authorities were unlikely to handle him again in such a clumsy, heavy-handed way. Even in a Siberian cell he wasn't shut away from the outside world. "I feel that I am supported," he told me. "And the authorities feel it too."

"NO ONE, INCLUDING ME,
BELIEVED THIS WAS POSSIBLE IN RUSSIA"

In the fall of 2010 Navalny went to Yale on a fellowship. One of his friends, a Russian journalist, told me that he hoped Yale would help smooth out Navalny's rougher edges. For many liberals in both Russia and the West, Navalny was hard to pin down. Sure, he was anti-Putin, anticorruption, and pro-shareholder. But there was also something about him that was raw, even a little threatening.

There were his appearances at the controversial Russian Marches, which were also attended by neo-Nazis, as well as a general concern among liberals that he had violent and racist streaks. There was the notorious video in which Navalny likened Caucasus militants to cockroaches. You can kill cockroaches with a slipper, but for humans, Navalny says, "I recommend a pistol."

Navalny tried to explain to me that Americans didn't understand Russian nationalism. "It's not about ideology," he said. "It's all about real problems, a real agenda." He brought up a current nationalist campaign that aimed to stop "feeding" the Caucusus. "It's all about disproportion of funding," he said. "We give to Chechnya billions, but we don't give these billions to Smolensk or some Russian regions."

Some suspected that Navalny actually harbored intolerance toward people from the Caucasus, as those attitudes were not uncommon among Russian nationalists. In December 2010 a soccer fan named Egor Sviridov was killed, allegedly by eight men from the Caucasus. After the killing, a gang of thousands, including soccer hooligans and nationalists, gathered to protest. According to Julia Ioffe in *The New Yorker*, the mob screamed, "Russia for Russians!" and attacked anyone who didn't look Slavic. Some of the thugs even went into the Metro and, screaming "white car!," proceeded to beat Caucasians and Central Asians until they were unconscious.

Navalny seemed dubious that this incident really happened as it was portrayed in the media. He also shot back, "Ah, come on. Look at the British football fans . . . They are much more racist. Come on, look at the meetings of Sarah Palin."

Navalny was also surrounded by the usual conspiracy murmurings that he was being backed by murky political or business interests. At first glance he seemed like your handsome golden boy, breezy and casual in an almost American way. But he also had a thick neck and steely eyes that would narrow and quickly scan his surroundings.

Navalny later told me that by giving him a stamp of approval, Yale saved him the trouble of having to explain his background. It became easier for him to get high-level meetings in the United States. "It was really annoying to explain who I am," he said. "Now, I am a Yale World Fellow. It's enough for them to understand that I'm someone they can deal with." Navalny appreciated the value of this. As he told me on countless occasions, he hated to waste time.

In November 2010 he used his newfound credibility to visit Washington and brief the Helsinki Commission, an independent government agency. The commission included members from the U.S. Senate, House of Representatives, and the Departments of Commerce, State, and Defense.

During his briefing, Navalny gave several examples of corruption in Russia's energy sector, such as questionably high gas pipeline construction costs and Transneft's mysterious charitable donations. Why should Americans care? He argued that corruption in Russia affects share prices for shareholders around the world, and U.S. funds have billions of dollars invested in Russian companies. Navalny hoped to see a reduction in damage to investors as well as to draw attention to human rights violations. He discussed the death of Sergei Magnitsky, expressing gratitude for the emerging congressional support for the Magnitsky Act. He mentioned the beating of Oleg Kashin, which had occurred the previous weekend.

Navalny said that better ratings from such agencies as Standard and Poor's would increase transparency and allow Russian companies to borrow money at lower rates. He recommended that if concerns arise about specific investments in Russia, investors should alert the appropriate American authorities so that they can investigate or take legal action. He also said that America needed a strategy for prosecuting corruption committed by Russians in the United States.

That same fall, I invited him to the White House for an informal meeting with Mike McFaul, then President Obama's senior adviser for Russia. I was working at the State Department at the time. Navalny arrived early to the meeting, looking elegant in a well-fitting suit. After only a few months at Yale he was making jokes in colloquial English. He asked if the password I used to enter the State Department was "666." In general, he didn't bother with unnecessary gravitas. "I like that you wear heels," he made a point of telling me. "Americans are always wearing these *flats*. In New Haven the only one who wears heels is my wife."

The meeting was my idea. I wanted to give McFaul, who later went on to become U.S. ambassador to the Russian Federation, a clearer picture of the role of activist bloggers in Russia. There was no other goal or agenda, and there were several other Russians at the meeting. As far as I know, it was the only time Navalny and McFaul had met.

Navalny's enthusiasm for the Web was stronger than ever. He said that the Internet was one area where "there is democracy," and that the Web was home to an "informal center for fighting corruption." His own experience continued to challenge the assumption that Russian citizens were apathetic about political or social change.

He described how he used his blog to draw attention to a suspicious competition held by the Russian Health Ministry. Potential contractors were challenged to design a social network for health workers. The contestants had to complete an expensive and complicated project in a little over two weeks. Navalny suspected that the competition was fraudulent and the winner had already been decided. He wrote about this on his blog, urging his readers to speak out. Soon after, he said, "the antitrust ministry called me and said, 'Please leave us alone. We just got sixteen hundred complaints.'" Less than a week later, the competition was withdrawn, and the director of the Health Ministry's IT department resigned.

Navalny found himself in a difficult situation. Upon witnessing his power and influence, ordinary Russians began turning to him for help with various problems. "Every single day I have twenty letters," he said. People sometimes got angry when he didn't have time to respond. He didn't want to be such a one-man show. Russia needed more Navalnys. But in the meantime, he said, "I need an electronic system to coordinate this." He complained that in Russia, there wasn't much technological support or funding for these kinds of Web-based social action projects.

What I remember most about that day is not the meeting itself. It was standing with Navalny at the back entrance of the White House's Old Executive Office Building. We stood atop a grand stairway. I remember emptiness around us, and white stone. Washington was beneath us. Standing on those stairs next to Navalny in his suit, I felt very powerfully that something was going to happen to him. But I couldn't say what it would be. He might be the future president of Russia. Or perhaps I was standing beside an eventual ghost.

What I never imagined was how soon the drama would begin. Neither of us could have predicted that less than eighteen months later, tens of thousands of Russians would take to the streets in the largest protests since the fall of the Soviet Union, and that one of the protest leaders would be Navalny himself.

Shortly after he left Washington and went back to Yale in the fall of 2010, I received an email with the memorable subject line "Holy War." The email began, "Hi Emily, last week I started another Holy War." Navalny alleged that, in cooperation with government officials, managers of the oil-transport monopoly Transneft embezzled about $4 billion from the company. The graft was linked to the construction of Transneft's East Siberia–Pacific Ocean pipeline. Navalny published some documents about the alleged corruption on his blog.

He told me in his email that he was preparing to sue the company and launch a criminal investigation of its managers. "The problem is the highest Russian officials were involved, so they are doing everything to squelch an investigation," he said. He included a link to a short YouTube video in which he explains the alleged graft.

The documents Navalny published attracted great attention on his blog and in the Russian media, making millions aware of the case. And a few weeks later he got something that looked like retaliation. A prosecutor's office in Kirov, where years earlier he had worked as a volunteer assistant for the governor, was reported to be investigating accusations that Navalny pressured an official to sell timber on unfair terms. In May, the Russian Investigative Committee opened a criminal case against him.

These allegations, which Navalny called "stupid," made his life more difficult. He was burdened with legal fees. He needed to get permission from his investigator to travel abroad. The investigation was also a warning. "They will try to find something more serious," Navalny said. "That's why I should be careful. I cannot afford to have operations with cash. It is my only option to be transparent."

But despite the legal headaches, he continued to build momentum. After the Health Ministry case, several of his readers alerted him to other suspicious competitions. Navalny wrote about one, and this competition too was canceled.

As his popularity rose, so did the demands on his time. He began getting so many requests that he couldn't personally address all of them. He needed to find another solution. Then, in August 2010, he described a letter that made him happy. It was from one of the readers of his blog, named Fyodor. Fyodor was fed up with the roads around his house, which were riddled with bumps and holes.

At one time, perhaps, Fyodor would have just learned to deal with it. But after reading Navalny's blog, he decided that he should be less passive. A quick Google search revealed that the holes in the road did not meet state standards. He wrote a letter to the local police, and the hole was repaired.

Navalny, telling this story on his blog, explained that Fyodor had actually scored a much larger victory. Authorities assumed that most people wouldn't bother complaining. Navalny wrote that people like Fyodor would force officials to spend "real money" on "actual repair" rather than just using road-repair funds for kickbacks. Navalny wrote playfully on his blog, "Raise your hand if you have a hole in the road next to your house. I see a forest of hands, thank you."

This kind of thing inspired Navalny to create his Rosyama site, which went live in May 2011. On Rosyama, Russians could post photographs of unfixed potholes, and complaints would be sent directly to the authorities. Thousands of road problems have reportedly been fixed as a result of the site.

Navalny kept aiming higher. In 2011 he started RosPil, a site that crowdsourced scrutiny over Russian government tenders. In an apparent attempt to crack down on corruption, the Russian government published tenders online. Requests for tender, or the documents in which government entities present potential bidders with their demand for particular goods or services, are posted on zakupki.gov.ru. The outcome of the bidding process is posted as well.

If anyone found a peculiar-looking government tender, they could fill out a form and explain why they found it suspicious. The information would then be posted on RosPil, and experts affiliated with the site and registered users could discuss the posted document. They could examine the price, delivery schedule, and criteria for the winning bid. If anything was deemed unreasonable, RosPil lawyers would send letters of complaint to the appropriate authorities.

RosPil made a splash in the domestic and international media. It was widely compared to WikiLeaks, which Navalny found irritating. "There's nothing in common with WikiLeaks," he told me. "I'm using open information from public reports." The point of RosPil was to take publicly available information and expose it to scrutiny.

In January 2011, for example, there was a request for tender posted for the Bolshoi Theatre website, which was to be launched in tandem with the theater's reopening after its restoration. The project cost more than $150,000. After members of RosPil submitted letters of complaint, the project was canceled. There was discussion about the fairness of the price and the project deadline, but the bottom line was that the request for tender violated regulations by indicating that a specific software package be used. This requirement limited the competition to one company. According to the official notice, the requester canceled the order because the assignment description was not clear regarding the nature of services to be provided.

Since RosPil launched, millions of dollars in suspicious contracts have been annulled. The success of RosPil was a critical turning point not only for Navalny's personal fame but for the expectations of ordinary Russians. "They are starting to believe in the power of collective action," Navalny said. RosPil also chipped away at the notion that Russians are apathetic and can't be bothered to make donations. Navalny used Yandex Money, a PayPal-like product of Russia's largest search engine, to raise money for RosPil. (Yandex ended up giving personal information about Navalny's donors to the FSB, Russia's security services.)

Still, he collected more than $100,000 in a week. Referring to the volume of donations, he said, "No one, including me, believed this was possible in Russia."

"YOU CANNOT BE A HERO FOR A LONG TIME ON THE INTERNET"

In October 2011, a few months before mass protests broke out in Russia, Navalny came back to Yale for a reunion. I went to New Haven to see him. He had initially told me that he would have a packed schedule, that he'd have very little time to spare for meetings unrelated to Yale, and that if anyone asked what I was doing with him, he would say I was a professor. He first told me to meet him at 16:15, explaining, "Since we fight for democracy, we should use military time!" After arriving at Yale, however, he decided that the scheduled events were wasting his time. We ended up meeting earlier, spending the better part of the day, a golden moment in mid-autumn, strolling leisurely through the campus and the streets around it. Our conversation was punctuated by the mellow chimes of university bells.

At one point during the day I randomly found a twenty-dollar bill on the sidewalk. Navalny glanced around and muttered something about cameras, but then he happily accompanied me to Blue State, a nearby café, to spend our windfall on lattes.

Navalny looked poised in a crisp white button-down and black pants. He had crossed a threshold. People on campus were starting to recognize him, and not just because he had spent time at Yale. RosPil had, in Navalny's own words, made him a "rock star." Although only a small minority of Russians knew who he was, his influence could be measured in other ways. A babushka in a small village, for example, may not have known Navalny's name, but she may well have heard Putin's United Russia party called "the party of crooks and thieves," a term Navalny had coined in a radio interview in February 2011.

The phrase quickly caught on. According to a Levada poll in April, 23 percent of Russians polled said that United Russia was "probably" the party of crooks and thieves; 8 percent said it definitely was. The phrase became so popular that if you typed "United Russia" into a Russian Google search box, "the party of crooks and thieves" would immediately follow.

Navalny was also more watchful than ever. As we sat on a bench, his eyes scrolled across nearly every person who passed by. There was an investigation against him. He had powerful enemies in government and big business. He also had more banal rivalries with less charismatic Russian activists who were jealous of his success. There were many people waiting for his downfall, and this affected our relationship as well.

"Listen, I'm not sure I understand what you do," he said to me shortly after we met up at Yale. "If there's anything I need to know, please tell me. It could cause real problems for me."

"I'm not in the CIA," I said. I told him I used to work in government, but now I was writing a book.

"So you don't have any stones?" he asked, playfully peering behind me. I looked at him blankly.

I later understood that this was a tongue-in-cheek reference to a bizarre incident in 2006, when the Russian security service discovered a fake rock in a Moscow park. Inside this "rock" was a communications device planted by British spies. Russian television had a field day with the rocks, showing videos of them being taken apart to reveal the transmitters inside. The British later took responsibility for the rocks, which really were used for espionage, with a former British official calling them "embarrassing."

Navalny seemed reasonably convinced that I wasn't in the CIA, although he never stopped jokingly referring to me as an agent. His caution was understandable. The chief executive of Transneft, Nikolai Tokarev, had already suggested that Navalny was working for the CIA to defame Russian companies like his own. Navalny's enemies were questioning his American connections, and if they couldn't find incriminating evidence, they would just invent it. He showed me a hilarious Web page that purported to be a Yale World Fellows site. It contained comments on Navalny from various Yale "instructors." One particularly Russian-accented entry read "He is doomed to failure as an active political leader in absence of outward aid, PR support or some other special technologies."

Navalny was under pressure, and much more than his personal reputation was at stake. After years of crippling apathy in Russia, he had become a test case for effective activism. "We really need success stories. That's why all these journalists are jumping and dancing around me. But I'm only one guy, and everyone expects miracles from me. I can't do miracles. I did a simple thing, I collected money without stealing it."

Beneath Navalny's humor was a wire of uncertainty. "You cannot support this kind of miracle," he told me. "People are getting disappointed. You cannot be a hero for a long time on the Internet. It's like in the music industry; you need a new album."

His most serious concern was determining if his support was virtual or real. He wanted to weed out "fake people" from the Internet. He said, "I write a post, and two hundred people write comments. How do you know if they are real?"

The problem of "fake people" was a serious one. In America, activists fight for online anonymity as a means to protect privacy. But in Russia this same anonymity undermines the opposition. Russian Internet sites have long been plagued by bots, or software applications that simulate human activity. These bots, which can be paid for by government or private entities, produce comments and posts. They make "friends" on social networks. Russia's bot invasion is significant: in 2012 VKontakte's deputy director Ilya Perekopsky said that up to 76 percent of all traffic to major companies was driven by bots.

Bots easily distorted the rankings of the most popular bloggers and topics. Navalny told me that these ratings were manipulated by pro-Kremlin youth figures whose preferred topics always seemed to score suspiciously high ratings. Other uses of bots were more inventive. Navalny's office said that his rivals paid for bots that actually supported him, with the intention of accusing Navalny of buying supportive bots. All of this created a sense of general confusion about who was really influential online.

Navalny was working with other activists, such as Leonid Volkov, an opposition politician in Yekaterinburg, to develop an online polling system that would use electronic signatures to verify users' identities. Navalny's ultimate goal was to create online polls and primaries to determine the leaders of the Russian opposition. He was convinced that electronic signatures would help Russia's opposition "believe in its own power" by proving that there were enough people to register for a party or participate in a major demonstration. When I asked Navalny if he wanted to be president himself, he demurred. In 2013, right before he went to trial, he publicly stated that he did.

But back in 2011 he had other reasons to doubt the depth of his support. His "comfortable way of struggle" approach was a double-edged sword. Yes, his followers were willing to fill out online forms. Some even donated money. But if necessary, would they actually take to the streets?

"I'm a little bit afraid," Navalny admitted. "People ask me, appeal to everyone to go to the street. But there is the chance, more than fifty percent, that after my appealing, I don't know, two hundred people will come. It would be a huge, epic fail. And I cannot afford it right now."

But Navalny also understood how quickly the situation could change. The mood in Russia was shifting. In September, Putin announced that he would run for president in the March elections. For many Russians, this was a blatant admission that Medvedev, with his iPhone and supposed reforms, was nothing more than a seat warmer. And a Putin run meant a Putin win.

A slow indignation was simmering, but the decisive moment would not arrive for another few months. Navalny knew that one event could change everything. The Arab Spring, he said, was started by the self-immolation of a Tunisian street vendor. "It's thin," he told me, "this barrier between stability and riot."

Navalny told me about meeting a Tunisian activist, also at Yale, in December 2010. The Tunisian told him, "In Russia you are so lucky, you have Twitter, Facebook, YouTube, and you can operate the opposition freely." Navalny remembered looking at the Tunisian protest movement and thinking, "How pathetic." To him it looked like a few people wearing T-shirts. A month later the regime of President Zine El-Abidine Ben Ali fell, ending a two-decade dictatorship. Even Tunisian activists were taken by surprise, Navalny said. "These people didn't believe in change."

"MY COUNTRY AND MY LIFE ARE DEPENDENT ON WHAT I DO"

Navalny visualized his Internet projects long before they were realized. He knew precisely what he wanted to achieve. There was just one problem: he was not a programmer. He had to enlist people with the technological capacity to bring his ideas to life, and in Russia this was not so easy to do. He initially made an appeal on his blog for help in building his road-repair site, Rosyama. He said that about twenty people replied, allowing him to create a team. But their work was not up to his standards, and he had to pay a (pricey) outside company to complete the task. He told me in 2011 that if he wrote one post calling for help, he would get "five projects, and all of them will be awful. And I will try to coordinate one project from these five, and they will all start arguing."

Navalny's conundrum highlighted a larger problem. Although there was no shortage of good programmers in Russia, they weren't necessarily inclined to spend their free time hacking away on a site for reporting potholes. It could be a challenge to find technological support for these kinds of "social responsibility" projects, as Navalny called them, especially for an opposition-minded activist without a lot of rubles to spare. "We don't have a lot of professionals in this area," he told me. "And those who are professionals don't want to work for free."

The creators of Russian-fires.ru, the crowdsourcing website that helped connect the needy with volunteers when Russian wildfires broke out in the summer of 2010, had a similar lament. The site, staffed entirely by volunteers, was based on Ushahidi crowdsourcing software. Ushahidi was created to map reports of 2008 postelection violence in Kenya. Since then, the open source software has been adapted for use all over the world. But Ushahidi did not always work so smoothly in Russia, said Alexey Sidorenko, one of the founders of the wildfires site. The site got hundreds of thousands of hits but also crashed several times.

"Although the initial installation was pretty easy, technical problems did arise later," Sidorenko wrote in a blog post. "Most of them had to do with internationalization and localization. Ushahidi is a great platform, but non-Latin implementations of it still need a lot of work."

In the United States, unlike Russia, the idea of hacking for social change was trendy. One initiative, called Random Hacks of Kindness—a partnership between Google, Microsoft, Yahoo!, NASA, HP, and the World Bank—would organize volunteer coding marathons to address such problems as disaster relief. In 2009 RHOK was held in Mountain View, California. The winners, a team from Carnegie Mellon University, developed "I'm OK"—a one-step method of sending an SMS to friends and family in a disaster situation, when cell phone networks were likely to be overburdened.

I wondered if it would be possible to convene this kind of hackathon between the United States and Russia. At the very least, it would provide a good excuse for Russian and American programmers to spend a couple of days working on common problems.

In the fall of 2010 I was well situated to work on such an initiative. I had just joined the U.S. State Department, where I was serving as a member of Secretary of State Hillary Clinton's Policy Planning Staff. My portfolio was technology, innovation, and twenty-first-century statecraft. This was a fairly new area of diplomacy, and Secretary Clinton had thrown her weight behind it. This meant that it was relatively easy to get political backing for out-of-the-box ideas.

I brought the idea for the hackathon to Mike McFaul at the White House, who was immediately supportive. But my colleagues in Washington were uncomfortable with the word "hackathon," probably because of the negative cybersecurity implications, and as a result, we went with the slightly more awkward "codeathon." USAID got on board, as did the U.S. embassy in Moscow. SecondMuse, the company that handled logistics for Random Hacks of Kindness, helped with the execution. We called the project Code4Country.

At the same time, my job at the State Department was somewhat of a liability. Russians were very sensitive to the perception of U.S. government "meddling" in political affairs. There was a real danger that a U.S.-Russia codeathon would be interpreted by the Kremlin as a "Trojan Horse" for helping opposition activists incite revolution. It was a running joke among the opposition that the State Department was behind all their activities.

USAID was also viewed with great suspicion. In its two decades of operation, USAID spent nearly $3 billion on programs in Russia that touched on issues ranging from human rights and democracy to fighting the spread of HIV. In 2012, a little over a year after Code4Country, USAID was thrown out of Russia, seemingly for meddling in the country's internal affairs.

The Internet was a particularly sensitive area, as evidenced by Russian media reactions to Secretary Clinton's Internet freedom speech earlier that year. The text, which I had advised on, had two references to Russia. One was in praise of the wildfires site, and the other was an announcement that the State Department was launching a Russian-language Twitter feed (in addition to feeds in many other languages). Somehow this very mild public diplomacy tool was construed by various Russian media and blogs as a means to inundate the Russian Internet with enemy information. They used such terms as "strategic Twitter offensive" and "Cold War 2.0."

Nor did the Russians react well to Clinton's announcement that the State Department would devote $25 million in funding to Internet freedom all over the world. Even Anton Nossik, considered to be a relatively liberal-minded Internet expert, wrote on his blog, "Every official that tries to rule the Internet, the national or international one, should be sent to hell immediately." In sum, it was not an ideal time to be working at the State Department, trying to drum up support for a U.S.-Russia Internet event.

Still, I sensed a flickering opportunity. President Medvedev was promoting technology, innovation, and especially "modernization." One of Medvedev's pet projects was to build a Silicon Valley in the Moscow suburb of Skolkovo. A project like a U.S.-Russia codeathon would need at least the tacit support of the Kremlin, and the Medvedev administration seemed like our best hope. Such a project would have to happen under the framework of the Bilateral Presidential Commission, which was launched by Obama and Medvedev. It would need a combination of U.S. and Russian funding and strong partnerships with Russian companies.

As it turned out, getting the Russians on board proved to be far easier than I ever would have imagined. The Skolkovo Foundation immediately expressed its willingness to be a partner, and Google Russia soon followed. Yandex, Russia's largest search engine, even offered to host the event at its Moscow headquarters.

We decided that the codeathon would be held simultaneously in Washington and Moscow, with coders working on software solutions to common problems of government transparency and anticorruption. Ordinary citizens and NGOs from both countries would suggest problem definitions on the bilingual Code-4Country website; programmers would decide which problems they wanted to address; and then the winners in each country would be decided by an independent panel of judges.

Up until the eve of the event, we wondered if people would actually show up. Would ordinary Russians really give up their weekend to code for something as abstract and seemingly unobtainable as "open government"? We also had been fairly light on publicity. The last thing we needed was a swarm of angry Russian bloggers misconstruing Code4Country as nefarious U.S. interference in Russian affairs. I was also worried that the Russian government would suddenly decide that it didn't want Code-4Country to happen.

I tried not to think about all the reasons why Code4Country was likely to fail. On one of my planning trips to Moscow, I bought a silly pink rubber bracelet that said "Pink Dreams," in Russian, an expression that roughly translates to "rose-colored glasses." It seemed the perfect mantra for a seemingly impossible situation.

On September 24–25, Code4Country launched in Moscow and Washington. I was in the Moscow location, at Yandex headquarters. A large screen allowed the Moscow participants to videoconference with programmers at George Washington University when they began coding hours later. All in all, there were seven Russian teams, with several programmers each. A young woman came from St. Petersburg to work on a program that would help disabled people find the most accessible parts of the city. The Russian programmers tended to wear jeans and bright T-shirts, except for one, who earnestly showed up in a suit and tie. They sprawled on colorful beanbag chairs and drank Red Bull. One programmer asked me if my job at the State Department was to "control the Internet." Some came to meet other coders, to interact with Americans, or simply out of curiosity. The mood was extraordinarily upbeat. In Washington, D.C., eight teams participated. We could watch them on the big videoconferencing screen, coding away. Occasionally Russian programmers would send a message over to their Washington counterparts, asking if they knew a particular coding language.

The prizes were determined by two panels of judges, one in Moscow and the other in Washington. In Moscow, third prize went to a program for tracking the assets and income of Russian officials. Second prize went to a program that created a clear and easy visualization of Russian government spending. And the first prize went to a team, which included participants from Yandex, for a prototype for an anonymous, fraud-proof, and verifiable e-voting program. In Washington, the winning team worked on a tool for connecting citizens to legislation relevant to their interests and helping them make sense of it.

Navalny was in Europe during Code4Country and wasn't involved in the event, though he did submit a problem definition for an online video portal for whistle-blowers. He later told me that Code4Country was so professional it looked as if it were backed by the CIA. It wasn't, of course, but in this instance I decided to take it as a compliment.

As Navalny had said, Russia desperately needed success stories. I hoped that Code4Country would at least show talented programmers that working on socially minded projects wasn't a total waste of their time. I later learned that some of the Code-4Country programmers went on to either develop their projects or work on different programs. Alexey Poimtsev, a cheerful, spiky-haired programmer who at the time of Code4Country worked for the Russian telecom company Beeline, became one of the developers of Web-Nabludatel, a cell phone app for reporting election violations.

Poimtsev later told me that Code4Country deeply affected him. "I've got a lot of new friends and business partners, and I understand that my country and my life are dependent on what I do."

"I WANT TO THANK YOU FOR CONSIDERING YOURSELF CITIZENS!"

As I was in Moscow, basking in the unlikely success of Code-4Country, the ground suddenly lurched beneath our feet. On September 24, 2011, at a party convention in Moscow, President Medvedev announced that he was stepping aside to allow Putin to run in the March 2012 elections. This essentially amounted to an official declaration that Putin would be in power for at least one, if not two, terms of six years each. I later heard that Russians started making agitated calculations along the lines of: if I'm thirty now, by the time Putin finally leaves office, I will be forty-two!

At the same time, the image of Medvedev as the great reformer crumbled into dust. Suddenly it looked as if he and Putin were co-orchestrators of a cynical ruse. Putin openly admitted that "an agreement over what to do in the future was reached between us several years ago." Those who had put aside their doubts to support Medvedev felt humiliated, as if they were being openly mocked by the Kremlin. As Navalny put it, "All the people who supported Medvedev, and who forced themselves to believe in Medvedev, became the worst enemy of Putin and Medvedev."

On September 24 the match was lit. But the fire didn't break out until the state legislature, or Duma, elections on December 4. Four hundred and fifty seats were up for grabs. Putin's United Russia party took 238 seats, a little over 50 percent of the total. More striking was the fact that United Russia conquered less than 50 percent of the popular vote. This was a stark contrast to the last Duma elections, in 2007, when United Russia took 70 percent of the seats and 64 percent of the popular vote. Suddenly Putin's party looked vulnerable.

Even Navalny hadn't expected that United Russia would take such a hit. He had predicted that the party would take at least

54 percent of the popular vote. Navalny interpreted the Duma election results as a sign that opposition efforts were working and that more ordinary people were starting to see United Russia as the "party of crooks and thieves." On December 5 he wrote on his blog that he was sick of the skeptics who claimed that he and his supporters were disconnected from the masses outside of Moscow. He resisted the idea that the battle against the party of crooks and thieves was being fought only by "net hamsters"—a derogatory Russian term for bloggers and social media users who "scurry" around the Web.

"We have built a new political space in the country: All together—against United Russia," Navalny wrote triumphantly on his blog. He concluded, "Thanks again to all who in any way participated in the campaign against the party of crooks and thieves. You—true citizens. The next step will be more difficult, but also more fun. Now we know that we can succeed. And win."

The Duma elections marked a critical turning point, and not just because of United Russia's relatively poor performance. Those still smarting from Medvedev's betrayal were humiliated anew. Many Russians assumed that their election process was marred by fraud, but in the Internet era, millions are able to witness suspicious election activity with their own eyes. In the days following the Duma elections, as Navalny put it, "the Internet was just bursting with cell phone videos."

One such video was uploaded to YouTube on December 4 and was viewed more than a million times shortly after being posted. Made by journalists and activists of the opposition Solidarity movement, the video opens with their successful attempt to have several people detained for ballot stuffing. The video also shows election observers who found a stack of ten ballots in favor of United Russia in the garbage can of a precinct bathroom. It documents Alexey Pomerantsev, a journalist from *Novaya Gazeta*, describing how he infiltrated a "carousel"—a group of voters who traveled from polling station to polling station, casting vote after vote for United Russia.

Pomerantsev explains that he was part of a group of about forty people who each earned 1,000 rubles for casting a total of seventy ballots. He says the carousel people were handed bags containing ballots, identifications of people who wouldn't vote, and a special document that signaled to those manning a precinct that they were colluding with United Russia. The video was posted on Navalny's blog and on the Ekho Moskvy site.

Another video looks down on a gray-haired man who turns out to be the chairman of the election commission, calmly filling out ballots himself. The video was shot by Yegor Duda, a thirty-three-year-old volunteer election observer who promptly posted his findings on YouTube. The head of the Moscow City Elections Commission, Valentin Gorbunov, said that Russian investigators had opened a case into the tampering at the polling station depicted in the video. A separate video documented a cardboard ballot box with large, open gaps (ostensibly to allow for ballot stuffing). Yet another video from Yekaterinburg documented people seemingly preparing ballots the day before the elections.

One particularly memorable video documents observers from the opposition Yabloko Party scribbling with the blue-ink pens supplied by a Moscow polling station. All you see is hands, ink, and scrap paper. The person then takes the other side of the pen, rubs the blue ink with it, and the ink slowly vanishes. Votes could apparently disappear. During the presidential elections in March, I heard of at least one Russian guy who took the precautionary measure of bringing his own pen to the polling station.

The substance of the videos was supported by other evidence. Election observers from the Organization for Security and Cooperation in Europe (OSCE) cited election irregularities, including the stuffing of ballot boxes. The state-owned news agency Ria

Novosti reported more than a thousand official complaints of irregularities. In some cases the polling results were suspicious in and of themselves. In Chechnya, for example, support for United Russia somehow exceeded 99 percent. But in Navalny's view, the Moscow results (46 percent for United Russia) really enraged people the most. "It was very humiliating for the people in Moscow," he told me. "No one votes for them here."

On December 5 Navalny put a call for action on his blog. "The blatant and total fabrication of elections in Moscow requires us to prove our citizenship and protest what is happening. We must not remain silent when these bastards . . . just throw our votes in the trash." He told his readers to come at 7:00 p.m. that same evening to Chistye Prudy, where the opposition group Solidarity had obtained the city's permission to hold a protest. Navalny hardly expected a huge turnout for a political demonstration. This was Russia, after all. But when he got out of the Metro station at Chistoprudny Boulevard, he knew something was different. It was dark, and all he could see were people.

The protest took a while to start, as police blocked the paths of streams of people who were trying to enter the rally area. People yelled, "Russia without Putin!" while others, held back near the Metro, yelled, "Let us through!" Some people helped each other climb over a fence to get to the rally. Even the protest speakers had to climb over a fence because there was no other way to get to the area without confronting the police. People held signs that said THE ELECTIONS ARE A FARCE and DOWN WITH FAKE ELECTIONS.

But neither the police nor the pouring rain deterred those who crowded the streets or even hung from lampposts. Then Navalny climbed onto the stage, wearing jeans. The atmosphere quivered with rage. The Duma elections were, as Russians like to say, the last drop of water that causes the cup to overflow. Several months earlier, Medvedev had blithely handed power back to Putin. If this wasn't bad enough, the Kremlin then proceeded to ridicule those who exercised their right to vote. The deception was so blatant, so obvious, that it wasn't simply a matter of the government not respecting or listening to the people. It was as if the citizenry didn't exist.

Navalny started his speech on a light note. "While climbing over the fence to get to this rally, I forgot everything I wanted to say," he said to laughter around him. Then his tone hardened. He held the microphone with both hands. "I want to thank you," he told the audience. He addressed the voters in the crowd: "I want to thank you for considering yourself citizens!" The people cheered. *"Spacibo!"* he spat out. "Thank you for telling the bearded Churov [head of the election commission] and his bosses that *my sushchestvuem*—We exist!

"We exist!" Navalny bellowed, and the crowd roared its approval. "They can hear us; they are afraid," he said, waving his finger in the air.

"They can call us microbloggers and network hamsters," Navalny cried, reclaiming the derisive term for bloggers. "I am a network hamster," he declared, "and I will gnaw through those bastards' throats!" The crowd was electrified. "We'll do it together," Navalny added, pumping his fist, "because we exist!"

He led his followers toward the Central Electoral Commission, which was almost a mile away. They passed through a row of soldiers but were eventually blocked by the OMON, the helmeted riot police. Navalny later said that they might have had enough people to overwhelm the OMON, but the crowd was too spread out. So instead of going to the CEC, he and hundreds of others were arrested and packed into buses.

But he still had his cell phone. From the police bus, he shared a photo with his followers on Instagram of a dozen activists in a police van, grinning and thrusting two-fingered victory signs toward the camera. The photo caption read, "I'm sitting in a police bus with all the guys. They all say hi." Throughout the night, dozens waited by the police precinct where Navalny was rumored to be held. One of his supporters filmed the protest, and thousands watched the video online. Navalny was ultimately given fifteen days of jail time for defying a government official.

"I would advise to everyone to spend ten days in jail," he later told me. "You start to evaluate very simple things like boiled water, socks, to be without an Internet, and listen to radio again." In fact, his first tweet after leaving prison was the following: "Hey, I'm with you again in the world where shoes with laces are allowed."

Navalny's prison stint was useful in other ways as well: the arrest elevated his status and heightened his popularity. When he was released on December 21, a crowd of supporters gathered in the snow to wait for him. Thousands more watched the live video of his release. But by that point the protest movement had taken on a life of its own. In the fifteen days he had spent in jail, Russia experienced its largest protest since the mass demonstrations of the 1990s that led to the breakup of the Soviet Union. As Navalny put it, he went to jail "in one country and came out in another."

"SO, IS IT YOU WHO IS ORGANIZING THIS REVOLUTION IN RUSSIA?"

With Navalny behind bars, an unlikely segment of Russian society sprang into action. They were the hipsters and "net hamsters" who seemed more at home at Starbucks than at a political rally. One of these self-described hipsters was the twenty-four-year-old

Ilya Klishin, who created the Facebook page that helped bring thousands of people to Bolotnaya Square on December 10.

I first met Klishin at a Dunkin' Donuts on the commercial and charmless Novy Arbat Avenue. When I asked if Dunkin' Donuts had Wi-Fi, he said, "Yes, or I wouldn't be here." He was wearing slim jeans and a winter scarf that was smartly tucked into his gray overcoat. Pinned to his coat was the white ribbon that had become the symbol of the Russian opposition movement. Save for the ribbon, Klishin looked like someone who might be sitting across from you on the L train to Williamsburg, Brooklyn. "The generation of hipsters is like the first totally Western generation," he told me. "I was born in 1987. I don't remember the Soviet Union."

Klishin attended the December 5 protests as well as the unsanctioned protest on Triumfalnaya Square that took place the following day, leading to hundreds of arrests. He said that he chatted with a lot of people at the demonstration. Everyone was talking about a protest that was supposed to take place on December 10, but nobody had any specifics. Where would this protest be, and at what time?

Klishin lived nearby, five minutes away from Mayakovskaya Square. He went home and read an Internet news report that said rallies were sanctioned by Moscow City Hall for December 10 at Revolution Square. The opposition activist Sergei Udaltsov had secured a protest permit. Klishin thought about all the people who were wondering where to go. He asked himself, what is the easiest way to tell everyone?

He decided to create a Facebook event page, which in Russia was usually used for "birthday parties," he said with a laugh. In this case, Klishin chose to create a public event page that could be seen, shared, and commented on by everyone. "I just created the event with no specific goal, just to inform people. I didn't plan for it to be the major tool of organizing," he said. He posted about the event on his personal Twitter feed and Facebook account. He also sent messages to prominent journalists and bloggers to draw their attention to the event.

On December 6, after creating an event called "Saturday on Revolution Square," Klishin went to sleep. When he woke up, he saw that some ten thousand people had already signed up. "I keep refreshing the page, and I see every second it's growing and growing . . . I start writing about it in Twitter, everyone retweets it, then it becomes a piece of news itself: ten thousand people signed up for the meeting!" At that point the Revolution Square protest was sanctioned for only three hundred people. But the numbers on Facebook kept growing. Klishin said that some liberal media sites linked to the event page. He heard that some people registered for Facebook just to sign up for the event.

Navalny, meanwhile, was monitoring the situation from jail. "We heard it on the radio. And it was a kind of, you know, this story, wow, how many people will join this Facebook group tomorrow, and how many of them will come in reality?" Navalny said to himself, Please, please, let at least ten thousand people come to this rally. A small turnout would just confirm the assumption that people are perfectly willing to attend a protest on Facebook but have no interest in showing up in real life.

The opposition also used social media to gauge public opinion. One Facebook poll asked, among other things, what the rally's demands and slogans should be, and which people should speak. The most popular demand was to cancel the results of the December 4 Duma elections, and the number one choice of speaker was Yuri Shevchuk, an opposition-minded rock musician. The total number of votes was close to forty-five thousand. Klishin also created a twelve-person, invitation-only Facebook chat to discuss event logistics. It was made up of such well-known journalists as Oleg Kashin and Yuri Saprykin. "I came into the circle as the stakeholder of the first Facebook page," Klishin explains. "I was considered the person who knows the social media secret to get tens of thousands of people."

There was also a page on VKontakte, the Russian version of Facebook. On VKontakte, the organizers posted a link to a blog that offered legal advice to protesters and a file with flyers that people could print and hand out, as well as a link to a Facebook poll.

By the morning of December 9, more than 33,000 people had indicated on Facebook that they would attend the December 10 rally; around 10,000 said that "maybe" they were attending. On VKontakte, 18,600 said they would attend. The psychological impact of these numbers cannot be underestimated. Social media such as Facebook indicated to individual Russians that if they went to the streets, they wouldn't be alone. The social media response swayed officials as well. On December 8 Moscow authorities suggested that the protest be moved from Revolution Square to Bolotnaya Square, since so many people had expressed their willingness to participate. The new number of permitted participants jumped to thirty thousand.

Klishin and his friends thus had to figure out how to inform tens of thousands of people of the rally's new location. This was made difficult by the bots that attacked the Facebook page with messages saying that there were tanks in the streets and snipers on the roofs, and that the document with permission to hold the rally was fake. The organizers had to manually delete the spam. There were also fake Facebook pages and communities, but according to Klishin, these were generally less populated and easy to spot.

On December 9 one of the organizers, Ilya Krasilshchik, wrote on the wall of the VKontakte page: "Friends, this is an important point. Do not break up the meeting into two parts under any circumstances. Do not come to Revolution Square. Do not march in processions. This is a peaceful rally. Under no circumstances should you allow run-ins with the riot police, that is very dangerous. Facebook is a thing that no one can control. If there is blood, we will all be responsible for it."

Meanwhile, Klishin, who had set up the first Facebook event, had fallen into the international spotlight. He said that foreign media called him with such questions as "So, is it you who is organizing this revolution in Russia?" He also eventually came onto the radar of the FSB, Russia's security service. Authorities called his mother and invited her to come in for an interrogation. Klishin told her not to go without a written notification. His father got such a notification from the local anti-extremism center. "They asked my whereabouts," Klishin said, "which was just a kind of pressure. Everyone in Moscow knows my phone number. It's on my Facebook page." He said that his parents were scared at first, but later joked about it. Meanwhile, he decided to make his intimidation public. "They are trying to pressure me by scaring my parents," he wrote on his Facebook page. "It seems that it's linked with the fact that I have and continue to organize protests in support of honest elections through social networking sites."

In any event, locating and intimidating protest leaders was not the most effective tactic. Navalny, the closest thing to the figurehead of the opposition, was in jail and couldn't have stopped the protests even had he wanted to. For the December 10 protests, there were dedicated social networking groups in eighty-two Russian cities and thirty-six cities abroad.

In the social media era, unlikely figureheads emerge. In Egypt, an ordinary tech geek named Wael Ghonim started a Facebook page that helped pave the way for the collapse of a thirty-year dictatorship. Ghonim certainly had good social media and networking skills, but other than that, his fame was somewhat accidental. This was true of Klishin as well. "I was just at the right place at the right time," he admitted. "The good thing is that you can't stop the movement that is headless. It's kind of like the

Occupy Wall Street movement; you can't stop the movement that's organized by no one."

Klishin had long been interested in politics and social media. Upon graduation from university, he said, "I just started to look for job offers with words like 'Facebook,' 'Twitter,' 'LiveJournal.' I was surprised to find that there were jobs like that." He ended up taking a job at an advertising agency, helping corporate clients bolster their Facebook presence. He also did a several-month stint at Skolkovo. "People were arguing about whether there were clashes between the Putin and Medvedev teams. I got the offer from so-called Medvedev guys," Klishin said. He said they told him, "We understand your opposition. We need guys like that. We need fresh ideas." "I was really intrigued," he continued. "Maybe it was naive."

Klishin's friends gave him grief for working for Skolkovo, which was essentially akin to working for the Russian government, but he kind of believed in the Medvedev reform story. "These Medvedev guys seemed nice," he said. "I felt they were thinking the way I was thinking. They didn't seem old-fashioned, conservative. That's where they got me." Skolkovo wanted to attract the next Steve Jobs, so Klishin tried to submit draft proposals about how to make Skolkovo, which aimed to be the nexus of Russian innovation, appeal to the hip urban set. He says he proposed ideas about how to make Skolkovo look cool and organic rather than like a top-down innovation project. After his suggestions were summarily rejected, he decided to move on. It was mid-September 2011, and he had lasted at Skolkovo only two months.

But he had other things to do. In 2010, while he was still working in advertising, he and two friends had started a blog called *Epic Hero*. The majority of posts were written by Klishin, Roman Fedoseev, and Yury Bolotov, but they were not signed. The idea of *Epic Hero* was to make politics appeal to Russian hipsters, a relatively new demographic. In the early 2000s there were no hipsters,

Klishin said. "There were golden youth. They wore expensive clothes, but this went out of fashion. You don't want to wear expensive clothes, you just want to be hip." By around 2009 the Russian "hipster" identity came with its own cluster of clichés, including Ray-Bans, skinny jeans, Starbucks coffee, Apple products, and Moleskine notebooks.

Klishin said the term "hipster" eventually broadened to encompass urban youth in their twenties. In Russia, hipster "means young bourgeois guy," he explained to me, "similar to your 'yuppie.'" One of the goals of *Epic Hero* was to show this demographic that it was cool to be engaged in politics. Klishin's audience were those Russians who couldn't imagine life without the Internet. Thus the Internet was the perfect place to create a new social group—the "political hipster," a concept that didn't exist, at least among Klishin's peers. "Among your friends, when you start talking about politics, they would be like, oooh, it's not interesting, let's talk about something else," he said. Klishin knew that earnest calls to political activism would not appeal to them. So *Epic Hero* tried to use a light, humorous tone, playing on hipster clichés. "We'll write about things, but ironically. I'm a big fan of the Jon Stewart show. Not the fake news, but the attitude," Klishin said. Reports of political protests would thus include tongue-in-cheek complaints, such as "There were riot police; we almost lost our iPads!"

Epic Hero launched with a call to participate in the Triumfalnaya protests on October 31, 2010. These were similar to the protests I had witnessed on July 31, when the police swooped in on a tiny group of protesters who were just standing around. In October, however, the city government decided to authorize the protests for the first time. "We often regret that all significant events took place before us," *Epic Hero* wrote. "We didn't get to take down the Berlin Wall, and we didn't get to stand at the [Russian] White House in August '91 . . . This day will go into history textbooks, and in twenty years our children will ask: were you on Triumfalnaya Square on October 31, 2010? And today everyone decides for himself what he will answer them then."

The post continued with prose that was tailor-made for the hipster set: "It is cold today, so dress warmer, and pick up a Starbucks or McDonald's coffee near Triumfalnaya. In your hands the logos of these brands will be better than any political banner. See you at six on Triumfalnaya."

The day after the protests, there was a victorious post on *Epic Hero* called "the hipster breakthrough." It described the previous day's events on Triumfalnaya.

> We read enough on Twitter about how guys there were getting harassed while we were getting bored near the stage. We understood that we had to go help them. A battlefield vanguard of 200 hipsters carried the full group of Epic Hero editors to the front of the forceful confrontation with the cordon . . . And so we fought—two hundred frail guys and young women in keds and coats shouting "Freedom!" against an equal number of skinny soldiers. Finally, we broke through and flowed with cries of "Hurray!" to the steps of the concert hall. There we screamed out our bourgeois and generally democratic demands.

The post also implored the opposition to be more respectful of the hipster aesthetic. Quit playing "cheesy songs." Instead, "have elegant slogans, stylish clothing, cheerful faces and indie rock. Civil protest should be beautiful."

Epic Hero encouraged young Russians not to succumb to apathy. As Klishin described it to me, "We say okay, we understand, you don't like politics; we understand the elections are rigged, the TV channels are censored. But here's something you can do. You can at least go to elections, it doesn't hurt. You can go to your local elections."

Epic Hero reportedly got ten thousand hits a day. More well known was *Afisha*, a biweekly entertainment magazine that focused on art, culture, entertainment, and good food. In 2012 *Afisha* editor in chief Yuri Saprykin told me that *Epic Hero* was for years seen as an "art project," with a relatively small following. "It's a weird political blog with very strange ideas about hipster politics. In many things they were right. I thought it was funny and naive," he said.

In November 2011 the OpenSpace media group bought *Epic Hero*. Klishin and his friends were allowed to maintain its brand and their team, as well as to focus on the blog full-time. The audience of *Epic Hero*, Klishin said, was the base he appealed to when he created the Facebook page for the Bolotnaya protests. He also posted the event on the Facebook account of *Epic Hero*, whose readers he described as "the core social media audience" for the Facebook event that advertised the protests. They were the people to whom he "didn't have to explain why" they should attend the protests. With *Epic Hero*, Klishin explained, "what we were doing is telling those guys who went to Bolotnaya Square is that one day they would go there."

"WE EXIST!"

Medvedev's September announcement gave rise to another unlikely opposition figure: Rustem Adagamov, or Drugoi, Russia's most popular blogger. The last time I had seen Adagamov, he told me that in Russia, there was no point in engaging in politics. When I saw him in Moscow in March 2012, he seemed completely transformed. He had hoped that Medvedev would run for a second term and emerge as a true leader. "I thought he wants to be a real politician, not a paperboy," Adagamov told me angrily. He felt personally betrayed by Medvedev's transfer of power back to Putin. "I talked with him. I supported him on my blog. I have no words to show to what degree I'm disappointed."

Despite his previous skepticism, Adagamov now publicly expressed support for Navalny. "I have also been impressed by Alexey Navalny's potential, and think he may have a big future in front of him," he wrote in a March 1 article. "If, as the Kremlin maintains, Navalny is a project of the U.S. State Department, I can only congratulate the Americans for doing such a good job!" Adagamov was now deeply engaged in Russian politics, and the Russian companies that sponsored his blog took note. He told me that recently MegaFon had asked him to temporarily remove its logo from his blog.

Adagamov had considerable broadcasting power. And now he intended to use that platform for political mobilization. On his blog, he had implored people to attend the December 10 protest: "Let's just go there and look at each other—how many of us are there, citizens who don't like it when we are lied to, when we are taken for silent cattle, or, as is said in certain circles, for dandruff. We are not dandruff, we love our country and want it to be better, freer, more honest."

Adagamov later called the December 10, 2011, protest at Bolotnaya "one of the most wonderful days of my life." He remembered walking from Revolution Square alongside nationalists and opposition activists. It took him an hour to make his way through the crowd to the stage at Bolotnaya. He later told me, "A lot of people came to this meeting because of me. Because I asked them to come. It's a real contract between me and my readers . . . They told me, thank you. Some of them hugged me. Clapped me on the shoulders. I go through these people with tears in my eyes."

When Adagamov got to the stage where other opposition figures were assembled, one of the organizers informed him that fifty thousand people had attended the protest. By the start of the rally, not only was the square full, but so were all the embankments and roads leading to it. And these weren't typical Russian demonstrators. There were people who worked in such industries as science, architecture, finance, insurance, and engineering; there were university students and retirees. There was an owner of a chicken farm. Katya Parkhomenko said that in the past she would go to a protest and see everyone she knew. On December 10, she said, "I was shocked by all the people I am seeing for the first time in my life."

Another unlikely opposition figure at the December 10 protest was Ksenia Sobchak, the daughter of Anatoly Sobchak, the first democratically elected mayor of St. Petersburg, who is credited with launching Putin's political career. Sobchak had made her name as a television host, entertainment journalist, and socialite. She starred in her own reality series and hosted the long-running reality show *Dom-2*. She is often referred to in the media as the "Paris Hilton" of Russia. She transitioned to more serious work around 2010 and eventually became one of the most visible figures in the opposition movement. She pointed to the Duma election falsifications as her tipping point, saying that reality hit her as she was watching the election videos posted online.

The December 10 protest took place in the dead of Russian winter: the trees were brown and bare, the sky a pale gray. People bundled into hats, scarves, and fur-lined hoods. They brought white flowers and white ribbons, which Putin nastily said reminded him of "condoms." One protest organizer, Ilya Krasilshchik, wrote on the VKontakte page: "Today I saw the city of my dreams. There are a lot of beautiful, cheerful and different people in it. There are polite policemen in it."

Many people brought their children to the protest. Young women handed flowers to the police. Attendees peacefully chatted with officers, who complained about being cold and having been up since 5:00 a.m. Young people handed out whistles and encouraged people to whistle as loudly as possible. They even ran up to the police, trying to get them to take the whistles and join in. A wedding party showed up. The bride said, "Our wedding is for honest elections!"

People weren't calling for revolution; they just wanted a fair system. Katya Parkhomenko perhaps best summed up the protest movement: "They are not fighting for power, they are fighting for rules." Yet despite the almost utopian atmosphere, Klishin described the protests as fundamentally pragmatic. "Those protests back in the 1980s, they were like, you know, idealistic," he told me. They wanted democracy and a market economy, he said, but "generally speaking, they didn't know what democracy is, actually, because they never had it." Today's generation thinks in more concrete terms. The reason Navalny is popular is that "he speaks in terms of taxes, we are all paying taxes to government, and here is what they do with our taxes."

Navalny, meanwhile, was in jail on December 10. He was thrilled to hear the reports on the radio: "There is a full square," he said. "There hasn't been anything like this since the 1990s. Everyone said wow, we can do it!"

Some will point out that the protests of the late 1980s and early 1990s took place without the aid of social media, which is of course true. But one of the main differences in these new protest movements was the speed of their growth. In the twilight of the Soviet era, it took many months for popular protests to gain serious momentum. In the 2011 protests, there were ten thousand people in the streets the day after the Duma election. Five days later, there were tens of thousands more.

One activist, Alexander Daniel, also noted that the democratic movement of the late 1980s had clear leaders, unlike the 2011 protests. "For the youth that gathered on Bolotnaya on the tenth . . . there are no parties, no political movements," he said. "There are only two parties—the party of Facebook and the party of VKontakte."

On December 10 Oleg Kashin published a letter said to be written by Navalny, which concluded, "All people of dignity must feel solidarity with each other. No matter where they are at the moment, out in the square, in their kitchens or in a jail cell. We feel our solidarity with you and we know that we shall triumph. It simply cannot be otherwise. We say: One for all and all for one!"

Unlike previous opposition protests, the December 10 event was so big that it crossed over from the Internet to the mainstream media. Information on social media was picked up by radio and print media. The protests were so significant that they even made it to state television. On the evening of December 10 Alexey Pivovarov, an anchorman for the government-owned NTV, made a surprising announcement: "Tens of thousands of people came out to register their disagreement with the results of recent parliamentary elections, which they said were rigged in favor of United Russia." The announcement was unusual because an anchor for a major Russian television station not only was reporting the protests, but he was doing it in a fairly objective way.

It was later leaked to the media that Pivovarov would have quit NTV if he wasn't allowed to report the protests, making the anchorman an unlikely hero of the opposition. Pivovarov later told me, "When the protest happened, I felt like I could not be on air and not tell the story of these protests." He said his motivation was purely professional. "You can't work for a news organization and not cover the major news. My boss understood that as well."

Pivovarov said that several days before the protest, it was evident that the numbers would be huge. "In my circle, everyone was on Facebook, and all anyone discussed was how to go and where to go. When it became evident that the authorities would let the protest go ahead and it would be on Bolotnaya, everyone understood that there would be many people there." It was easy enough for state television to overlook the protests that had only a couple of thousand people, but "when it became obvious that the opposition became tens of thousands, they couldn't be ignored."

I went back to Russia right before the March 2012 presidential elections. The air was cold and fresh, with a delicate glitter of snow. I met with Katya Parkhomenko in the same Le Pain Quotidien where two years earlier she had enthused about the blue bucket protests. There were the same wooden tables; Katya smoked her cigarettes as usual. But there was one major difference between this meeting and the last. "Everyone around us is talking about politics!" Katya exclaimed.

The momentous December 10 protests, it turned out, were only the beginning. On December 24 tens of thousands gathered again. The police said there were 30,000 people, while organizers claimed the number was closer to 120,000. Even in February, I saw scenes I never could have imagined. Joyous protesters gathered on the Garden Ring, which stretches some ten miles and encircles the center of the city. Strangers held hands to create an enormous white circle. Cars honked their support; people carried white flowers and balloons. The atmosphere was light: I saw a mustachioed man whose white cat, which sat on his shoulder, wore the opposition white ribbons. The man held a sign with a play on the popular slogan "If not Putin, then who?" He had replaced the Russian word "*kto*" (who) with "*kot*" (cat). So his sign said IF NOT PUTIN, THEN CAT.

Yet for the most part, December's euphoria had faded. I didn't meet a single person who doubted that Putin would win the March 4 elections. These elections, too, were expected to be marred by fraud. One sign that things had changed, however, was that thousands of eager volunteers went to the polls to monitor the election.

The authorities were anticipating a big protest for March 5, the day after the election. Russian officials could no longer rely on public apathy, so they tried to instigate fear. Buses of riot police swarmed the city. On election day some of these riot police formed a human wall on the streets near the Kremlin while others came into the Starbucks where I was sitting and perused the pastries behind the glass.

Nobody knew what would happen if people decided to protest on election day, but I knew at least a few Russians who were afraid to find out. There were concerns that once Putin was solidly back in power, he would strike hard against dissent. One of my friends thought about attending the March 5 protests, but his wife wouldn't let him. Meanwhile, paranoia threatened to reach Soviet levels. American journalists I knew said that their phone lines went dead after they uttered the word "Navalny."

Navalny himself was clearly under pressure. When I went to see him at his modest law office in central Moscow, a dark-haired man opened the door and narrowed his eyes at me. Then several other equally unfriendly men came to the door and looked at me suspiciously. Finally they let me in and led me upstairs, where I found Navalny looking more exhausted than I had ever seen him. "Welcome to Russia," he said. In a photo I took that day he was hunched over his desk, glaring at the camera, clutching his iPhone like a weapon.

We went into his office, where he sat on a black couch. Next to him was a large framed photo of Putin embracing Gaddafi. Someone from his office brought me tea and dry, sugary wafers. Navalny told me that he now had bodyguards and no longer went out alone. People had been harassing his wife, which she found more annoying than scary. Nor did they seem very impressed by the sophistication of the surveillance attempts. Navalny said that one car lay in wait in front of their house for some time, until it finally got too obvious and was replaced by a different car. But the second car had the same license plate as the first.

Navalny was gaining momentum but also attracting the skepticism of liberals I knew in Moscow. They thought his tone was too aggressive and nationalistic. At the December 24 protest he publicly observed that there were enough people present to "storm the Kremlin," though he didn't advocate doing so. When I saw him in March, he told me that he wasn't about to apologize for his style. The potential danger to the Kremlin "should be real," he said. "All the protests, it shouldn't be like hipster stuff—hello, we have funny posters! . . . Because you can do nothing with just people who are ready to sit in Starbucks and drink coffees."

Putin won the election. And the much-anticipated protest came with its fair share of arrests but no major drama. The protest numbers had been getting smaller since December, but the opposition understood that their future would not lie in street demonstrations. Navalny was already working on building an alternative network of information. He had online contests for anti-Putin videos, songs, and posters. He was also developing a strategy to reach the non-Internet population and tell them what he saw as the truth about United Russia. And he was working with Leonid Volkov and others to hold a secure online election for the opposition. None of this would be easy. The Kremlin now understood that the Internet was a political threat, not just a playground for hipsters. Officials were going to put up a fight.

And that they did. As many predicted, once Putin solidified his power, he began systematically cracking down on dissent. Dozens of activists were arrested. The most famous case was that of Pussy Riot. In February 2012 the female punk rock band staged a music video in Moscow's Cathedral of Christ the Savior. The video—"Punk Prayer—Mother of God, Chase Putin Away!"—spread quickly on YouTube. Three members of the group, Nadezhda Tolokonnikova, Maria Alyokhina, and Yekaterina Samutsevich, were convicted of hooliganism motivated by religious hatred, and each was sentenced to two years in jail. Despite the huge international outcry that followed—Madonna, Paul McCartney, and other celebrities took up their cause—the Kremlin stood its ground. Samutsevich was freed on probation, but the other young women remained behind bars.

Nonprofit groups that received funding from abroad became required by law to identify themselves as "foreign agents." The Duma passed a law allowing the government to block Internet content, ostensibly in an attempt to protect children. A new Russian law would impose severe fines on those organizing or participating in unsanctioned demonstrations. Not long after Rustem Adagamov became politically active, his ex-wife accused him of sexually abusing a young girl when he lived in Norway fifteen years earlier. RT, a Kremlin-controlled television channel, published an online interview in which Adagamov's ex-wife detailed the allegations.

There were some victories, however. In October 2012 the opposition held online elections to select the forty-five members of the new Opposition Coordinating Council. More than eighty thousand people participated in the poll. The process was far from perfect, but still marked a landmark event for the opposition movement, which demonstrated it was capable of holding its own election. In the spring of 2013 Navalny himself went on trial. The timber case that had haunted him at Yale came back. He was charged with embezzling half a million dollars from a state-controlled timber company in Kirov. Prosecutors had dismissed the case, which pertained to Navalny's role as an adviser to the Kirov regional governor in 2009. The case was widely viewed as politically motivated, a suspicion officials didn't try to dispel.

"If a person tries hard to attract attention, or if I can put it, teases authorities—'look at me, I'm so good compared to everyone else'—well, then one gets more interested in his past and the process of exposing him naturally gets faster," said Vladimir Markin, spokesperson of the Investigative Committee. In many ways, it was the perfect charge: get the anticorruption hero on charges of corruption.

Navalny thought he would lose the case. He talked about the clothing he would bring to jail. He said he planned to read a lot of books. Nor could he guarantee that people would rally around him. The atmosphere had changed, and people were getting scared. But over the longer term, he said, "I see there is a large number of people who support me, and I am sure we will win. I am absolutely sure." So instead of keeping his head down, Navalny proceeded to run for mayor of Moscow.

The December 2011 protests had proved Navalny's point. He had spent years fomenting the comfortable way of struggle. Online, his followers slowly got over their apathy. And when the moment came, their new determination spilled over into real life. Along with thousands of others, they took to the streets to demand their rights. When Navalny was convicted in 2013, thousands of supporters protested again. The numbers were smaller than in 2011 but, given the atmosphere of fear, still substantial. In part due to those protests, Navalny was released from police custody to wait for his appeal. Then he continued with his mayoral campaign. He lost the election, but his jail sentence was later suspended on appeal.

In Navalny's last blog post before the verdict was announced, he made one final plea against apathy. He lauded his supporters for their success thus far. "We now know how to investigate, publish our own newspapers, organize protests, fundraise and conduct our own elections online," he wrote. "Therefore it is clear what to do, how to do it and how to pay for it," he said. "The main thing is to tap into the internal bravery, brush off laziness and just do it." He reminded his readers that there are no magic volunteers or contributors. "Understand this: there is no one but you," he wrote. And if you are at the point where you are already reading this blog, you are the "cutting edge." He ended his post with the words: "If you are reading this, you are the resistance."

Navalny described the December 10 protest as a "crucial moment." It challenged the Kremlin propaganda that its opponents were merely virtual. It also answered a key question about the opposition: "Are you real or just Internet hamsters?" Klishin also described December 10 as a psychological turning point. Russia's Facebook protesters proved that they were capable of putting boots on the ground. "It was important for the guys who went to the meeting that they saw each other," Klishin told me. "Like, I'm not alone. It was a message to the world and to themselves. Look, we exist. There's lots of us."

AFTERWORD

Isolation, fear, and apathy have long been the most effective weapons of authoritarian regimes. Now the Internet is helping ordinary people transcend these paralyzing emotions. The question is, what's next?

Predicting revolution is often a fool's errand. Revolutions need a spark, often in the form of a political or economic crisis. Social media alone will not light that spark. What the Internet does create is a new kind of citizen: networked, unafraid, and ready for action. These citizens will transform their countries whether a revolution takes place or not.

It's also not evident that revolution is the ideal scenario for China, Cuba, or Russia. As we saw in Egypt, mass uprisings that are organized online tend to be leaderless and decentralized. They have neither a plan nor unity of vision. This can be key to a revolution's success, as it makes it much more difficult for governments to cut off the heads of a protest movement. But leaderless revolutions can yield a great deal of chaos if and when a revolution succeeds.

In Egypt, after the celebratory mood wore off, the world criticized the revolutionaries for not having a master plan. But they never did. Wael Ghonim, the Google executive who administered the Facebook page that helped organize the game-changing January 25 Egyptian protest, never fancied himself a leader. Any revolution organized by the personalities in this book would have similar strengths and weaknesses to the one we saw in Egypt.

Some Russian activists are aiming for evolution, not revolution. They want to make the system more fair, not overhaul it entirely. In Cuba, Laritza and Yaremis are busy educating Cubans about their legal rights, not plotting to overthrow the Castro regime. And in China, netizen opinion is deeply divided between such people as He Caitou, who tries to work within the Communist system, and Michael Anti, who believes that the Party has to go. But at this point few are seriously calling for a Chinese revolution, given the inevitable chaos, turmoil, and violence such an event would entail.

That doesn't mean we won't see major changes in these three countries. Reality looks static until it's not. The Mubarak regime looked as if it would stay in charge forever, until it no longer was. In the nearly two decades since I have been watching China, I have seen various realities. The Party would appear to loosen the reins; then it would suddenly clamp down. Then it would loosen up again.

In a much shorter period of time, from 2010 to 2013, I have seen three completely different Russias. The first was a country mired in apathy. You could say what you wanted online, but what would be the point? The second Russia, which came to life in late 2011, was one where thousands of people took to the streets to demand their rights. And the third Russia, which emerged once the excitement of the protests wore off, was one of fear and oppression. This just proves that beneath a seemingly constant surface are different versions of the current reality.

Cuba, of all these three countries, sometimes seems to have changed the least. The transition from Fidel Castro to his brother Raúl has hardly brought liberty to the masses, but there is a general sense that the Cuban regime's days are numbered because their model simply doesn't work. Despite various economic reforms, Cuba is plagued by economic need, which the government conveniently blames on the U.S. embargo. Although the embargo certainly isn't helping matters, it is not solely to blame for the failures of the socialist model.

If the Chinese economy were to collapse and the government could no longer promise upward mobility, and if oil prices were to plummet and the Russian government could no longer offer social welfare, then the potential for unrest in those two countries would be great. In Cuba, however, the government has long ago failed to fulfill its side of the economic bargain, yet the people sit placidly and wait. The Cuban government is largely protected by the paralysis of the people. But what happens when people are no longer afraid?

China, Cuba, and Russia are shaped by the legacy of communism, where the collective whole was supposed to take precedence over individual rights. Now, largely thanks to the Internet, ordinary citizens are discovering their voices. They are finding their comrades. And they are fighting back.

NOTES

Introduction

3 *densely networked*: For more on social media and Egypt's revolution, see Rasha A. Abdulla, "The Revolution Will Be Tweeted," ww.aucegypt .edu/gapp/cairoreview/pages/articledetails.aspx?aid=89, and Zeynep Tufekci, "New Media and the People-Powered Uprisings," www.tech nologyreview.com/view/425280/new-media-and-the-people-powered -uprisings/.

3 *"Egypt Dissent Yet"*: Shaimaa Fayed, "Egypt Dissent Yet to Get from Face-book to the Streets," Reuters, November 21, 2010.

5 *"virtual nations, a place"*: Rasha A. Abdulla, "How Online Social Network-ing Systems Create Virtual Political Entities: The Federal Democratic Republic of Facebook," *Democracy*, April 1, 2009.

6 *"a reflection of the"*: Gene Sharp, *From Dictatorship to Democracy* (The New Press, 2012), 31.

6 *In eighteenth-century France*: For more on the spread of poetry in eighteenth-century France, see Robert Darnton, *Poetry and the Police* (Belknap Press of Harvard University Press, 2010).

7 *mimeographs and cassette tapes*: Madeleine Korbel Albright, *Poland: The Role of the Press in Political Change* (Praeger, 1983).

7 *"isolating and suppressing dissidents"*: Albert Wohlstetter, unpublished speech for the Prague Conference, July 23, 1990. First published in Robert Zarate and Henry Sokolski, eds., *Nuclear Heuristics: Selected Writings of Albert and Roberta Wohlstetter* (Strategic Studies Institute, 2009).

8 *"The first lesson"*: *Democracy Now*, January 18, 2011, www.democracynow.org /2011/1/18/egypt_based_political_analyst_the_first.

10 *"The Internet is not"*: Wael Ghonim, *Revolution 2.0* (Houghton Mifflin Harcourt, 2012), 51.

"Now I know who my comrades are"

17 *Falun Gong, a religious group*: For details on Falun Gong, see work by Ian Johnson, www.pulitzer.org/archives/6463, accessed May 30, 2013, and also Ian Johnson, *Wild Grass: Three Portraits of Change in Modern China* (Vintage, 2005).

"Chinese people don't read personal stories"

19 *responsible former Chinese officials*: Emily Parker, "The Cultural Revolution: Painters Revisit Their Pasts," *The Wall Street Journal*, September 16, 2008.

20 *A middle-aged administrator*: Kang Zhengguo, *Confessions: An Innocent Life in Communist China* (W. W. Norton, 2004), 178–79.

20 *"Human relationships are impermanent"*: Kang, *Confessions*, 86–87.

20 *"idealistic group-mindedness"*: Kang, *Confessions*, xiv.

20 *"It focused sharply on"*: Ibid.

20 *"are isolated as individuals"*: Ibid.

"I support the Party . . . but what about other people?"

22 *The 1989 Tiananmen demonstrations*: For more on the Tiananmen crackdown, see Antony Thomas (director), "The Tank Man," *Frontline*, aired April 11, 2006.

23 *"Hundreds of people, most"*: Jay Mathews, "The Myth of Tiananmen," *Columbia Journalism Review*, June 4, 2010, www.cjr.org/behind_the_news /the_myth_of_tiananmen.php?page=all.

24 *"There is no massacre"*: Nick Kristof, "China Update: How the Hardliners Won," *The New York Times*, November 12, 1989.

"My world was so small"

27 *"the despairing looks on"*: Yu Hua, "China's Forgotten Revolution," *The New York Times*, May 30, 2009.

28 *In 1995 China's GDP per capita*: For Chinese GDP data, see http://nyti.ms /UPyrIB, http://data.worldbank.org/indicator/NY.GDP.PCAP.CD, and http://data.worldbank.org/indicator/NY.GDP.PCAP.CD?page=3.

28 *"Across the Great Wall"*: Gady Epstein, "China's Internet: A Giant Cage," *The Economist*, April 6, 2013.

28 *He heard that his former high school classmate*: For Bei Zhicheng's description of the Zhu Ling incident, see http://beizhicheng.blog.caixin.com /archives/29696.

30 *"Hi, This is Peking"*: www.csc.pku.edu.cn/art.php?sid=2830.

31 *"there can't be any"*: http://laiba.tianya.cn/laiba/CommMsgs?cmm=15984 &tid=2554801196548232283.

31 *The letter was transmitted*: For details on Zhu Ling, see Malcolm Mc-Connell, "Rescue on the Internet," *Reader's Digest*, August 1996.

33 *"With the help of"*: www.csc.pku.edu.cn/art.php?sid=2830.

33 *"I sit here at"*: Xin Li, John W. Aldis, Daniel Valentino, "The First International Telemedicine Trial to China: ZHU Lingling's Case," http://web.archive/org/web/20050408214735/http://www.radsci.ucla.edu/telemed/zhuling/preface.html.

"I thought, I can really control the world"

36 *In January 1999*: Michael S. Chase and James C. Mulvenon, *You've Got Dissent! Chinese Dissident Use of the Internet and Beijing's Counter-Strategies* (Rand, 2002).

36 *By mid-2005*: "Surveying Internet Usage and Impact in Five Chinese Cities," Research Center for Social Development, Chinese Academy of Social Sciences (October 2005).

36 *"young, male, well educated"*: Ibid.

36 *By the end of 2007*: www.cnnic.cn/hlwfzyj/hlwxzbg/ncbg/201208/P020120917540818669915.pdf.

36 *By the end of 2012*: www.chinainternetwatch.com/whitepaper/china-internet-statistics/.

36 *The Great Firewall of China*: For details on the Great Firewall, see James Fallows, "'The Connection Has Been Reset,'" *The Atlantic*, March 1, 2008.

37 *"approximately 20,000–50,000"*: Gary King, Jennifer Pan, and Margaret E. Roberts, "How Censorship in China Allows Government Criticism but Silences Collective Expression," *American Political Science Review* 107, no. 2 (May 2013): 1–18, http://gking.harvard.edu/files/gking/files/censored.pdf.

37 *"About 80 percent"*: Monroe E. Price, Stefaan E. Verhuist, and Libby Morgan Routledge, eds., *Routledge Handbook of Media Law* (Routledge, 2013).

37 *a more recent report*: Katie Hunt and CY Xu, "China 'Employs 2 Million to Police Internet,'" CNN, www.cnn.com/2013/10/07/world/asia/china-internet-monitors/.

37 *complex system of laws*: For details on Chinese censorship and Internet regulation, see "Internet Filtering in China in 2004–2005: A Country Study," OpenNet Initiative, April 14, 2005, https://opennet.net/studies/china.

38 *"Normally, the great snake"*: Perry Link, "China: The Anaconda in the Chandelier," *The New York Review of Books*, April 11, 2002.

38 *"When the Chinese people"*: King, et al., "How Censorship in China Allows Government Criticism but Silences Collective Expression."

39 *"Bei.Da" and "Bei2Da"*: Guobin Yang, "The Internet and Civil Society in China: A Preliminary Assessment," *Journal of Contemporary China* (August 2003): 460, www.asc.upenn.edu/gyang/Civil%20society%20web.pdf.

"Put any good guy in a bad system, and he will act very bad"

42 *What made Anti finally become Christian*: Anti on Christianity, see http://m.xici.net/d25144.htm?ref=1566&sort=date.

45 *"It changed my view"*: Emily Parker, "Who Will Tell the Story of China," *The Wall Street Journal*, September 23, 2006.

45 *When he was growing up*: Anti's Children's Day post: www.xici.net/d17792.htm.

"Nothing is impossible to a willing heart"

47 *His* Manual for New Journalists: www.globalmediawatch.org/6/post/2010/02/3.html.

"The people won't forget you, history won't forget you!"

51 *My inaugural column*: For details on Dick Cheney in China, see Emily Parker, "China vs. the Internet," *The Wall Street Journal*, May 3, 2004.

51 *"rising prosperity"*: For details on Cheney in China, see Joseph Kahn, "Chinese Gave Cheney Speech Their Own Form of Openness," *The New York Times*, April 19, 2004.

52 *"Comrade Zhao Ziyang died of illness"*: news.xinhuanet.com/english/2005-01/17/content_2469618.htm. For comments on Zhao Ziyang, see Emily Parker, "Cracks in the Chinese Wall," *The Wall Street Journal Asia*, January 26, 2005.

53 *"Comrade Zhao Ziyang committed serious mistakes"*: www.chinadaily.com.cn/english/doc/2005-01/29/content_413413.htm.

"Who are our enemies? Who are our friends?"

56 *"There is no point"*: For a translation of Han Han's writing, see http://zonaeuropa.com/201112a.brief.htm#009.

"I tried to organize"

62 *"The world is not far away"*: www.zonaeuropa.com/20050904_1.htm.

62 *Microsoft's move*: For more on Microsoft in China, see Rebecca Mac-Kinnon, http://rconversation.blogs.com/rconversation/2006/01/microsoft_takes.html. For more on U.S. companies and Chinese censorship, see Rebecca MacKinnon, *Consent of the Networked: The Worldwide Struggle for Internet Freedom* (Basic Books, 2013).

62 *signed a pact to promote "self-discipline"*: "The basic principles of self-discipline for the Internet industry are patriotism, observance of the law, fairness and trustworthiness," China's state media reported. http://english.peopledaily.com.cn/200203/26/eng20020326_92885.shtml.

62 *"While this is a complex and"*: Tom Zeller, Jr., "China, Still Winning Against the Web," *The New York Times*, January 15, 2006.

63 *The most egregious example*: For details on Shi Tao, see Joseph Kahn, "Yahoo Helped Chinese to Prosecute Journalist," *The New York Times*, September 8, 2005, www.nytimes.com/2005/09/07/business/worldbusiness/07iht-yahoo.html.

63 *local staff reportedly worked*: http://nytimes.com/2006/02/12/weekinreview/12kahn.html.

63 *"Launching a Google domain"*: http://googleblog.blogspot.com/2006/01/google-in-china.html.

64 *"Our continued engagement"*: Ibid.

64 *"sickening collaboration"*: Tom Zeller, Jr., "Web Firms Are Grilled on Dealings in China," *The New York Times*, February 16, 2006, www.nytimes.com/2006/02/16/technology/16online.html.

64 *"But still, I will appreciate"*: www.pbs.org/moyers/journal/09122008/profile3.html.

"I speak in complicated sentences that my comrades can understand"

65 The President Is Unreliable: Lin Da, *Zongtong shi Kaobu Zhu de: Jinjuli Kan Meiguo 2* (Beijing: Sanlian Bookstore, 1998).

"I express what they want to say but cannot write down"

67 *China's biggest publicly listed*: Paul Mozur, "China's Tencent Aims Mobile App at U.S. Markets," *The Wall Street Journal*, March 5, 2013.

"Just like in a jailbreak, there's a hole in the wall"

76 *"The Endless Road"*: www.hecaitou.com/blogs/hecaitou/archives/122059 .aspx.

"We are like plants without roots"

78 *Since 2001 Beijing*: Amy Cortese, "Before the Olympics, A Parade of Companies," *The New York Times*, March 30, 2008.

79 *He felt this dislocation acutely*: For He Caitou on Kunming, see www .hecaitou.com/blogs/hecaitou/archives/134160.aspx.

"I caused a lot of fights on the Internet"

81 *When this post was criticized*: For more on Charlie Custer's argument with He Caitou, see http://chinageeks.org/2009/03/racism-in-china/ and http:// chinageeks.org/2010/02/hecaitou-on-race-in-china/.

82 *Several people asked Chen Yi*: Some background and details on Chen Yi from Guobin Yang, *The Power of the Internet in China* (Oxford University Press, 2009), 176–80.

83 *"Many commentators said"*: Yang, 178.

83 *"This is the Chinese Internet's"*: http://bbs.tianya.cn/post-free-363962-1.shtml.

84 *access to thallium*: Andrew Jacobs, "Poison Attack Revives Fury in China Over '95 Case," *The New York Times*, May 10, 2013.

85 *brown-and-white kitten*: Tom Downey, "China's Cyberposse," *The New York Times Magazine*, March 3, 2010.

"They want to know they are not so lonely on this planet"

87 *"jump off a building"*: www.hecaitou.com/blogs/hecaitou/archives/122201 .aspx.

88 *"When I tearfully"*: www.shu0.net/?m=20100809.

"This is how I imagine the feelings of the guards"

91 *As of December 2012, Tencent*: www.tencent.com/en-us/at.abouttencent.shtml.

"You have to play by certain rules"

95 *Fanfou was founded in 2007*: For more on Wang Xing, see Gady Epstein, "The Cloner," *Forbes*, April 28, 2011.

95 *"We cut Internet connection"*: http://news.xinhuanet.com/english/2009-07 /07/content_11666802.htm.

"I'm a journalist and I know not to call for action"

100 *Authorities reacted swiftly*: For more on Beijing's war on jasmine, see Andrew Jacobs and Jonathan Ansfield, "Catching Scent of Revolution, China Moves to Snip Jasmine," *The New York Times*, May 10, 2011.

101 *"I didn't care about jasmine at first"*: http//articles.washingtonpost.com /2011-04-03/world/35229738_1_chinese-artist-china-researcher-chinese -human-rights-defenders.

"Twitter is everything about me"

103 *"Coders in China"*: Emily Parker, "Leaping the Great Firewall of China," *The Wall Street Journal*, March 24, 2010.

104 *"Twitter, whose servers"*: michaelanti.com/archives/37.

105 *The story began after Chen Guangcheng*: For details on Twitter and Chen Guangcheng, see Emily Parker, "How the Obama Administration's Narrative About Chen Guangcheng Unraveled, One Tweet at a Time," *The New Republic* online, May 4, 2012.

"If I don't stand up for Zhu Ling, who will stand up for me?"

108 *"If you have ten million followers"*: http://read.dangdang.com/book_14028 and http://jpkc.fudan.edu.cn/picture/article/215/87/f7/72763e9a48fc8e a6ec29122eebb4/bed7c33f-8895-4ed6-b81f-4407a3a01d03.pdf.

110 *Furthermore, eight officials*: "Mapping Digital Media: China," Open Society Foundations, www.opensocietyfoundations.org/reports/mapping-digital -media-China.

110 *a $32,000 reward*: "Gu Yongqiang, "In China, Water You Wouldn't Dave Swim In, Let Alone Drink," *Time*, March 6, 2013.

110 *"How is the river"*: www.techinasia.com/deng-fei-launches-weibo-campaign -share-images-water-pollution/.

110 *Chinese authorities measured pollution*: http://blogs.wsj.com/chinarealtime /2011/11/08/internet-puts-pressure-on-beijing-to-improve-air-pollution -monitoring/.

111 *Zhu Ling's poisoning case*: For details on Zhu Ling, see Emily Parker, "The 20-Year-Old Crime That's Blowing Up on Chinese Social Media," *The New Republic* online, May 4, 2013.

"You never know who is who"

119 *"When I made the decision to write"*: www.desdelahabana.net/de-internet-y
-la-seguridad-del-estado/.

122 *In 2009 the private sector*: Victoria Burnett, "Slowly, Cuba Is Developing
an Appetite for Spending," *The New York Times*, July 6, 2013. For more on
Cuban economic reforms, see Julia E. Sweig and Michael J. Bustamente,
"Cuba After Communism: The Economic Reforms That Are Transforming the Island," *Foreign Affairs*, July/August 2013. For more background
on Cuba, see Anne Louise Bardach, *Cuba Confidential: Love and Ven-
geance in Miami and Havana* (Vintage, 2003). See also Daniel P. Erikson,
The Cuba Wars: Fidel Castro, the United States, and the Next Revolution
(Bloomsbury Press, 2008).

122 *A typical Cuban day*: www.cubanet.org/articulos/vivir-a-lo-cubano/.

123 *"Laws Made to Be Broken"*: http://leyesdelaritzaen.wordpress.com/2009/09
/06/laws-made-to-be-broken/.

123 *"I write a blog because"*: www.cpj.org/blog/2009/04/a-cuban-blogger
-confronts-cubas-silent-repression.php.

"Resignation became my only comrade"

124 *In an admiring blog post*: Iván García on Laritza, www.penultimosdias
.com/2009/08/25/hija-de-la-revolucion/.

125 *Gorbachev announced that*: Julia Sweig, *Cuba: What Everyone Needs to
Know* (Oxford University Press, 2009), 127.

126 *"Today I have a degree"*: Laritza's blog in translation, http://leyesdelaritzaen
.wordpress.com/2009/11/02/what-made-me-a-dissident/.

127 *In 1960 he created*: For details on CDR, see Isabel Sanchez, "Cuba's
Neighborhood Watches: 50 Years of Eyes, Ears," AFP, September 7, 2010.

127 *"In the face of the imperialist"*: www.cnn.com/2010/WORLD/americas/09
/28/cuba.castro/index.html.

128 *"Keep your position"*: http://leyesdelaritzaen.wordpress.com/category/laritza
-diversent-translated-from-the-spanish/page/36/.

"The world knows the name and face of dissidence"

129 *In today's interconnected world*: For background on the Cuban Internet, see
special report by the Committee to Protect Journalists, "Chronicling
Cuba, Bloggers Offer Fresh Hope," 2009.

129 *According to some 2012 estimates*: For official Internet statistics, see www

.one.cu/publicaciones/06turismoycomercio/TIC%20en%20Cifras%20Cuba
%202011/TIC%20en%20Cifras%20Cuba%202011.pdf.

129 *periodically have access*: See "Freedom on the Net 2012," www.freedom
house.org/report/freedom-net/2012/cuba#_ftn2.

130 *"In a free country"*: Manuel Roig-Franzia, "Havana's 148 Flags Prove Might-
ier than the Billboard," *The Washington Post*, May 13, 2006.

"You see agents or informers everywhere"

138 *"The whole country is permeated"*: Jose Prieto, "Travels by Taxi, Reflections
on Cuba," *The Nation*, December 14, 2009.

"I comport myself like a free man"

143 *Did Obama consider*: www.desdecuba.com/generationy/?p=1179&cp=all.

"I knew everything was bad, but I had to write that everything was good"

146 *Reinaldo was born*: For more on Reinaldo Escobar, see Iván García, "¿Quién
es Reinaldo Escobar?" *Elmundo.es*, November 12, 2009, www.elmundo.es
/america/2009/12/11/cuba/1260543291.html.

"The fear of those who learn their lessons through the trauma of others"

149 *"pena ajena"*: www.desdecuba.com/sin_evasion/?p=1762.

149 *"the fear of those"*: Reinaldo's blog in translation, http://desdeaquifromhere
.wordpress.com/2008/01/.

151 *Development Alternatives Inc.*: Mary Beth Sheridan, "Maryland Contractor Alan Gross Draws 15-Year Sentence in Cuba," *The Washington Post*,
March 13, 2011.

151 *"subversive project"*: Nicholas Casey, "Cuba Sentences U.S. Contractor,"
The Wall Street Journal, March 12, 2011, http://online.wsj.com/article
/SB10001424052748704838804576196784145868002.html.

152 *"The agents quickly closed"*: http://elyuma.blogspot.com/2011/05/this-will
-be-your-last-time-reflection.html.

154 *"At any site in Santiago"*: Reinaldo's blog in translation, http://desdeaqui
fromhere.wordpress.com/2009/02/04/at-the-foot-of-the-mountain/.

154 *"fear, the father"*: www.desdelahabana.net¿por-que-los-cubanos-no-protesta
mos/comment-page-1.

155 *That year the festival*: Emily Parker, "For Most Cubans, Film Is the Only Way to Travel," *The Wall Street Journal*, December 16, 2008.

"People have to search for their own voice because they never had one"

157 *He was reminded*: Reinaldo Escobar on Cienfuegos, Reinaldo's blog in translation, http://translatingcuba.com/which-party-owns-this-yacht-now-reinaldo-escobar/.

157 *They didn't bother*: www.desdecuba.com/generation/?p=2739.

161 *"That means a worker"*: www.cnn.com/2008/WORLD/americas/02/07/cuba.videos/.

"I want my lawyer, and *nada más*!"

168 *"The housing situation"*: Yaremis's blog post in translation, http://translatingcuba.com/that-old-newspaper-yellowed-with-age-laritza-diversent/.

172 *"There is also no"*: Laritza's blog in translation, http://translatingcuba.com/cuban-ministry-of-interior-authorizes-murder-suspect-to-leave-the-country-laritza-diversent/.

"When someone is detained, everyone knows about it"

173 *Yaremis Flores had been arrested*: Committee to Protect Journalists (CPJ) report on Yaremis, "Cuban Reporter Flores Arrested on Anti-State Charges," November 9, 2012.

177 *Yaremis had similar feelings*: For Yaremis's description of her time in jail, in translation, see http://translatingcuba.com/number-54033-part-1-cuban-legal-advisor-yaremis-flores/.

"People were silent and kept the constitution over their heads"

187 *The demonstrators were wedged*: Richard Boudreaux, "Russia Breaks Up Protests, Arrests Leaders," *The Wall Street Journal*, July 31, 2010.

188 *An oft-cited survey*: www.levada.ru/archive/gosudarstvo-i-obshchestvo/grazhdane-i-vlast/mogut-li-takie-lyudi-kak-vy-vliyat-na-prinyatie-.

188 *"Someone gets to stand"*: Translation by Kevin Rothrock, www.agoodtreaty.com/2010/06/08/oleg-kashin-on-strategy-thirty-one/.

"You have to propose to people the comfortable way of struggle"

190 *"My laptop—that's"*: Paul Sonne and Alexander Kolyandr, "Russia Activist Facing Trial Discusses Personal Toll," *The Wall Street Journal*, April 15, 2013.

191 *Not only a blogger*: For details on Navalny and Surgutneftegas, see Carl Schreck, "Russia's Erin Brockovich: Taking on Corporate Greed," *Time*, March 9, 2010.

192 *Mezhregiongaz*: www.vedomosti.ru/newspaper/article/2008/12/24/175138, subscription only, accessed through factiva.

192 *The intermediary later*: For details on Navalny and anticorruption, see Julia Ioffe, "Net Impact: One Man's Cyber-Crusade Against Russian Corruption," *The New Yorker*, April 4, 2011.

192 *suspicions against Igor*: www.vedomosti.ru/newspaper/article/2009/08 /07/208743, subscription only, accessed through factiva.

192 *"The Interior Ministry has"*: http://navalny.livejournal.com/398936.html.

193 *A descendant of*: For details on Gazprom and Putin's Russia, see Angus Roxburgh, *The Strongman: Vladimir Putin and the Struggle for Russia* (I. B. Tauris, 2012).

194 *over $150 million*: navalny.livejournal.com/411199.html.

194 *"I am confident that"*: http://globalvoicesonline.org/2010/10/27/russia -blogger-alexey-navalny-on-fighting-regime/.

195 *With Daimler, the U.S. Department of Justice*: Department of Justice document on Daimler, www.justice.gov/criminal/fraud/fcpa/cases/daimler/03-24 -10daimlerag-agree.pdf and www.justice.gov/criminal/fraud/fepa/cases /daimler/03-24-10daimlerag-agree.pdf.

196 *"I urge all to show citizenship"*: http://navalny.livejournal.com/446841.html.

197 Vedomosti *reported*: www.vedomosti.ru/newspaper/article/274054/sekretnye _podozrevaemye.

"We have our own words"

198 *When Navalny talks about*: 1976–1982 LiveJournal page, http://76-82 .livejournal.com/.

199 *the Soviet Union's first McDonald's*: For the McDonalds story, see http://76 -82.livejournal.com/4544054.html.

199 *the country's first telethon*: For the telethon story, see http://76-82.live journal.com/4517085.html.

200 *Encyclopedia of Our Childhood*: www.76-82.ru/project/.

"The problem is that people don't search for it"

202 *In the fall of 2010, 40 percent*: http://bd.fom.ru/pdf/Bulliten_31_osen_2010_short.pdf.

202 *However, more than 90 percent*: http://company.yandex.ru/researches/reports/internet_regions_2011.xml.

202 *In 2010 about one-quarter*: http://runet.fom.ru/Mobilnye-tehnologii/10228.

203 *more than double*: For more Internet statistics, see www.comscore.com/Insights/Press_Releases/2010/10/Russia_Has_Most_Engaged_Social_Networking_Audience_Worldwide and http://download.yandex.ru/company/figures/yandex_on_twitter_march_2010.pdf.

203 *"First attempt at writing"*: Robert Greenall, "LiveJournal, Russia's Unlikely Internet Giant," *BBC News*, February 29, 2012, www.bbc.co.uk/news/magazine-17177053.

205 *a 2010 report*: 2010 Levada poll, www.levada.ru/books/vestnik-obshchestvennogo-mneniya-4106-za-2010-god.

205 *"The Web That Failed"*: Floriana Fossato and John Lloyd with Alexander Verkhovsky, "The Web That Failed: How Opposition Politics and Independent Initiatives Are Failing on the Internet in Russia," Reuters Institute for the Study of Journalism, 2008, https://reutersinstitute.politics.ox.ac.uk/fileadmin/documents/Publications/The_Web_that_Failed.pdf.

"In Russia, change never comes from the bottom"

210 *"The abundance of gold"*: "Kremlin Invites Top Blogger to Cover Russian Leader," AFP, September 4, 2009, www.google.com/hostednews/afp/article/ALeqM5jTdbSfxaRDjvX8NedDFt3nnXJw_Q.

210 *"Beaten, mutilated, half-dead"*: http://drugoi.livejournal.com/2099678.html.

210 *charitable acts*: For charity figures, see www.cafonline.org/pdf/world_giving_index_2011_191211.pdf).

211 *Adagamov used his blog to direct readers*: http://drugoi.livejournal.com/3436535.html?thread=368531703.

"You can keep silent, you can emigrate, or you can stay here and fight"

214 *"widely accepted"*: archives.republicans.foreignaffairs.gov/news/story/?2401.

215 *"was effectively prevented"*: Other Politkovskaya details from Masha Gessen, *The Man Without a Face: The Unlikely Rise of Vladimir Putin* (Riverhead Books, 2012), 212–13 and 219–20.

216 *"an unacceptable crime"*: www.nytimes.com/2006/10/10/world/europe/10iht -germany.3102737.html.

216 *"The impunity the masterminds"*: Nina Ognianova, "Despite Progress, Impunity Still the Norm in Russia," Committee to Protect Journalists, 2012, www .cpj.org/2012/02/attacks-on-the-press-in-2011-in-russia-pr-is-bette.php.

217 *the journalist Mikhail Beketov*: For more on the Beketov case, see www.cpj .org/killed/2013/mikhail-beketov.php and www.nytimes.com/2010/05/18 /world/europe/18impunity.html.

218 *"I have ordered"*: www.opendemocracy.net/od-russia/mikhail-zakharov /oleg-kashin-words-that-cripple.

"We didn't apply to the authorities, we appealed to the people"

222 *identified witnesses*: For details on the accident, see Bruce Etling, Karina Alexanyan, John Kelly, Robert Faris, John Palfrey, and Urs Gasser, "Public Discourse on the Russian Blogosphere: Mapping RuNet Politics and Mobilization," *Berkman Center Research Publication* No. 2010–2011, October 19, 2010.

222 *"Get out of my way"*: Alexander Osipovich, "Russian Rap Inspires a Movement," *The Wall Street Journal*, July 24, 2010, http://online.wsj.com/article /SB10001424052748704518904575365892029763162.html.

223 *"I can imagine"*: http://cook.livejournal.com/131226.html.

"Rights are not given, they are taken"

231 *In 2006 Max Neroda*: http://tayga.info/details/2006/06/28/~89584.

231 *OBERIU (meaning the Union of Real Art)*: For details on OBERIU, see Eugene Ostashevsky, Matvei Yankelevich, Thomas Epstein, Ilya Bernstein, and Genya Turovskaya, *OBERIU: An Anthology of Russian Absurdism* (Northwestern University Press, 2006), XVI–XX, accessed through Google Books.

232 *"Many said it was pornography"*: Miriam Elder, "Political Expression in Russia," *Global Post*, July 2, 2009, http://www.globalpost.com/dispatch /russia-and-its-neighbors/090602/art-politics?page=full.

234 *"black magic, the Constitution"*: http://kissmybabushka.com/?p=1942.

234 *"Rights are not given"*: http://kissmybabushka.com/?p=1988.

"Bloggers have nothing to fear from publicity"

236 *While they were investigating*: For some details and background on Artem's arrest, see Miriam Elder, "Political Expression in Russia," *Global Post*, June 2, 2009, www.globalpost.com/dispatch/russia-and-its-neighbors/090602/art -politics.

237 *"Participate in events"*: http://songs-of-moors.livejournal.com/26244.html.

238 Sekstremizm: http://dw.de/p/imm5.

240 *He posted the recording*: http://kissmybabushka.com/?p=3392.

"No one, including me, believed this was possible in Russia"

243 *"I recommend a pistol"*: Ellen Barry, "Rousing Russia with a Phrase," *The New York Times*, December 9, 2011.

243 *Navalny tried to explain*: For more background on Navalny and nationalism, see Kevin Rothrock, "Navalny's Nationalism," www.agoodtreaty.com /2011/04/22/navalnys-nationalism/.

243 *"Russia for Russians!"*: Julia Ioffe, "Race Riots in Russia," *The New Yorker* online, December 16, 2010.

248 *"I see a forest of hands"*: http://navalny.livejournal.com/498772.html.

"You cannot be a hero for a long time on the Internet"

251 *23 percent of Russians*: www.levada.ru/press/2011050501.html.

252 *"embarrassing"*: Janet Stobart, "British Admit Using 'Embarrassing' Fake Rock to Spy on Russians," *Los Angeles Times*, January 20, 2012.

253 *in 2012 VKontakte's*: http://lenta.ru/news/2012/04/18/brandbots/.

"My country and my life are dependent on what I do"

256 *"Although the initial installation"*: http://globalvoicesonline.org/2010/08/10 /russia-russian-fires-ru-the-first-ushahidi-experience/.

257 *The Internet was a particularly*: On Russian Internet reactions to Internet freedom agenda: http://globalvoicesonline.org/2011/02/26/russia-internet -freedom-as-cold-war-2-0/.

"I want to thank you for considering yourself citizens!"

261 *"an agreement over what"*: www.nytimes.com/2011/09/25/world/europe /medvedev-says-putin-will-seek-russian-presidency-in-2012.html ?pagewanted=all.

262 *"We have built a new"*: navalny.livejournal.com/2011/12/05/.

263 *Another video looks down*: Michael Schwirtz and David M. Herszenhorn, "Voters Watch Polls in Russia, and Fraud Is What They See," *The New York Times*, December 5, 2011.

264 *a thousand official complaints*: http://ria.ru/politics/20111220/521735637 .html.

264 *"The blatant and total"*: http://navalny.livejournal.com/656297.html.

265 *blocked by the OMON*: www.esquire.com/blogs/politics/alexei-navalny interview-6628420.

266 *"in one country"*: Julia Ioffe, "The End of Putin," *Foreign Policy* online, December 28, 2011, www.foreignpolicy.com/articles/2011/12/28/the_end _of_putin.

"So, is it you who is organizing this revolution in Russia?"

269 *18,600 said*: www.forbes.ru/sobytiya/lyudi/77323-miting-10-dekabrya-na -bolotnoi-ploshchadi-vse-podrobnosti.

269 *"Friends, this is an important"*: http://vk.com/wall-32872901_24269.

270 *"It seems that it's linked"*: Miriam Elder, "Russian Police Accused of Scare Tactics Before Anti-Putin Rally," *The Guardian*, February 2, 2012.

270 *eighty-two Russian cities*: ria.ru/analytics/20111223/524124814.html.

272 *"We often regret"*: http://epic-hero.ru/2010/10/31/31/#.

273 *"the hipster breakthrough"*: http://newtimes.ru/articles/detail/29793.

"We exist!"

275 *"I have also been impressed"*: Rustem Adagamov, "Moscow on the Eve of the Presidential Election," opendemocracy.net, March 1, 2012.

275 *"Let's just go there"*: http://drugoi.livejournal.com/3665097.html.

276 *"Today I saw the city"*: http://vk.com/wall-32872901_25856.

277 *In the twilight*: Mark R. Beissinger, *Nationalist Mobilization and the Collapse of the Soviet State* (Cambridge: Cambridge University Press, 2002).

278 *"For the youth"*: Москва революционная, Arthur Solomon, *Novaya Gazeta*, December 23, 2011.

278 *"All people of dignity"*: J. David Goodman, "Updates on Protests in Russia," nytimes.com, December 10, 2011.

278 *"Tens of thousands"*: Michael Schwirtz, "On Russian TV, a Straightforward Account Is Startling," *The New York Times*, December 10, 2011.

282 *Not long after Rustem Adagamov*: For more on Adagamov, see Allan Cullison, "Russia Investigates Allegations Against Opposition Blogger," *The Wall Street Journal*, January 11, 2013.

282 *"If a person"*: "Russian Official: Putin Foe Targeted for Probe," Associated Press, April 12, 2013.

283 *"I see there is a"*: Ellen Barry, "Russian Activist Aleksei Navalny: 'I Am Absolutely Sure We Will Win,'" nytimes.com, April 16, 2013.

283 *"Therefore it is clear"*: http://navalny.livejournal.com/823602.html.

ACKNOWLEDGMENTS

First, thank you to the amazing people who contributed research to this book: Natalya Berenshteyn, Kirsten Berg, Haowen Chen, Pavel Reznikov, Becky Shafer, and Ting Zhao. I am in awe of your intelligence and professionalism. To the bloggers and activists who put up with my endless questions and years-long intrusion into your lives. To the New America Foundation, for providing me with an incredible community, as well as the time and space to write, with special thanks to Anne-Marie Slaughter, Steve Coll, Rachel White, Andres Martinez, Faith Smith, and Madeline McSherry. To the Carnegie Moscow Center for bringing Russia into my life, and to the Russia hands James Collins, Masha Lipman, Matt Rojansky, Vyacheslav Bakhmin, and Esther Dyson. To Sam Greene, for your support at Carnegie and also at the Center for New Media and Society. To my fellow China hands Orville Schell, Ian Johnson, Lijia Zhang, Brendan O'Kane, and Hugo Restall. To Stephanie Huezo, Pedro Freyre, Carlos Lauria, and Alvaro Vargas Llosa for your help with Cuba. To the Council on Foreign Relations for providing me with an International Affairs Fellowship, and to Asia Society's Center on US-China Relations for your early support of this project. To my former colleagues at *The Wall Street Journal*'s editorial page, and to Mike Gonzalez for knowing that the Internet in China would become a major global story. To Leslie Gelb, J. Stapleton Roy, Tunku Varadarajan, and Minky Worden for supporting my career in all kinds of ways. It has been an honor to work with the truly awesome team at FSG, with special thanks to Sarah Crichton, Sarah Scire, Devon Mazzone, Dan Piepenbring, and Tobi Haslett. To Diane Parker for being a brilliant reader, Mel Parker for your sage advice and deep understanding of the publishing industry, and David Parker for, among other things, being a fantastic companion in Moscow and St. Petersburg. To the friends and family who lived through this with me: Veronika Belenkaya, Nila Dharan, Ronna Gradus, Elizabeth Kendall, Hilary Winston, and Safi, Nabil, and Ameer Saleh.

And, finally, to Kareem Saleh, because nobody believed in this book more than you.

A NOTE ABOUT THE AUTHOR

Emily Parker is a digital diplomacy adviser and senior fellow at the New America Foundation. Previously, she was a member of Secretary of State Hillary Clinton's policy planning staff, where she focused on digital diplomacy, Internet freedom, and open government. Before joining the State Department, Parker was an op-ed editor at *The New York Times* and an editorial writer and op-ed editor at *The Wall Street Journal* in Asia and the United States.

Printed in the USA
CPSIA information can be obtained
at www.ICGtesting.com
LVHW091137150724
785511LV00005B/371

9 780374 535513